THE SCOTTISH EXPERIENCE

THE SCOTTISH EXPERIENCE

A Prose Anthology

Oliver & Boyd

Oliver & Boyd
Robert Stevenson House
1–3 Baxter's Place
Leith Walk
Edinburgh EH1 3BB
A Division of Longman Group Limited

ISBN 0 05 003454 5

Printed in Singapore by
Singapore Offset Printing Pte Ltd.

Contents

Acknowledgments

The editors and publishers would like to thank the following for permission to publish copyright work:

John Calder (Publishers) Ltd for the extracts from George Friel's *Mr Alfred MA* and Robert McLellan's *Jamie the Saxt* both published by them; Curtis Brown Ltd for the extract from Edwin Muir's *Scottish Journey* (Heinemann); David Higham Associates for the extracts from George Blake's *The Ship Builders* (Collins); Faber & Faber Ltd for the extract from Hugh MacDiarmid's 'Growing up in Langholm' published by them in *Memoirs of a Modern Scotland* edited by Karl Miller; Ian Hamilton Finlay for 'The Potato Planters and the old Joiner's Funeral'; Gerald Duckworth Ltd for the extract from R.B. Cunninghame Graham's 'Beattock for Moffat' (from *Scottish Short Stories* 1932); Granada Publishing Ltd for the extracts from Hugh MacDiarmid's *The Uncanny Scot* published by them; Dairmid Gunn for the extract from Neil Gunn's *Highland Pack*; Clifford Hanley for the extract from *Dancing in the Streets* (UR Books); Hogarth Press for the extracts from George Mackay Brown's *Greenvoe* and *A Calendar of Love* and Edwin Muir's *Autobiography*, all published by them; Hutchinson Publishing Group Ltd for the extracts from Lewis Grassic Gibbon's *A Scots Hairst* and *Cloud Howe*, and Archie Hind's *The Dear Green Place*, all published by them; Robin Jenkins for the extract from *The Changeling*; Liz Lochhead for 'A Protestant Girlhood' from *Jock Tamson's Bairns* edited by Trevor Royle (Hamish Hamilton); Longman Group Ltd for the extract from Donald Cameron's *The Field of Sighing* published by them; Lord Tweedsmuir (through A.P. Watt Ltd) for the extract from John Buchan's *Montrose* (Nelson); James Reid for the extract from his Rectorial Address to Glasgow University, 1972; The Society of Authors as the literary representative of the Estate of Sir Compton Mackenzie for the extract from his Rectorial Address to Glasgow University, 1932; Souvenir Press Ltd for the extract from Neil Gunn's *Morning Tide* published by them; Victor Gollancz Ltd for the extracts from Iain Crichton Smith's *Consider the Lilies* published by them.

This book is published in association with Strathclyde Regional Council Education Department, Glasgow Division.

Introduction

This anthology is intended primarily for students in the Fifth and Sixth Years of Scottish secondary schools. These senior pupils deserve the experience of exposure to and study of as wide a range of prose as possible, and in particular the prose of their own country. It is to fulfil such a need that the anthology has been compiled by a small group of teachers of English in Glasgow.

We believe that this volume will be attractive in its own right, simply for the interest and enjoyment to be had from reading the various passages. As a sample of the huge range of good Scots prose that exists it may also prove to be informative. In addition, however, we hope that the book will have considerable practical value for students who have examination goals to achieve.

Obviously there is the Literature element in all English papers, but every other part of the Higher and Sixth Year Studies English examination can also be involved. The variety of passages offered here can afford a strong stimulus to the candidates' own writing in the various forms called for in the examinations. Again, the Higher Interpretation paper in recent years has shown a tendency towards greater variety of passages than in the past, and some blurring of the previous distinctions between various sections of the paper has taken place. With the introduction of prose passages to the Practical Criticism section of the Literature paper that blurring now extends even further. As a result we can find over both papers three prose passages, all varied in style, purpose and tone, and all demanding the same close observation on the part of the candidate. In Sixth Year Studies, of course, Paper III has always involved close comparative reading of several substantial prose extracts.

Any experienced Examiner will testify that our senior pupils are all at least competent writers, and the best of them are brilliant. Almost all are reasonably skilled in expressing a personal response to what they have read, at least in broad general terms. Where they are weakest is in the close reading of texts, especially prose texts, with awareness of meaning, style, tone, language features, technique etc. Too often in the past their training in this area has been so closely tied to S.C.E. examinations that their close reading has been virtually confined to passages taken from past papers. Even here all too often the passages have been used not so much for close study and group discussion as for individual practice in answering examination questions. The range of texts included here can provide a nourishing diet to make good these former deficiencies.

During the initial selection of extracts for this anthology a rough thematic pattern soon became apparent and this was adopted as a framework, though there is considerable overlapping of themes. Because of constraints of space, selection was for the most part confined to late nineteenth- and twentieth-century writing, though there is a brief sampling of older texts dating from the sixteenth century, which are included to show that there is some continuity in the Scottish prose tradition. The whole range of writing in Gaelic has been ignored, though there are glancing references to the Gaelic culture. Where it was practicable a few pieces were chosen in their entirety, but most texts had to be represented in extract. In most such cases the titles under which they appear are not the authors' but the compilers', and they apply to the extract only, not the complete text. Fiction predominates, naturally enough, but there is a fair representation of other forms of prose: biography, reminiscence, descriptive writing, discursive prose, even a snatch of drama. An enormous variety of style and language is displayed. Standard English is the norm (sadly, some may think), but there is no shortage of Scots of various regions and periods.

It would be presumptuous of us to suggest classroom methods for using this book. We are confident, however, that there is ample material here to provide a varied and valuable set of language experiences for all Fifth and Sixth Year students.

Jack O'Neill
Adviser in English,
Glasgow

1 · Childhood

The faithful re-creation of early experience has always been a challenging task for the writer. In this opening section some highly skilled writers present various aspects of childhood memories.

Edwin Muir (1887–1959) was the son of an Orkney farmer who moved to Glasgow when the writer was fourteen. On leaving school he worked as a clerk in a bottling factory and later in a factory which converted bones into grease — a far cry from his former Orcadian surroundings. For Muir, 'the slums seemed to be everywhere around me, a great spreading swamp into which I might sink for good.' Nevertheless he did survive and *An Autobiography* (1954), an extended version of which first appeared as *The Story and the Fable* (1940), is often lighthearted, humorous and reflective. Muir is also a major figure in Scottish poetry of this century.

Hugh MacDiarmid (Christopher Murray Grieve) was born in 1892 and spent his early years in Langholm, Dumfriesshire. After entering journalism he served in the First World War. In the period immediately following the war he was to play a prominent part in what became known as the Scottish Renaissance. Largely through his influence Scottish poetry changed direction — more radical experimentation in the use of 'braid Scots', a much wider range of subject matter, the re-connection with European literary movements and thought. He died in 1978. In the extract from *Memoirs of a Modern Scotland* which is presented here he reveals a deep and sympathetic awareness of his natural surroundings.

J. McDougall Hay (1881–1919) was the author of the novel *Gillespie*. This is a powerful study in social disintegration and in this respect has much in common with *The House with the Green Shutters* by George Douglas. Hay's portrayal of the small community being manipulated and relentlessly dominated by one man, the self-made Gillespie Strang, is masterly: does this have a peculiarly Scottish interest? McDougall Hay, born at Tarbert, Loch Fyne, eventually became a minister of the Church of Scotland. For a man of the cloth to produce such a 'strong' book as this in 1914 was quite remarkable.

With his writings encompassing 800 years of Scots, English and French history, Sir Walter Scott (1771–1832) was indisputably the leading European writer of his time. The key to the passage included here is to be found in Scott's boyhood experiences. Saturating himself in tales of older days, his landscapes with their strong sense of myth and legend are filled with romance and daring. Scott's use of language is interesting in this extract — the serious, even sonorous tone, the slow stately tempo in keeping with the theme.

Robin Jenkins was born in 1912 in Cambuslang, near Glasgow. He is possibly one of the most sensitive observers of relationships in his own part of the country. *The Changeling* (1958), perhaps his best novel, portrays Charles Forbes, a teacher with liberal ideas, who wishes to take one of his working-class pupils on holiday with his own family. The pupil, Tom Curdie, an intelligent if cynical youngster, finds the problems of accepting this offer, with all its implications, insurmountable; in many ways the ensuing tragedy is a comment on the central dilemma of modern industrial society.

Neil M. Gunn (1891–1973) was born in Caithness into a society of crofters and fishermen. After thirty years in the excise service, he abandoned this in his mid-forties and retired to the Highlands to devote his time to writing. *Morning Tide* presents a picture of a boy growing up in a crofting and fishing society, sensitively aware of all the physical features of the landscape around him. Not just boyhood, however, but a whole way of life, with all its values, is portrayed.

As a Child

My first definite memories are connected with the Bu; but there is one composite one which may conceivably go back to the house where I was born, it brings such a sense of timelessness with it. I was lying in some room watching a beam of slanting light in which dusty, bright motes slowly danced and turned, while a low murmuring went on somewhere, possibly the humming of the flies. My mother was in the room, but where I do not know; I was merely conscious of her as a vague, environing presence. This picture is clear and yet indefinite, attached to one summer day at the Bu, and at the same time to so many others that it may go back to the day when I first watched a beam of light as I lay in my cradle. The quiet murmuring, the slow, unending dance of the motes, the sense of deep and solid peace, have come back to me since only in dreams. This memory has a different quality from any other memory in my life. It was as if, while I lay watching that beam of light, time had not yet begun.

My first definite memory is of being baptized. Why I was not baptized in Deerness, where there were two churches, I have never been able to find out; but the ceremony was postponed for some reason until I was three years old. I was dressed for the occasion in a scarlet suit with petticoats instead of breeches, for boys were not given boys' clothes then until they were five. The suit was made of some fine but slightly rough material like serge; the sun must have been shining that day, for the cloth seemed to glow from within with its own light; it was fastened with large glittering golden buttons. I think it must have been the first time that I saw the colour of gold and of scarlet, for it is this suit that makes me remember that day, and it still burns in my memory more brightly than anything I have ever seen since. In the afternoon my father and mother led me by the hand to the school, where Mr Pirie, the minister of Rousay, had come to baptize me. Some people had gathered. I was lifted up by my father, face upward; I saw Mr Pirie's kind face with its thin beard inclined diagonally over me (for he had a glass eye and looked at everything from the side), then I felt the cold water on my face and began to cry. As if the baptismal water had been a deluge, all the rest of that day is damp and drowned, the burning scarlet and the gold sunk in darkness.

Most of my childhood is drowned as deep as the rest of that baptismal day; I have no recollection of the routine of my first seven years, though it was there, giving me my first realization of order in the world. A fragment of that age swam up recently after being lost for more than sixty years. It was another suit of clothes, and it returned by a curious road. I was down in Edinburgh a few years ago with some time on my hands. I went into a tea-room, and after having my tea looked round to see what the hour was, but there was no sign of a clock. As the waitress was giving me the bill I asked her the time; she glanced at a wrist-watch she was wearing, and told me with a condescending air that it was a quarter to six. As I still had some time left I went to the Café Royal for a drink. Where I sat I was directly facing the clock set in the wall above the buffet, a round, plain clock with a face like that of an old-fashioned watch very much enlarged. My mind returned to the waitress; I remembered an evening in Prague when my wrist-watch had been stolen from me in a tramcar without my noticing it. My thoughts wandered on, and I found myself thinking that I was too old now for a wrist-watch; for some reason this seemed a perfectly sensible notion. But in that case — I was still paying very little attention to my thoughts — what sort of watch should I wear, for it was inconvenient to be without a watch? Then I saw dangling in the air a big, heavy watch such as the ploughmen used to wear when I was a boy. This troubled me, for what pocket could I keep it in? The watch settled the matter by dropping into my breast pocket, where it attached itself by a black, twisted cord to the top buttonhole of my coat, under the lapel. But this is a very juvenile arrangement, I told myself, wakening into another layer of daydream, though not into complete awakeness. Then, as if all these windings had been deliberately leading up to it, all at once I saw a boy's blue sailor suit with a yellow twisted hempen cord loosely knotted round the collar, and at the end of it a canary-yellow wooden whistle. The sailor suit startled me so much that I did not know what to do with it. Next moment I realized that I had worn it once; I could remember distinctly the feel and the smell of the smooth wooden whistle; it had a faint, fragrant smell. But I could not say when I had worn that suit, and the fact that after being buried for all these years it should come back now by such a tortuous and yet purposive road struck me as very strange. Yet it seemed still stranger that it could have disappeared at all, for the yellow whistle must have been one of the things which I loved most as a child, since even in memory I could feel the delight it had given me. Could some disaster have befallen the yellow whistle, so that I put it so completely out of my mind that it had never returned since? If that could happen once it might have happened hundreds of times.

I can still see the scarlet dress and the sailor suit; I can see the rough grey stones spotted with lichen on the top of the Castle, and a bedraggled gooseberry bush in a corner of the garden whose branches I lovingly fingered for hours; but I cannot bring back the feelings which I had for them, the sense of being magically close to them, as if they were magnets drawing me with a palpable power. Reasonable explanations can be found for these feelings: the fact that every object is new to a child, that he sees it without understanding it, or understands it with a different understanding from that of experience — different, for there may be fear in it, but there cannot be calculation or worry; or even the fact that he is closer to things, since his eyes are only two or three feet from the ground, not five or six. Grass, stones, and insects are twice as near to him as they will be after he has grown up, and when I try to re-create my early childhood it seems to me that it was focused on such things as these, and that I lived my life in a small, separate under-

world, while the grown-ups walked on their long legs several feet
above my head on a stage where every relation was different. I was
dizzily lifted into that world, as into another dimension, when my
father took me on his shoulders, so that I could see the roof of the
byre from above or touch the lintel of the house door with my
hand. But for most of the time I lived with whatever I found on the
surface of the earth: the different kinds of grass, the daisies, butter-
cups, dandelions, bog cotton (we did not have many flowers), the
stones and bits of glass and china, and the scurrying insects which
made my stomach heave as I stared at them, unable to take my
eyes away. These insects were all characters to me, interesting but
squalid, with thoughts that could never be penetrated, inconceivable
aims, perverse activities. I knew their names, which so exactly
fitted them as characters: the Jenny Hunderlegs, the gavelock, the
forkytail, the slater — the underworld of my little underworld,
obsessing me, but for ever beyond my reach. Some were not so
horrible, such as the spider, impersonal compared with the others,
whose progress was a terrifying dart or a grave, judge-like, swaying
walk. Unlike the others, he was at home in the sun, and so did not
need to scuttle; I thought of him as bearded and magistral. I could
never bear to touch any of these creatures, though I watched them
so closely that I seemed to be taking part in their life, which was
like little fragments of night darting about in the sun; they often
came into my dreams later, wakening me in terror. How many
hours I must have spent staring with fixed loathing at these creatures! Yet I did not want to know anything about them; I merely
wanted them away. Their presence troubled me as the mind is troubled in adolescence by the realization of physical lust. The
gavelocks and forkytails were my first intimation of evil, and
associations of evil still cling round them for me, as, I fancy, for
most people: popular imagery shows it. We cannot tell how much
our minds are influenced for life by the fact that we see the world
first at a range of two or three feet.

The insects, of course, were only a small part of that three-foot
world; I think I must have passed through a phase of possession by
them, comparatively short. The grass was a reliable pleasure; the
flowers were less dependable, and after I picked a dandelion one
day and found it writhing with little angry, many-legged insects,
the faces of the flowers took on a faithless look, until my mother
taught me which could be relied upon. The crevices in stone walls
were filled with secrets; a slab of hard cement on the wall of the

house had a special meaning. Mud after new rain was delicious, and I was charmed by everything that flew, from the humble bee to the Willie Longlegs. At that stage the novelty of seeing a creature flying outweighed everything else.

My height from the ground determined my response to other things too. When my father and Sutherland brought in the horses from the fields I stood trembling among their legs, seeing only their great, bearded feet and the momentary flash of their crescent-shaped shoes flung up lazily as they passed. When my father stopped with the bridle in his hands to speak to me I stood looking up at the stationary hulks and the tossing heads, which in the winter dusk were lost in the sky. I felt beaten down by an enormous weight and a real terror; yet I did not hate the horses as I hated the insects; my fear turned into something else, for it was infused by a longing to go up to them and touch them and simultaneously checked by the knowledge that their hoofs were dangerous: a combination of emotions which added up to worship in the Old Testament sense. Everything about them, the steam rising from their soft, leathery nostrils, the sweat staining their hides, their ponderous, irresistible motion, the distant rolling of their eyes, which was like the revolution of rock-crystal suns, the waterfall sweep of their manes, the ruthless flick of their cropped tails, the plunge of their iron-shod hoofs striking fire from the flagstones, filled me with a stationary terror and delight for which I could get no relief. One day two of our horses began to fight in the field below the house, rearing at each other like steeds on a shield and flinging out with their hind-legs, until Sutherland rushed out to separate them. A son of our neighbour at the Haa had a crescent mark on his forehead where a horse had kicked him; I stared at it in entrancement, as if it were a sign in the sky. And in a copy of *Gulliver's Travels* which my eldest brother had won as a school prize there was a picture of a great horse sitting on a throne judging a crowd of naked men with hairy, hang-dog faces. The horse was sitting on its hindquarters, which had a somewhat mean and inadequate appearance; its front hoofs were upraised and its neck arched as if to strike; and though the picture was strange and frightening, I took it to be the record of some actual occurrence. All this added to my terror of horses, so that I loved and dreaded them as an explorer loves and dreads a strange country which he has not yet entered.

Edwin Muir, *An Autobiography*

Growing Up in Langholm

After journeying over most of Scotland, England and central, southern and eastern Europe, as well as America, Siberia and China, I am of the opinion that 'my native place' — the Muckle Toon of Langholm, in Dumfriesshire — is the bonniest place I know: by virtue not of the little burgh in itself (though that has its treasurable aspects, and on nights when, as boys, we used to thread its dim streets playing 'Jock, Shine the Light', and race over the one bridge, past the factory, and over the other, with the lamp reflections wriggling like eels at intervals in the racing water, had an indubitable magic of its own), but by virtue of the wonderful variety and quality of the scenery in which it is set. The delights of sledging on the Lamb Hill or Murtholm Brae; of gathering hines in the Langfall; of going through the fields of Baggara hedged in honey-suckle and wild roses, through knee-deep meadow-sweet to the Scrog Nut Wood and gathering the nuts or crab-apples there; of blaeberrying on Warblaw or the Castle Hill; of dookin' and guddlin' or making islands in the Esk or Ewes or Wauchope and lighting stick fires on them and cooking potatoes in tin cans — these are only a few of the joys I knew, in addition to the general ones of hill-climbing and penetrating the five glens which (each with its distinct character) converge upon or encircle the town — Eskdale, Wauchopedale, Tarrasdale, Ewesdale and, below the town Carlislewards, the Dean Banks.

As we grew up, too, we learned to savour the particular qualities and rites of Langholm in comparison with other Border burghs: the joys of Langholm Common Riding compared with those at Selkirk or Hawick, for example; the peculiar shibboleths of local pronunciation; the historical associations of our corner of the 'Ballad-land' rife with its tales of raidings and reivings and with the remnants of peels; the wealth of local 'characters' who were still about.

As I grew into my early teens I ranged further afield, and soon all the Borders were within my ken. Many places had their special beauties or points of interest and advantage; but none had the variety of beauty centred round Langholm itself — none seemed so complete a microcosm of the entire Borderland. I knew where to find not only the common delights of hill and forest and waterside (and chiefest of all these to me were the chestnut trees at the saw-mill — even now it thrills me to remember the beautiful chestnuts, large and luxurious as horses' eyes, which so surprisingly displayed themselves when we cracked open the prickly green shells, and I remember many huge strops of them I strung and many a fierce competition at Conquerors), but also the various kinds of orchises, and butterwort, sundew, and the like; the various nests — including Terrona crags where ravens nested; how to deal with adders and smoke out wasps' 'bikes', and much other lore of that sort. In short, a boyhood full of country sights and sounds — healthy and happy and able to satisfy its hunger with juicy slices of a big yellow neep stolen from an adjoining field.

I never made any conscious decision that I should be a writer. That was a foregone conclusion from my very early life. I don't know if it originated with myself. When I was nine or ten my teachers seemed to realise that writing was going to be my destiny and I may have absorbed the idea from them. Certainly from a very early age I had begun to try to write for the local paper at Langholm, where my father was the local postman. We lived in the Post Office buildings. The library, the nucleus of which had been left by Thomas Telford, the famous engineer, was upstairs. I had access to it, and used to fill a big washing-basket with books and bring it downstairs as often as I wanted to. There were upwards of 12,000 books in the library, and a fair number of new books, chiefly novels, was constantly bought. Before I left home (when I was fourteen) I could go up into that library in the dark and find any book I wanted. I read almost every one of them.

My grandfather, John Grieve, was a power-loom tuner in a Langholm tweed mill. I only remember seeing him once — shortly before he died, when I was about four years old. An alert 'jokey' little man, I remember he wore a transparent, butter-coloured waistcoat or linen jacket; and on the occasion I recall I caught him in the act of taking some medicine of a vivid red colour, and somehow or other got it into my childish head that he was drinking blood, and thought of him with horror — not unmixed with envy — for years afterwards. I resemble him physically (in point of leanness and agility, though I am considerably taller) and facially (a big brow and all the features squeezed into the lower half of my face); but when I was a lad the older folk used to tell me I took after him in another respect: 'just like your grandfather,' they used to say, 'aye amang the lassies.' As boys my brother and I wore the Graham tartan. Our mother was Elizabeth Graham. If my father's people were millworkers in the little Border burghs, my mother's people were agricultural workers. My alignment from as early as I can remember was almost wholly on the side of the industrial workers and not the rural people. I have never had anything but hatred and opposition for deproletarianising and back-to-the-land schemes; my faith has always been in the industrial workers and the growth of the third factor between man and nature — the machine. But even as a boy, from the steadings and cottages of my mother's folk and their neighbours in Wauchope and Eskdalemuir and Middlebie and Dalbeattie and Tundergarth, I drew the assurance that I felt and understood the spirit of Scotland and the Scottish folk in no common measure, and that that made it possible that I would in due course become a great national poet of Scotland. My mother's people lie in the queer old churchyard of Crowdieknowe in the parish of Middlebie.

There was certainly nothing 'lowering', in Lawrence's sense of the word, in Border life when I was a boy. Langholm was full of genial ruffians like the employer to whom, communist though I am, I look back with the utmost relish, who, after carefully instructing a workman whom he was sending up Westerkirk way as to what he was to do, ended: 'and just call in when you come back and I'll gie you the sack!' Border life was raw, vigorous, rich, bawdy, and the true test of my own work is the measure in which it has recaptured something of that unquenchable humour, biting satire, profound wisdom cloaked in bantering gaiety, and the wealth of mad humour, with not a trace of whimsy, in the general leaping, light-hearted, reckless assault upon the conventions of dull respectability.

My first introduction to my native land was when my mother wrapped me well in a Shetland shawl and took me to the door to see — but, alas, my infant eyesight could not carry so far, nor if it could have seen would my infant brain have understood — the most unusual sight of the Esk frozen over so hard that carts and horses could go upon it for twenty miles as upon a road and the whole adult population were out skating upon it all day, and by the light of great bonfires at night. That, I think, has not happened since — nor anything approaching it.

These were indeed the champagne days — these long enchanted days on the Esk, the Wauchope and the Ewes — and the thought of them today remains as intoxicating as they must have been in actual fact all those years ago. I have been 'mad about Scotland' ever since.

There were scores upon scores of animals and birds I know far better than I now know the domestic cat, which is the only specimen of the 'lower animals' of which I see much. My eyes may, perhaps, still seek out and recognise and appreciate a dozen or so wild flowers in the course of a year, but my memory recalls — with a freshness and a fullness of detail with which such living specimens cannot vie at all — hundreds I have not seen for over thirty years. My poetry is full of these memories: of a clump of mimulus 'shining like a dog's eyes with all the world a bone'; of the quick changes in the Esk that in a little stretch would far outrun all the divers thoughts of man since time began; of the way in which, as boys, with bits of looking-glass, we used to make the sun jump round about us. Above all, when I think of my boyhood, my chief impression is of the amazing wealth of colour. A love of colour has been one of the most salient characteristics of Scots poetry down to the best work of our contemporary poets, and I have celebrated it again and again in my own work.

Many great baskets of blaeberries I gathered on the hills round Langholm. Then there were the little hard black cranberries, and — less easy to gather since they grow in swampy places — the speckled cranberries, but above all, in the Langfall and other woods in the extensive policies of the Duke of Buccleuch, there were great stretches of wild raspberry, the fruit of which the public were allowed to pick, and many a splendid 'boiling of jam' I gathered there — gathering more than the raw material of jam, too.

I would come cycling back into Langholm down the Wauchope road with a pillowslipful of crab-apples (as at other times a basket of plovers' eggs) on my carrier; and again there was the Scrog Nut wood, shaking its bunches of nuts like clenched fists in the windy sunlight. I have nowhere seen loveliness so intense and so diverse crowded into so small a place. Langholm presents the manifold and multiform grandeur and delight of Scotland in miniature — as if quickened and thrown into high relief by the proximity of England.

There is a place at Langholm called the Curly Snake where a winding path coils up through a copse till it reaches the level whence, after passing through a field or two, it runs into the splendid woods of the Langfall. It has always haunted my imagination and has probably constituted itself as the ground-plan of my mind, just as the place called the Nook of the Night Paths in Gribe-Shov, the great forest north of Hillerod, haunted Kierkegaard's.

My boyhood was an incredibly happy one. Langholm was indeed — and presumably still is — a wonderful place to be a boy in.

Scotland is not generally regarded as a land flowing with milk and honey. Nevertheless, it can do so more frequently than is commonly understood. It certainly did so in my boyhood — with a bountifulness so inexhaustible that it has supplied all my subsequent poetry with a tremendous wealth of sensuous satisfaction, a teeming gratitude of reminiscence. I still have an immense reservoir to draw upon. My earliest impressions are of an almost tropical luxuriance of nature — of great forests, of honey-scented heather hills, and moorlands infinitely rich in little-appreciated beauties of flowering, of animal and insect life, of subtle relationships of water and light, and of a multitude of rivers, each with its distinct music.

Hugh MacDiarmid

Rejection

The burn divides Brieston, in respect of its armies — the Barracks Boys north and west of the burn; the Quay Boys south and east.

The legions drilled, one at the old Castle behind the Quay, and the other at the Barracks. Their swords were laths which the luggage steamer brought in bundles for Toddle Peter, slater and plasterer, himself a lath of a man.

The Captain of the Quay army had little appearance of a warrior, being small, thin-faced, pale, meagre in look, long-haired. His eyes were arresting: quick and sharp, they burned with internal fires. The spey-wife, whose husband, a MacCann from Ardmarkie, had deserted her and three children, and who made a living by selling cockles gathered in West Loch Brieston to Gillespie, observed the boy's eyes upon her as she counted her cockles in the store.

"He's got an eye like a traivellin' rat," she said to Gillespie, with one of MacCann's Irish oaths.

"A chip o' the auld block," Gillespie answered.

The boy, secretly pleased, from that moment practised the battery of his eyes in drilling and in fighting, because he had an itch to excel.

Gillespie was at the back of the store searching for a bag to hold the cockles, and the boy heard the cockle-wife sigh as she straightened her back. She saw compassion in his eyes.

"Ay! Tam's taen up wi' another wumman in Ardmarkie, an' the ault mear's left to bear the burden." She told him to be good to his mother. Another sorrow was added to the boy's life. He was finding

that in the world there is much cruelty and heartache, and because
he could not analyse the causes of things, and his lively imagination
fed superficially on what he saw, he wasted an enormous amount of
pity, and was tortured in the silence of his breast. Only last week
he had suffered in another fashion. On his way to school he had
been cajoled into his father's slaughter-house. It was a back yard
littered with empty boxes and straw behind MacCalman's Lane
where Gillespie housed the country vans. Big Jumbo the butcher
was standing in the midst of the yard lighting a blackened cutty, his
hairy arms naked and rusty with gore. Having lit his pipe he led out
from the shed a famished beast, brick-red, with fallen flanks, and
broken kneed. Its coat was muddy, its tail worn, its horns stumps
— "one of Gillespie's beasts." It stumbled and stopped, sniffing
among the straw, and was dragged forward by a rope twisted about
its stubby horns. Suddenly it cried. It was not a bellow, not a bleat,
but a half-human cry, as if knowledge of its doom had come upon
it. It was trailed forward with its fore-knees raking the ground. The
bovine wail reached the heart of the boy, who in that moment recal-
ling what he had read in the Bible — "He can send legions of
angels" — prayed silently for these angels of flame to come and
blast this devil, who, coolly smoking, was trussing up the beast's
feet. It lay on its flanks, its cheek flat on the straw, the weight of
its head pressing on the stubbed horn. The great brown eyes, the
boy imagined, were looking into his with a liquid sob of fear. They
gnawed him in mute appeal; they were as darkened windows out of
which gloomed the horror of a great gulf of darkness. The muddied
flank, with the hollow in the side, so pitiably shrunken, was heaving and falling with deep pants, and the tail whisking feebly, like
the hand of a little child beating gently as it falls asleep. The boy
wanted to cry out for mercy; it was his father's cow, let the butcher
spare it. But there was a crowd gathered. He was afraid of crowds,
afraid they would see his quivering body.

"Any one like to try his hand wi' the hammer?" this fiend was
saying; "a tap is a' she needs."

As the boy turned his eyes away from the terrified innocence at
his feet, he felt something hard thrust into his hand, and looking
down saw the blackened polished haft of the slender hammer.

"Here, young 'un; now's the time to learn."

He felt petrified: the haft dropped weakly from his hand.

"No muckle o' Gillespa' aboot you." The boy blushed at the
insolence. The butcher spat in his hands; and Eoghan, Gillespie's

son, turned his head away and closed his eyes. He heard a dull thud. When he opened them again a black moist muzzle pointed skywards, and a glaze like thin grey mud was gathering over the brown eyes. Something beautiful had been ruthlessly stamped out there. A flame of anger surged over him. Big Jumbo was bending over the dying beast. Running up to him Eoghan swung his leg viciously, and blindly kicking the butcher on the ankle, turned and fled through the yard. As he gained the entrance gate he felt the air suddenly blow icily cold about his cheek, and almost instantaneously the hammer-head crashed on the gable wall in front of him. With his blood on fire now he swerved, and picking up the hammer fled down MacCalman's Lane, past the Bank, and through the Square to the breast-wall, where, planting his feet with his back to the sea, and whirling the hammer around his head as he had seen athletes do at the Regatta Sports, he swung it out in a flying curve into the Harbour. A thrill went through him at the "plout" with which it took the sea, and his eyes danced at the jet of foam it flung up. Lust and cruelty, rapine and crime, were buried in the cool oblivion of the cleansing water, which closed down over the horror of pain, darkness, and death which he had seen through the fathomless windows of a cow's eyes.

At four o'clock he crept home quaking with his bundle of books. At the tea-hour Gillespie stood tweaking his ear.

"Let him be, Gillespie," pleaded his mother.

Gillespie frowned on her. "I'm no' goin' to alloo such wastery."

The boy made no external sign that he was suffering even when he thought his father would tear the ear from his head. His thin face turned the colour of clay.

Gillespie suddenly pushed him violently against a chair. "Ye'll tak' to the wulks every day the school comes out, an' on Setturdays, till ye mak' up the price o' the hammer."

The boy, devouring his mother's face with his eyes, felt himself strangling for the pain that he saw there. He made no answer to his father.

"Do ye hear me, Eoghan?"

"Ay."

"Weel, keep guid mind o't. Lonen's no deid when you're leevin'; gang noo an' greet behind your mother's bratty."

"I winna greet for anything ye can do," the boy shouted, and bolted from the kitchen.

J. McDougall Hay, *Gillespie*

The Dying Outlaw

"Kenneth," said the old outlaw, "hear the last words of the sire of thy father. A Saxon soldier and Allan of the Red-hand left this camp within these few hours, to travel to the country of Caberfae. Pursue them as the bloodhound pursues the hurt deer — swim the lake — climb the mountain — thread the forest — tarry not until you join them;" and then the countenance of the lad darkened as his grandfather spoke, and he laid his hand upon a knife which stuck in the thong of leather that confined his scanty plaid. "No!" said the old man; "it is not by thy hand he must fall. They will ask the news from the camp — say to them that Annot Lyle of the Harp is discovered to be the daughter of Duncan of Ardenvohr; that the Thane of Menteith is to wed her before the priest; and that you are sent to bid guests to the bridal. Tarry not their answer, but vanish like the lightning when the black cloud swallows it. And now depart, beloved son of my best beloved! I shall never more see thy face, nor hear the light sound of thy footstep — yet tarry an instant and hear my last charge. Remember the fate of our race, and quit not the ancient manners of the Children of the Mist. We are now a struggling handful, driven from every vale by the sword of every clan, who rule in the possessions where their forefathers hewed the wood and drew the water for ours. But in the thicket of the wilderness, and in the midst of the mountain, Kenneth, son of Eracht, keep thou unsoiled the freedom which I leave thee as a birthright. Barter it not, neither for the rich garment, nor for the stone roof, nor for the covered board, nor for the couch of down — on the rock or in the valley, in abundance or in famine — in the leafy summer and in the days of the iron winter — Son of the Mist! Be free as thy forefathers. Own no lord — receive no law — take no hire — give no stipend — build no hut — enclose no pasture — sow no grain; let the deer of the mountain be thy flocks and herds — if these fail thee, prey upon the goods of our oppressors — of the Saxons, and of such Gaels as are Saxons in their souls, valuing flocks and herds more than honour and freedom. Well for us that they do so — it affords the broader scope for our revenge. Remember those who have done kindness to our race, and pay their services with thy blood, should the hour require it. If a MacIan should come to thee with the head of the King's son in his hand, shelter him, though the avenging army of the father were behind him: for in Glencoe and Ardnamurchan we have dwelt in peace in the years that have gone by. The sons of Diarmid — the race of Darnlinvarach — the riders of Menteith — my curse on thy head, Child of the Mist, if thou spare one of those names when the time shall offer for cutting them off! and it will come anon, for their own swords shall devour each other, and those who are scattered shall fly to the Mist, and perish by its children. Once more, begone — shake the dust from thy feet against the habitations of men, whether banded together for peace or war. Farewell, beloved! and mayst thou die like thy forefathers, ere infirmity, disease, or age shall break thy spirit — Begone! begone! — live free — requite kindness — avenge the injuries of thy race!

The young savage stooped and kissed the brow of his dying parent; but, accustomed from infancy to suppress every exterior sign of emotion, he parted without tear or adieu, and was soon beyond the limits of Montrose's camp.

Sir Walter Scott, A Legend of Montrose

An Outcast

An aesthete, as well as its humanitarian owner, would have been shocked had Mr. Fisher's pet tiger wandered into Donaldson's Court. There its sleek skin, indigenous to jungle striped with sun and shadow, would have been shamed, and its fastidious paws polluted, by the garbage, filth, and overflow from broken privies. The splendour and beauty of the great beast would have been extinguished. In the same way, of course, it could be and often was objected that the more intricate, more fragile, and diviner beauty of the human body and mind was also shamed and polluted by such surroundings. But the humans had the advantage in that, being domiciled there for generations, they had undergone a debasement that softened the contrast. Newly-born babies in their prams, if washed, looked pathetically alien there; but in a short time, in two years or less, they had begun to acquire the characteristics which would enable them to survive amidst that dirt and savagery, but which naturally detracted a great deal from their original beauty. By manhood or womanhood they were as irretrievably adapted to their environment as the tiger to his. Hence aesthetes, humanitarians, moralists, and politicians, whilst still appreciating the tragedy, had it presented to them in a tolerable manner. Slumdom was hideous; but then the people who lived there were slum-dwellers.

On a wet afternoon two days after Mr. Forbes had made his vow, through the pend that led into Donaldson's Court, walked one of its inhabitants, distinguishable from most by his bright, wary, uncommitted eyes. He was Tom Curdie. In one pocket he had a letter from Forbes addressed to his mother although she could hardly read, and in another an apple lifted from a box outside a fruiterer's; this was for his brother Alec who had been off school that day through illness.

There was another inhabitant in the pend. An old black cat crouched in a hole against the wall, sheltering from rain and cruelties. It seemed afraid to close its eyes, and kept shivering as if in a nightmare of gigantic rats.

It had been kicked out by someone. Soon it would be found dead and its carcase swung by the tail by boys to make girls scream, before being tossed into some dustbin where the scavengers would discover it with oaths of outrage.

Tom went over, squatted, and, heedless of the scabs visible under its fur, stroked it. Suspicious of kindness, it mewed in misery at being too weak to slink away. He did not speak either to reassure or sympathise. Pity was never shown by him, only comradeship. For any creature whom he accepted as his comrade he would lie, steal, or suffer. This old cat was such a comrade. Recognising its hunger, and having only the apple reserved for Alec, he did not know what to do. Then, biting off a piece, he placed it under the cat's mouth. It mewed and sniffed, but did not eat. He knew that his presence, his human smell threatening treachery and cruelty put it off. He rose up, therefore, and padded out into the rain. There he looked back. The cat, not much liking apple, was nevertheless eating. He smiled in approval. Never to whine; to accept what came; to wait for better; to take what you could; to let no one, not even yourself, know how near to giving in you were: these were his principles by which he lived, and he honoured them in this old dying cat.

To reach his house, two storeys up, he had to climb a common stair wet with overflow from a privy. A stench of damp, decay, and urine, lay sour and thick on the air. He was passed by an old man, snivelling and squeaking, whose face looked like an apple out of which several bites had been taken. He was nearly blind. It was his custom to swing a blow at any person passing him, and when he missed, as he usually did, he broke into a horrible weeping and struck at himself. He drank methylated spirits and melted boot polish, and was crazy.

Tom easily dodged aside, without laughing, as some did, or swearing, like others. He gazed after the sobbing old man without fear, anger, or disgust. There were many such persons in the Court and the surrounding tenements. He knew them and their vices and despairs. He passed no judgment, but they were not his comrades. They had all long ago given in, and wanted him to give in, too.

It was Alec who opened the door. As soon as he saw Tom he began to whimper. He had a large sore at the side of his mouth, and looked ill.

Apparently not heeding the self-piteous whines of his brother, Tom entered the single-roomed house. No one else was there. His mother, with his half-sister of three, was out visiting; she would be drinking beer and playing cards.

Alec had been alone in the house for three hours; now he followed his brother about, as plaintive and possessive as a kitten.

'Did you bring me onything?' he asked. 'You said you would.'

Tom handed him the apple.

'I don't like aipples very much,' whined Alec.

'It's good for you.'

'There's a bite oot o' it.'

'I wanted to see if it was sweet.'

'Is it sweet?'

'Aye.'

Alec took a bite. 'It's no' very sweet,' he grumbled. 'Did you steal it, Tom?'

'I took it.'

'Shoogle says taking's juist the same as stealing.'

Shoogle was their foster-father. Imposed on him as an infant, the nickname had come to be used even by his mother, and now his three-year-old daughter lisped it. He worked in a rope factory.

'Shoogle's feart for you, Tom.'

Alec hee-hee'd at that astonishing fear inspired by his brother who was smaller even than Shoogle and not so strong.

'Will I read a comic to you?' asked Tom.

Alec agreed eagerly; he could not read himself well enough to enjoy it.

They sat side-by-side on a chair whose stuffing and springs were visible. Soon Alec was laughing as his brother read about the antics of the characters in the comic. But Tom's own mind was only partly on what he was reading. He was also wondering what Forbes's true reason was for so strange an invitation. The teacher had spoken about good food, fresh air, and scenery; he had said they would do Tom good, physically and morally. Tom had understood very well what he had meant, but he could not see what Forbes hoped to get out of it. He knew that Forbes was supposed to be conceited and rather stupid, and that other teachers laughed at him behind his back. Was this invitation then just an act of conceit and stupidity? Or was Forbes really trying to be kind?

Once before Tom had been befriended by a teacher. It was in the Primary. Miss McIntosh, who was always bothering him with kindness, one day brought clothes for him; they had belonged to her young brother. Tom had accepted them, but he had taken them straight after school to a junkshop where the man had given him ninepence for them. Next morning, when Miss McIntosh had whispered why he was not wearing them, he had announced, loudly so that all the class would hear, what he had done with them. He had expected her to strike him with her hand or the strap; indeed, he had wanted her to. Instead she had just stood and stared at him, with tears in her eyes. She had not reported him to Mr. Black the headmaster. He had been nine then. Even now he could not forgive her for her pity. She had come nearest to coaxing him to give in.

Forbes was different: he could be laughed at. Besides, it was more likely that Forbes was offering to take him just to show off, to prove that he was better than the other teachers who would never think of taking with them a boy from Donaldson's Court. From many things Forbes had said in class, and from overhearing remarks passed by other teachers, Tom knew that the fat English master was conceited about his championing of people oppressed, such as slaves, boy chimney sweeps, women in mines, foxes hunted by hounds, boys severely strapped, and children living in slums. He would hold up a lesson to display his indignation at those oppressions. It was always an opportunity for some boys to read comics under their desks, or do next day's Latin exercise, or just doze. One of the commonest charges against Forbes by his pupils was that he wasted such a lot of time.

Tom knew very well that the majority of children were far more fortunate than he, but he had never envied them. Envy, like pity, was not in his creed. What he hoped to do or to become was apart altogether from what others did or became. To have been envious would have been to become involved and so weakened. His success, if ever it came, must owe nothing to anyone. So far he had preserved this lonely independence. Not even Alec, or Peerie Whitehouse and Chick Mackie, the two members of his gang, had been allowed to violate it. Shame had no breach in him: he had none, neither for himself nor for others. For instance, he knew that the mothers of the other boys in his class wore hats and silk stockings and did not get drunk. His own mother, on the contrary, wore her hair lank and lousy about her ears and sometimes over her eyes. Usually her legs were bare, mottled with dirt and varicose veins. She was fat like Forbes, with her belly swollen and her breasts shrunken, so that when she stripped to the waist to wash at the sink she did not look like a woman at all. When she spoke she slavered, so that every three or four words she had to suck in and swallow. Several of her teeth were missing, making those oral noises of fatuous sorrow and mirth all the louder. She often made foolish jokes and wept silly tears, especially when drunk; then she would lament the early days of her marriage before her two sons were born, and before fat, like a curse from heaven, had fallen upon her, driving away her man who had disliked fat, even on ham. Such was his mother, but Tom was not ashamed of her; neither was he fond or proud. She was a phenomenon he had known since birth. All he owed her was life, a gift shared by lice and rats. If she gave him an order which he thought foolish, inconvenient, or unnecessary, he would ignore it; as he would any appeal which it did not suit him to answer. She might wheedle, threaten, or cry she was going to commit suicide, it made no difference. Since the age of five he had pleased himself.

As for her bedmate, Shoogle Kemp, he was of no account.

That left Molly his half-sister, who was the only creature Tom feared; not because of her vicious little nails which could cause suppurating scratches, or her shrieking rages, but because she had once been a chuckling baby whom he had liked to push about in a battered pram.

He was diverted from these thoughts by Alec tugging peevishly at his arm.

"You're no' reading, Tom. Whit's up?"

"I was thinking."

"Whit aboot, Tom?"

It was then that the idea came into Tom's mind. Merely to go with Forbes to Towellan would be purposeless. Why not then take

Alec with him, and Peerie and Chick? They could sleep in the gang's tent. No shopkeeper there would know them. There would be farms with henhouses, fields with potatoes, the sea with fish. It would pay Forbes back.

But some money would be needed.

Robin Jenkins, *The Changeling*

Confrontation

As Hugh went on alone he felt confident and happy. For a few steps he ran, but the bag bumped and slewed round, nearly choking him. He would drop it presently when no one would see that he had to take a rest.

With loud chatter, some boys loomed round a bend. The Seabrae boys going home from football. Hugh walked calmly, like a man.

"Ha! ha! here's Hugh!" cried Rid Jock, son of Magnus.

The other boys also cried the same thing.

Hugh's manner was quiet. "Coming home from the football?" he asked.

"Why didn't you come? You said you'd come in the morning."

"I said I might," corrected Hugh mildly.

"You didn't. You said you would," corrected Jock positively.

"Yes, I heard you," piped little Dannie. And the others piped the same thing. 'I heard you say it! I heard you say it!"

"You didn't," said Hugh.

"Am I a liar?" asked Jock.

"You are, if you say that," said Hugh.

"Oh, I am, am I?" asked Jock. "Ho! ho! I'm a liar, am I?"

"You are," repeated Hugh, who had not yet raised his voice.

"Say that again," threatened Jock loudly.

Hugh, ignoring him, took a step on. Immediately his bag was tugged from behind. He swung round. Dannie scampered off, and from a safe distance shouted, "Does your mother know you're out?"

The other boys laughed loudly as they backed a step or two.

"His mother wouldn't let him to the football — in case he would fall!" All the boys laughed and jeered, repeating the final insult in sing-song. Hugh made no move. This inaction at once frightened and goaded them.

It was nothing that this very morning at school he had been on ,easy terms with them all. A roving homeward band had happened on a solitary doing something different from themselves, and their minds immediately became excited and cruel. Moreover, this solitary did not belong to Seabrae. He was a bee from another hive, a gull from another rock.

"Mamma's pet!" shouted a voice, and encouraged by the sally, Jock suddenly hit Hugh's unprotected face.

In the same instant the bag dropped and Hugh sprang at him. Self-consciousness got blotted out in fury. He saw nothing but the blur of Jock's face and lashed at it. Nothing would stop him so long as he could see and stand. His fury was destructive and primal. Blows rained on his own face. They merely made his fury red. Something had to give way. It was Jock, because Jock, though a good fighter, could not be possessed by a demon.

The little band with their leader broke and fled, shouting insults. Hugh leapt after Jock and tripped him as he ran, so that Jock fell headlong on his face. Hugh sprang on his back. Jock covered up his face and squawked his fear and rage. Hugh, pinning down the neck with his left hand, walloped the head with his right, shouting, "Get up! get up!"

Some of the other boys came back.

"Get off him!" they yelled threateningly. He ignored them. One boy tried to kick him. He leapt from Jock's back. A stone hit him on the breast. All the boys, including Jock, retreated. Stones fell around him, where he stood stock still on the middle of the road, quivering.

"Never mind; you blooded his nose!" said a consoling voice in the distance to Jock, whose face was damaged more by the gravel of the road than by Hugh's fists.

Automatically Hugh's fingers came up to his nose and touched there the slime of blood. He peered at the reddened tips. He now felt the blood running down his upper lip. It was also trying to slide down the back of his throat. The taste of it was salty and sticky in his mouth. Drops fell on the back of his hand. They had been falling upon the breast of his jersey. He pressed his knuckles against his nose, and his throat swallowed a lot of the blood before he could stop it. He held his head back, and then the blood went down his throat freely. You always have to hold your head back when your nose is bleeding. It's the only way to stop it. But you should always at the same time hold something cold to the back of your neck.

He stumbled over the edge of the road holding his head back, over the grassy bank and down to the edge of the river or burn. He was not thinking of anything but the blood. All his flesh was trembling. He was not really frightened of the blood. Here he was with his nose bleeding after a fight, and he was calmly stretching backwards against the bank and pressing a cold stone to the nape of his neck.

He lay quite still, his eyes to the pale stars. There were not many; one here and there. The sky was very very far away. It was quiet, too. It was high and dark, and the stars were lonely in it. He had to swallow every now and then. The blood was stopping. It was strange and lonely on your back, looking at the stars, down by the burn. He was doing all this by himself. He had fought Jock — the whole of them — and sent them flying. His teeth closed and his face went cold. His face felt like a cold wedge and his eyes glittered relentlessly.

One could weep through sheer rage. But not even that would he do again. No matter what happened to him in the world, never would he cry more. He had conquered — and sent them flying. Everyone knew that the fight with Jock had to take place, and now it was all over and he was lying here. His nose had been blooded, but – that often happened at a fight. He had seen it happen once with grown men. But when a grown man had his nose blooded, he did not stop fighting for that. Only boys stopped fighting when they saw blood. Once Fred Munro was winning a fight when someone cried that his nose was bleeding. When Fred saw that it was bleeding, he started howling and weeping and running away. Everybody laughed. Fred was only eleven past, of course, but still .... And once a piper's nose had started bleeding. It was at that Games. The blood kept trickling down on to his white front. Everyone was silent, looking at the trickling blood with twisted faces. Then the judge had gone forward and stopped him. The piper was astonished, and did not know his nose had been bleeding. He got third prize. Some said he got it for consolation. But Hector the Roadman, who was the finest piper in the district, said that the man had shown by the bit he had played that he was the best piper there. "I knew it by the way he tuned his pipes," said Hector. So it was good of the judge to give him third prize. He needn't have given it to him. It was fine, therefore, of the judge that he did.

It was nothing to have your nose blooded — once it had happened. They couldn't crow over him for that. He had sent them all flying. The whole of them. He fought them with his nose bleeding — and sent them flying. Swallowing, he found that there was nothing more to swallow. He waited for a little longer to make sure, then very carefully sat up with a finger lightly against his nostrils, waiting. No blood came. He breathed slowly, mouth shut. The inside of his nose was cold and stiff. Still keeping his head tilted, he went to the water and very carefully began washing himself. They would not need to know at home.

Voices came from the road, and footsteps. Listening, he remembered his bag of mussels. It must be right in the way. Lightly he climbed up the bank. A man and a woman were close at hand. The black hump of the bag was lying by the edge of the road where the man was walking. Unless the man was looking where he was going . . . . The woman laughed. It was the voice of his sister Grace. At that moment the man tripped on the bag and kept himself from falling flat by splaying his hands on the road. "Blast it!" he said. As he rubbed his hands free of gravel he kicked the bag. "Who left this lying here?"

Hugh went forward a step or two uncertainly. You could hardly make out anyone's face clearly, because it was so dark.

"So it's your bag, you little devil!" said the man.

Hugh knew who he was, but he did not know Hugh, who was waiting for his sister to say something.

"You shouldn't leave a bag lying like that, you know," was what his sister said. Her voice was not angry. Yet its gracious reproof was curiously cold. In a moment Hugh understood that she was not going to know him, because she was with this particular man.

"Oh, it's nothing," the man said. "But don't you do it again!" He chuckled. His voice was rather kind, after the surprise of the first moment.

"Yes, but it was silly of him leaving it there," said his sister as they moved off. The reproof was still in her voice, but it was laughing and kind under the man's.

"Oh, I don't know . . . ." The man's chuckling excuses faded out.

Tears welled up into Hugh's eyes where he stood. His jaws were shut tight, but the tears brimmed over and ran one after another down his cheeks. His eyes floated, his sight grew blurred. Still he made no move. Behind his clenched teeth his throat choked — and swallowed tears that were hot and raw. His misery became too much for him. It rose up and up in a swelling spout, drowning even the clenched teeth. Stumbling, blinded, he dragged the bag off the roadside and threw himself down over the crest of the bank. Crushing his face into the grass, he sobbed harshly. His shoulders heaved, his body writhed. He was defeated utterly.

The agony of the defeat passed into a profound misery as his sobs died down and his eyes grew hot and burned. It was not what had been said to him — that was nothing; it was the two who had said it.

Not now that he minded them. He cared for nothing now. Nothing in the world mattered. There was no good doing anything more. He would lie out here in the dark. Lie for hours until the cold froze him, until he grew stiff perhaps and dead. They would find the bag — and then him lying here dead. His father would be amazed at seeing the bent body lying with its white dead face on the grass. His look would grow wild and scared, and his voice would come quick and queer, as he stooped and picked up the body. Then his mother would give a little husky scream that was like something clutching at your heart, and the scream would go searching round like a moan, as she herself went searching round, not being able to stand still. Oh-h-h-h . . .

One or two tears came again and he swallowed them quietly. But not before he had seen, behind his mother, the white scared face of his sister Grace, and the wondering face, serious and a little scared too, of the man who had been with her.

He sat up and slowly rubbed his eyes with the back of his hand, faintly embarrassed by his vision. The crushing of his hand against his eyes was like the half-shy crushing of himself away from his embarrassment. It had hardly been right to see his mother like that. Only once had he heard her cry — quick and husky-sharp as from a stab by a knife — going on, twisting on itself, as though the knife wouldn't come out.

He was a little ashamed of thinking it over again. A judgment might come on him. And not only on him.

Slowly he looked around at the deepening night, at the uncaring sky. Nothing cared. What if a judgment did come on him? Well — let it!

But in his defiance was a suppressed fear. His teeth chittered and he shivered all over. If it wasn't that his father was waiting for the mussels, he mightn't go home at all.

With a dour grace he got to his feet. A hand struck against the tangles in his pocket, but he ignored them. The memory of the fight came upon him with satisfaction but no warmth. He felt cold towards the boys concerned, cold and hostile. He would not get hot with fury if he was fighting Jock again. He would fight him, cold as death. He would meet him with a smile of disdain. Jock — who was Jock? To think that he had often trembled in secret at the thought of the unavoidable fight with him! He could always beat Jock now. And Jock was thirteen and a half.

He shouldered the bag with such violence that he staggered, and then went evenly on his way.

Neil M. Gunn, *Morning Tide*

Suggestions for Further Reading

Neil Gunn's work offers a rich source of insights into the world of the child. In particular, *Highland River* and *The Silver Darlings* can be recommended.

Robin Jenkins, too, has much to offer apart from *The Changeling* — for example *Gaily Sings the Lark* and *Guests of War*.

Charles Dickens was not a Scot, of course, but many of his novels contain portraits of children: *Oliver Twist, Great Expectations, The Old Curiosity Shop*, to name but a few. To modern taste, his idealised portrayals are perhaps too cloying, but the early parts of *David Copperfield*, based partly on his own experience, still ring true.

Still away from Scotland, James Joyce's *A Portrait of the Artist as a Young Man* shows that childhood in Dublin in the late nineteenth century was not different in kind from what is described here.

Molly Weir's autobiographical books describing her early years in Glasgow (particularly *Shoes Were for Sunday*) present a realistic description of childhood among the tenements.

Jock Tamson's Bairns, a collection of autobiographical essays edited by Trevor Royle, includes many fascinating reminiscences, one of which, by Liz Lochhead, appears in a later section of this book. Liz Lochhead in her collection *Memo for Spring* has several poems which touch on childhood.

William Wordsworth's long poem, *Ode on the Intimations of Immortality*, also can offer the discerning reader many fruitful insights into the nature of childhood experience.

2   Family and Home

The six passages in this section all examine aspects of family life. Although pictured at different periods and in different circumstances, some of the pleasures and tensions of family life presented here will be recognisable across barriers of time and class.

The first passage comes from *Mr. Alfred M.A.* by George Friel (1972). Because of trouble caused by her mother and her brother Gerald, Senga has lost the friendship of her school friend Rose. Unhappy at this and at her mother's favouritism towards Gerald, she retaliates against them both.

Following this passage comes another short one, from Lewis Grassic Gibbon's *Smeddum*. Here favouritism is again in evidence, but Mistress Menzies displays a different attitude towards her children from that she shows to her husband. The passage gives a portrait of a woman — wife and mother — with a passion for work. The assessment of this particular family situation is made either by local gossip or by the reader.

The third short passage is taken from Cliff Hanley's *Dancing in the Streets*. A happier family, this, that appears cohesive and harmonious. The atmosphere is one of warmth and protection, and the youngest Hanley is not isolated like Senga. Douglas Gifford, writing about Hanley (in *Scottish Writers and Writing*, ed. Wilson, The Ramsay Head Press, 1977), says he 'genuinely touches the real humour of working class life.'

It is a far cry from the east end of more-or-less modern Glasgow to family life in the Gaelic-speaking Highlands at the beginning of the nineteenth century, when the notorious Clearances took place. This is what Iain Crichton Smith, a modern poet, novelist and dramatist who writes in both English and Gaelic, describes for us in the extract presented here from his novel *Consider the Lilies*. An old widow, Mrs. Scott, threatened with eviction, reflects on her own family upbringing, her brief marriage, and the home she made for her son.

The next passage comes from Robert Louis Stevenson's *Weir of Hermiston* and illustrates how neglect does not always have to be of a physical nature. Here we find a father/son relationship where each seems unable to communicate with the other: an austere relationship, with little outward sign of parental or filial affection.

In contrast to this passage is the final one, taken from Donald Cameron's *The Field of Sighing*. This describes a country childhood, and a wartime one, with a sense of contentment evident in this family's home life that contrasts with the bleakness of some of the others included here. The general events of the 'real' world begin to impinge on the boy's particular and personal consciousness as he grows and develops.

Different families, different homes. Looking at these passages makes development to adulthood appear less accidental than these lines might suggest:

'Do you know who made you?'
'Nobody as I knows on,' said the child, with a short laugh.... 'I 'spect I growed.'

Favoured Son

Still a bitterness stayed with Senga. She had sued for peace with Rose, but she waged a civil war at home. The cause of it was never alluded to by either side, though both knew what the other was thinking. The week she was in disgrace with Rose she went on a modified hunger-strike to annoy her mother. It comforted her to refuse food from an adverse party. She never missed a chance to be sarcastic. She had come to have a sharp tongue, and she used it to cut those who wounded her. Perhaps it was guilt kept her mother from using heavy artillery to discourage these bayonet-charges. Anyway she got away with them. Even Gerald had nothing much to say for a time. Senga didn't enjoy her victories. They were too easy. She wanted stiffer opposition, then she would really show what vengeance could be.

She criticised Gerald's clothes and the shoes he wore. She derided his haircut, even his walk. She mocked the way he spoke. His enunciation was poor. He swallowed half his words, he used a glottal stop, and he spoke so quickly that every sentence came over like one enormous agglutination of syllables. It pleased Senga to make him repeat what he said the few times he dared speak to her.

"Pardon? What did you say?"

She gave a demonstration of clear speech in her very question.

"We'll have less of your airs, madam," said her mother. "Don't you try and make a monkey out of Gerald."

"If people can't speak properly they can't expect to be understood," said Senga.

"Feudcleanyurears," said Gerald.

"Pardon," said Senga.

"Do you think there's nothing wrong with the way you speak?" said her mother, crushing her with tone and glare, ironing handkerchiefs for Gerald. "You should hear yourself sometimes. But we're not good enough for you. Oh no! You're that superior."

"To him and his pals anyway," said Senga. She was loaded with venom, ready to strike.

"There's nothing wrong with Gerald's pals," said her mother.

"Not much," said Senga. "Crowd of apes."

"Hoosapes?" said Gerald.

"And he's in a gang," Senga tossed at her mother.

"Hoosnagang?" Gerald shouted.

"You are," Senga turned, shouting back.

"Oh, hold your tongue, you little besom," said her mother. "You're aye nagging. What shirt do you want to wear tomorrow, Gerald?"

"Mayella," said Gerald.

"You don't like the truth," said Senga. "Either of you."

"Gerald sees his friends after a hard day's work," said her mother. She flattened the last handkerchief, stacked the lot. "They go out and enjoy themselves, and you choose to call it a gang."

"Because so it is," said Senga. "He's in a gang all right. I'm telling you. You'll find out."

"What gang?" her mother demanded. Voice raised. Angry. "You let your imagination run away with you, you do."

"Just ask him," said Senga. "Ask him what they call his gang."

"Amnoinanygang," said Gerald.

He rushed across the kitchen with fist raised to thump his sister as he used to do.

George Friel, *Mr. Alfred M.A.*

Mother

She'd had nine of a family in her time, Mistress Menzies, and brought the nine of them up, forbye — some near by the scruff of the neck, you would say. They were sniftering and weakly, two-

three of the bairns, sniftering in their cradles to get into their
coffins; but she'd shake them to life, and dose them with salts and
feed them up till they couldn't but live. And she'd plonk one down
— finishing the wiping of the creature's neb or the unco dosing of
an ill bit stomach or the binding of a broken head — with a look
on her face as much as to say *Die on me now and see what you'll
get!*

Big-boned she was by her fortieth year, like a big roan mare, and
If ever she was bonny 'twas in Noah's time, Jock Menzies, her
eldest son would say. She'd reddish hair and a high, skeugh nose,
and a hand that skelped her way through life; and if ever a soul had
seen her at rest when the dark was done and the day was come he'd
died of the shock and never let on.

For from morn till night she was at it, work, work, on that ill bit
croft that sloped to the sea. When there wasn't a mist on the cold,
stone parks there was more than likely the wheep of the rain,
wheeling and dripping in from the sea that soughed and plashed by
the land's stiff edge. Kinneff lay north, and at night in the south, if
the sky was clear on the gloaming's edge, you'd see in the sky the
Bervie lights come suddenly lit, far and away, with the quiet about
you as you stood and looked, nothing to hear but a sea-bird's cry.

But feint the much time to look or to listen had Margaret Menzies of Tocherty toun. Day blinked and Meg did the same, and was
out, up out of her bed, and about the house, making the porridge
and rousting the bairns, and out to the byre to milk the three kye,
the morning growing out in the east and a wind like a hail of
knives from the hills. Syne back to the kitchen again she would be,
and catch Jock, her eldest, a clour in the lug that he hadn't roused
up his sisters and brothers; and rouse them herself, and feed them
and scold, pull up their breeks and straighten their frocks, and polish their shoes and set their caps straight. *Off you get and see
you're not late*, she would cry, *and see you behave yourselves at
the school. And tell the Dominie I'll be down the night to ask him
what the mischief he meant by leathering Jeannie and her not well.*

They'd cry *Ay, Mother*, and go trotting away, a fair flock of the
creatures, their faces red-scoured. Her own as red, like a meikle
roan mare's, Meg'd turn at the door and go prancing in; and then at
last, by the closet-bed, lean over and shake her man half-awake.
Come on, then, Willie, it's time you were up.

And he'd groan and say *Is't?* and crawl out at last, a little bit
thing like a weasel, Will Menzies, though some said that weasels

were decent beside him. He was drinking himself into the grave, folk said, as coarse a little brute as you'd meet, bone-lazy forbye, and as sly as sin. Rampageous and ill with her tongue though she was, you couldn't but pity a woman like Meg tied up for life to a thing like THAT. But she'd more than a soft side still to the creature, she'd half-skelp the backside from any of the bairns she found in the telling of a small bit lie; but when Menzies would come painching in of a noon and groan that he was fair tashed of his work, he'd mended all the ley fence that day and he doubted he'd need to be off to his bed — when he'd told her that and had ta'en to the blankets, and maybe in less than the space of an hour she'd hold out for the kye and see that he'd lied, the fence neither mended nor letten a-be, she'd just purse up her meikle wide mouth and say nothing, her eyes with a glint as though she half-laughed. And when he came home drunken from a mart she'd shoo the children out of the room, and take off his clothes and put him to bed, with an extra nip to keep off a chill.

Lewis Grassic Gibbon, *Smeddum*

Early Memories

A terrible thing the drink, and no defence for us against it except the Band of Hope chant... "honour my father and my mother and refrain from strong drink as a beverage..." But it wasn't the drink that led us into crime. We couldn't afford any kind of steady drinking on a halfpenny a week pocket money. We just turned naturally to law-breaking out of the badness of our hearts. Even I, essentially a sensitive, pure-minded keelie, was a hog for bad company. Something, I don't know, some original flaw in my character hurled me into the arms of any fast set who were up to something no good if it looked easy enough.

So maybe it's just as well we flitted. That old Hanley wanderlust was stirring in the family, and shortly after my fifth birthday I found myself in the middle of the delirious excitement of a flitting.

Everybody else seemed to be busy hauling chairs and ornaments about, but in the middle of this Mary found time to wash my face. A few minutes later Johanne noticed me under somebody's feet and for want of anything better to do with me she washed my face too

— "You want to look nice for the new house," she said. That was all right with me. When nobody bothered with me for ten minutes or so I went back to the jawbox and ran the tap over my head. I wanted to make a proper job of the thing while I was at it. The flitting was abandoned while half the team pulled me out from under the tap and dried me off, but nobody was much upset. One more little thing couldn't make any difference at a Hanley flitting. Soon afterwards I was hurried, wrapped like a mummy to keep the pneumonia out, downstairs, across Gallowgate and upstairs again. We had moved from the second floor flat on the south side to the second floor flat directly facing on the north side. We had begun to carve our way up through the amorphous social strata of the city, for there's no doubt that from the new windows, the old building was patently on the wrong side of the tracks. Instead of a long thin lobby the new house had a square hall; and a bath, in a dim dark room off the hall shaped like a three-decker coffin. We had a big, opulent front parlour too, with a vast oval table supported in a tentative manner by a three-legged curly mahogany thing. It was a splendid table with a heavy chenille mat draped over it, and it took us years to get rid of it — in the end, a friend and I carried it between us to a school jumble sale, dumped it in a corner and denied all connexion with it.

There was more room in the new parlour too for my musical experiments. No Hanley was ever entirely unmusical. We could all at least sing, and usually did, sometimes in opposition, though Flora was the only one who showed the distressing mannerism of joining in somebody else's song note-perfectly but in a different key, almost the most disquieting sound ever made. Harry even had a saxophone at the time, and there was a harmonium in the parlour I could practise on. It had to be pedalled all the time and I was too short to reach the pedals from a chair, but I could cling with the left hand to the underside of the keyboard to support my body, pedal like mad and play with my right hand. I don't know which I liked more — doing that or taking up the same position at the sewing machine and pedalling it. There were so many of us in the house that we had tea in two relays, and my finger was wandering idly over the mighty keys one evening as I waited for the kids' shift to start when Mary heard me and cried in amaze:

'Look at that! He's playing on the black notes as well!' And me only five.

We had a party in that house too, the first I ever remember in our own house. There was a lot of home baking and dishes of almonds and sweets on the oval table, and some neighbouring children came in and we roasted chestnuts at the fire. It was a warm, friendly feeling, and I still remember the feeling and the bright red of the big fire and everybody laughing, although I can't think what else we did.

Clifford Hanley, *Dancing in the Streets*

A Widow Remembers

As Mrs Scott lay half-dozing in the chair pictures swam in front of her closed eyes. Most were pictures from her youth for as one grows older one remembers most clearly the distant days, childhood and girlhood and wifehood. This particular evening there seemed to be more pictures than before. Pictures of her father, her mother, her husband. Not all were pleasant: many were not. But for some reason they emerged with a more prolific clarity. She remembered, for instance, the nights they used to dance to the music of the melodeon. This was before her mother had grown old and crabbed and half mad with fear. After all, her mother hadn't always been like that. She used to wear sweet-smelling clothes and aprons covered with flour. She used to stamp blankets in the white water — gaily as a girl. And there were the days they used to pick potatoes, the treasures of the earth, the white ones and the sliced rainbow-coloured ones.

Voices came and went behind her head in front of the flickering fire. And music, the music of the melodeon. The melodeon was played for the dances at night at the end of the road, when the red autumn moon was ripe in the sky, the moon of "the ripening of the barley". She could hear the sudden whoops of the dancers as they danced the eightsome reel, one of the commonest dances. At that time she would have been fifteen or sixteen. Surely there was no harm in the dancing? What other pleasures did they have, except the telling of stories in each other's houses, the ceilidhs? Her mother had put a stop to all that — the dances, the ceilidhs. No one could tell how she had become possessed by the fear of hell in her latter days. During her early years she had been on the whole bright and cheerful. People often became melancholy in their old age.

Towards the end of her life her mother read the Bible all the time, looking for signs and sayings. When her eyes had become too bad for reading she herself had to read chapter after chapter to her. This was the only way she could get her to sleep. For this reason she knew long snatches of the Bible by heart, all about Joseph and his brothers, and Ruth and Naomi, and Saul and David.

Her other sister had cleared off to get married, had left her to bear the burden alone. Not that she ever had any intention of laying down the burden. In the Highlands one got used to bearing burdens. In the morning she would milk the cow, bake bread, and make crowdie. Later she would make the dinner. After that she would clean the house and sometimes her mother in her shawl would come and sit in the chair by the fire. Latterly this didn't happen, and she would sometimes shout instructions to her from the bedroom. In the evening she would sit and listen to her mother's stories, disjointed bits and pieces which were difficult to follow since the characters would jump generations with no warning, and anyway she herself only half-listened. How could one pay attention to all that, endlessly? Her mother liked to talk, simply for the sake of talking. Sometimes a neighbour might come in the evening — Big Betty, for instance, jovial and ribald, and deaf enough for her to speak loudly to everyone, as if it were they who couldn't hear her.

At night she herself would lie in bed, listening to the music of the accordion and waiting for her mother's death. Her father had died some years before. One day he had come in from the field. Blood had begun to pour from his nose, after he had bent to take his boots off. The blood had poured down his beard and right down his jersey in an absolute river. He had taken to his bed, badly frightened, and had never risen from it. On a cold winter's night of a cold moon he had died. By that time his nose had turned thin and blue and his voice had become very gentle.

That left her with her mother who had died when she herself was twenty-nine. On the night of the day of her mother's burial, she went to bed and slept for twenty-four hours. The day had whirled round her, still lying in her bed, illuminating her pale hair and thin face. When she awoke and got up the house was empty. For hours she sat there waiting to hear her mother's call from the other room. No one came. Yet her mother's presence was absolutely palpable in the house. At night she was frightened to go to bed lest in the empty house at midnight she would see her mother in her nightgown standing furiously by the bedside. But she realised she must stay in the house all night and not be frightened. After the first night she relaxed more, though never completely.

Emerging into the day was like entering a hurtful world where the light hurt her eyes. In those first days she ate little and sometimes did without food altogether. She walked like a convalescent over an earth heaving at her feet. However, she was fortunate that it was the time for cutting the peats. Alasdair came over to do the cutting for her. He was four years younger than she, with a small head and moustache, and quick movements. She couldn't of course pay him in money but would herself help at carrying the peats home for Alasdair's family. She couldn't do the cutting herself: that was a job for the men.

Alasdair was for ever singing. In the morning with the ascent of the lark his voice could be heard raised in song all over the village. There had always been an adventurous quality about him, and he was given to the practical jokes common to all small villages. Like, for instance, the time he had driven Big Murdo's cart away in the middle of the night at Halloween and no one could find it. Later it appeared as mysteriously as it had disappeared.

It was strange and joyful to have someone young in the house again. She made him a good breakfast before he went off cheerily to cut the peats in his boots and neat navy blue dungarees, his hair sleeked back, his face with the cultivated moustache very bright. He ate well but rather hurriedly, she thought, not with the heavy deliberation of her father.

She followed him with her eyes as he strode over the moor in the early summer morning, heavy with dew. For some reason she thought of the nests of larks which they used to find quite easily near the tracks made by the carts: and of the yellow beaks of the nestlings. She heard herself singing as she made dinner for him. She went to the door to see him coming and was surprised to find him home earlier than she had expected. He had wrapped a handkerchief round his head because it was so hot — the sweat had been falling into his eyes — and clowned a little. She poured out cold water for him in a basin and took pleasure in watching him splash it on his head before he sat down to his dinner. She had put on her good dress, the black one that showed her pale hair and pale face.

At dinner time there was a little constraint but she piled more and more potatoes on his plate. The house seemed full of sun which laid squares of light on the floor and made yellow tracks across his hair. They talked of Norah who was getting married. He himself had two unmarried sisters in a small house. As well as that, his father and mother were alive.

She heard him saying, eating as he did so, "I suppose you've had a bad time," and longed to tell him about it but didn't because of her pride. Anyway, he was eating. He had very generous impulses. Sometimes she caught him looking around the house and down to the fields. After his dinner he took out his pipe and began to smoke. Again she thought he was unlike her father, who smoked very slowly. Alasdair smoked in quick puffs.

"It's going to be a good year for the crops," he said. It was indeed. After he had smoked a little he went off again, walking very quickly, wanting to be finished.

She had seen him often in church sitting up perfectly straight in his seat, always looking neat and perfectly aware of it. He laughed a lot when he got outside and made jokes.

In the evening she found herself thinking of him, for the house seemed even emptier than before, cold and silent. She ate very little, being on her own, and wondered what it would be like to be married. Not that this was the first time she had wondered this. But to be married was a happiness beyond her aspiration.

She looked in the mirror at her fair hair and pale face. She certainly wasn't ugly and the signs of suffering endured had made her face interesting and mature. No, she wasn't ugly but had he noticed that? Later he came with the "crew" to take the peats home. On that day there was much laughter as they gathered round the cart pitching the peats up. He — who else? — stacked them quickly and neatly, his hair stirring a little in the breeze, his face darkened by the peat dust. Big Betty made a few remarks about them which were received with much friendly laughter. She couldn't remember any of the remarks now, but she remembered the happy atmosphere of the day. They sat by the peat-stack dashing the midges out of their eyes. Their long skirts trailed the ground and their brows were wet and prickly with sweat. Little Iain was allowed to walk beside the horse and looked very important as he did so. They indulged their children, these women, but could be severe on them too.

As they made the dinner at her house for the "crew" she was told by Big Betty: "You two should get married."

She blushed but didn't say anything.

"What's the use of you sitting in this empty house alone?" said

Betty. "A house should have a man in it. A man to cut the peats and the corn, and to thatch the house."

True, it wasn't easy for a single woman. But what could she do? She couldn't go up to him and say: "Will you marry me?" He was always the life and soul of the party, singing as he caught the peats and composing spontaneous little poems. He looked all fire and energy as he stood there, high above everyone else, loving it in the sunshine.

After that they found themselves increasingly coming from church together. She liked going to church and always had done. Now that she was "free" she liked going more than ever. It was some time before she realised that one of the reasons why she liked it so much was because she wanted to get away from the empty house.

She knew, however, that Alasdair wasn't very interested in religion or prayer. He just liked going because he could put on his best suit and meet people. They would walk home together in the quiet of the evening. In the distance she could see the misty blue hills. She could hear the quiet murmur of the waters. It was all like a picture. One night he saw her home and standing by the door, his hat in his hand, he asked her to marry him.

"I'm getting to twenty-five, now," he said. "It's time I settled down." His eyes glanced at her sparklingly and restlessly. And he laughed gaily. She thought he laughed rather much for such a weighty matter, but at the same time she judged that he might be nervous. She had never been so happy in her life.

When she got inside she danced about the room. She picked up the picture of her father, gazed at it and laid it down again. Her heart was brimming like a cup which could hardly contain its happiness. Yet at the same time she knew she would never be so happy again.

That night she cleaned the whole house from top to bottom. She found at the bottom of an old chest a picture of her father and mother, her mother seated, her father standing behind her. His hands were big and he had a beard. She looked placid, her hands folded in her lap. Her smile was uncertain and hovering. The picture was brown with age. She put it away, then found a book which told of her father's sailing days:

"Conduct — Good."
"Conduct — Very Good."
"Conduct — Excellent."

The writing of this was blurred and the cover dog-eared. She found a ring belonging to her mother and a Bible, in the front of which were written various names:

"Georgina Scott — born 1701"
"Mary Scott — born 1730"

She even found her mother's bridal dress crushed under the heavy Bible, which was in double columns and had no pictures in it. She liked pictures in Bibles. It was a very big Bible. One could never dream of carrying it to church. It was too heavy for that.

She also found an old navy blue cap with braid along the edges. Funny how she had never examined the chest while her parents were alive. And there was a piece of carved wood which seemed to be a leg of something. At first she couldn't understand what it was, then realised it was one of the legs of a cradle. She left it lying on the top. After a while she closed the lid of the chest but cleaned the dust from it.

Then she made the bed all over again and changed the clothes. She cleaned the grandfather clock, and was interrupted once by a terrific boom which seemed to shake its old body to the very bones. She scrubbed the table and the chairs and the wood of the bed. She cleaned the bedroom window. All the while she hummed to herself. She even went into the barn and spoke to the cow, putting her arm around its neck while it gazed back at her with large liquid eyes. No, animals couldn't know such happiness.

All the night she tossed and turned and couldn't sleep. The house seemed to be full of vague moonlight presences. She thought of getting up and going for a walk but thought of her mother and didn't. The night was calm and the moon shone warmly all by itself in the empty sky. In the early hours of the morning she was still awake, as if waiting for a message from her parents. But there was none, and near dawn she fell asleep, to wake when the sun awoke her. She felt like a bird, the heart throbbing in her breast so that she had to put her hand on it to steady it.

But she didn't go and tell anyone of her happiness, for her nature was secretive. So she hoarded it like a pail full of sparkling water in a dark corner.

They were married and after that life began.

And she began to find out about a totally new person, one who had not grown with her, one who came from outside, from a similar yet totally different world. He was not at all like her father. He

was not deliberate and grave. He lived, unlike herself, from
moment to moment, flashing like water in the sunlight or like tears.
It was she who had to think what future they would have. He never
seemed to think of it at all.

But she found out soon enough that the dark years had cast their
shadow on her. In those long nights, when her mother fitfully
slept, she had taken to brooding about the future. She had wondered what would happen to her if, for instance, her mother lived
for another ten years. She had seen herself forever alone in an
empty house. And she had been, though not consciously, preparing
for those years. For instance, she spent little on herself and saved
all the money she could. She had trained herself too to save her
emotions. When her mother cried out of the dark, and in terrifying
moments called on her own mother, she had trained herself to rise
slowly and calmly from her bed. Sometimes she did not rise at all.
For what could she do? In self-defence she let a part of herself die.
How otherwise would she have survived?

But her husband had been playing football or going to dances
when she was struggling with these nightmares. Even yet if he had
a chance he would play with the "boys". The truth was she was
much older than he in suffering and her insight into the human
heart on the verge of madness. And in those days she was jealous
of him — jealous of his spontaneity and his forgetfulness, of his
seemingly motiveless swings from grave to gay and back again.
She found him as uncomplicated and natural as a child.

She thought marriage demanded a greater sense of responsibility
than this. She was, for instance, meticulous about the cleanliness of
the house. She wouldn't say anything directly to him when he
threw his boots under the table and flung his stained jersey on the
table. But her silences were meant to be disapproving. He would
stay in bed later than she liked, and go to it at night very late. She
had made a practice of going to bed at ten o'clock at night or earlier, for what was there to stay up for? Nevertheless, what had
begun as a reaction against emptiness remained as a habit which
had taken her to its heart.

When the child came he was very fond of him, and very proud.
He would lift young Iain to his shoulders and take him along in his
woollen dress to show to their neighbour, Donald Gunn. He would
boast, telling Donald how clever Iain was in comparison with
young Murdo Gunn. This, of course, was only friendly rivalry.
Nevertheless she disapproved of such excesses. And in those days

she was convinced that she was in the right, he in the wrong.

He would coddle the child but she was much sterner. Inevitably, the child preferred him to her. This rankled with her for she considered it very unfair. She was thinking more of its long-term interests. That was why as he grew up she didn't want him to run into danger, why she limited his expeditions, why she read to him from the Bible — while her husband would play football with him.

The first time she knew that something was seriously wrong was when Alasdair came in drunk. She ignored him in cold fury but he did not wish to be ignored. He kicked the door shut and stood in the middle of the room shouting. She had never seen anyone drunk in the house before. It was a different Alasdair she was seeing, not the bright clown but an almost crazy red-eyed drooling half-maniac. That was the night he had taken her father's picture from the wall and thrown it across the room.

"Can't stand it any more," he was shouting endlessly. "Can't stand it."

She put his plate of porridge before him, not speaking and not knowing what to do.

"You hate everybody. You hate to see anybody enjoying themselves."

Silence.

"Even children. You hate to see children enjoying themselves."

Silence.

"Not going to put up with it." Then, in a grotesque imitation of her voice: "Boots by the fire."

In another imitation: "You don't know you were born . . ."

Then he collapsed into silence, leaning back against the chair while he muttered to himself over and over: "You hate everybody."

After he had repeated that for a long time he fell asleep, snoring. She went to bed and left him there.

In the morning he was very repentant and kept looking at her as if wishing that he could be forgiven. She made no reference to the events of the previous night. Inside herself she was thinking: I wish I could tell him it's all forgotten. I wish I could show him I don't care. But that part of herself had been burnt out and she had lost the power of being spontaneous. But was it her fault? Could he not see what she had suffered all these years? But of course he couldn't, he hadn't experienced these sufferings. It was impossible for him to understand, though his wary glances sometimes suggested that there was something to understand. After all, he had had no responsibilities. It wasn't in him to sacrifice himself as she had done. He would have been unable and possibly unwilling to do it. As she saw him playing with the child she sometimes wondered whether his way was not the best after all. Shortly afterwards she would put that out of her mind as if it were a devilish thought.

One day he came in and said: "I'm going to join the Army."

And she knew within herself that this was what he would do, that this was what his whole life had been leading up to. He was too restless to stay in the one place all his life. Too adventurous, too irresponsible. Too much of a little boy. She imagined him in his proper place all dressed up behind the pipes and drums, letting the crowds admire him, living in the moment. It had taken him a little time to discover his place but now that he had he would wish to leave her.

Her first instinct was to keep him at home, for her will was stronger than his. She could calculate, and attack him at his weakest point. She could keep on and on. He wouldn't be able to do this to her. She had the child to bring up. It wouldn't be easy. And she foresaw clearly that as soon as he left home he would to all intents and purposes forget about her and it, no matter how gaily and affectionately he played with it now.

When it came into his head he would write "a few lines". Perhaps he would see someone who reminded him of her, some black-gowned foreign woman, and then he would say, "I must write". But as for keeping her continually in his mind she couldn't expect that of him. He would become completely involved in his soldiery, in the glitter and glamour of war. He would move into the future like a sparkling river, completely careless, not worrying where he was going, not even realising that he was falling from level to level, bemused by the sudden flashes and the wayward innocent sounds. All this she knew, yet let him go.

On the appointed day they went along with one or two others to the recruiting table. The Duke made a short speech. She listened but wasn't deceived by it. What were these countries to her? And that man on the white horse — what did she care about him?

But she saw that to Alasdair the words were like a trumpet call. He saw new countries ahead of him, new adventures. He was like a child wanting to do things which he wasn't sure were quite right, and looking for justification from his elders and superiors. And here was the Duke justifying in weighty terms the game he wished to play. He would be helping to save his country. It never occurred to either of them to ask why the Duke couldn't go himself. Dukes had their own purposes, their own ways. It wasn't for the likes of them to wonder about that.

Her son was gazing wide-eyed at the proceedings. He would remember this as one of the important and colourful incidents from his childhood. And Alasdair was pointing everything out to him, the Duke, the clerk, the massive castle towering high with the flag flying from the tower. He was doing this as if he were a little boy himself. Which was exactly what he was, and why she had to let him go.

The night before he left she read a section out of the Bible to him. She insisted on that. She deliberated a long time on the section she would read. Finally, she decided on the part which says: "Put on the whole armour of righteousness". But she knew that at best he was only half-listening. The thought that he might be killed never even entered his head. For he lived in an eternal present.

She saw this more clearly when he dressed up in his tartan, when he put on his sword. He paraded up and down, laughing heartily, and allowed young Iain to play with the ribbons on his stockings. He wanted to be off, having forgotten his home already.

As she watched him go she knew with a flash of clairvoyance (what she would call 'second sight') that she would never see him again. She wanted to shout after him, to call him back, to say that it was in her power to change herself, that she would become young again, or die. But she didn't say anything for she knew that all that was impossible. She simply took Iain's hand in hers and watched Alasdair go. He waved gaily but already he had become posthumous. She found it strange that he did not understand this himself, and followed him with her mind to tell him about it. But he turned a bend in the road, and it was as if he had stepped out of her mind as well.

She returned to the house with Iain, whose small hand was cramped in her convulsively tightening one, shut the door, and washed him.

Before she went to bed that night she read many pages of the Bible.

And six months later she received the notification and took it to the elder's house, when she had studied it. He read it and after some time said: "I'm sorry."

She only answered: "He shouldn't have gone," and then went home.

In a strange way she became rather proud of him and framed the notice. But she often wondered where he had been buried — if he had been buried at all.

In the six months she had received two letters from him. She gathered that he was enjoying himself and there were references to old Nosey: "Old Nosey will show them." But she couldn't understand whom he was showing what and why; and why her husband was there at all, except to escape from home. Once or twice between the lines she thought she detected some homesickness and was pleased about it. But perhaps it hadn't been there at all, and she had only wanted to believe it. Or perhaps it was true and he had found life in the army harder than he'd expected. She felt that the second of the two letters was more sober, less gay, and was sorry about that. For being who he was it was better for him to be gay.

Her own life continued. She brought up the child, sent him to school, made clothes for him, dared to speak once or twice to the schoolmaster about him. But young Iain wasn't particularly clever. He would not be a minister or a teacher.

She and Big Betty, who was older than her, became friends. Sometimes she had to borrow money from Big Betty, but always paid it back. She didn't need much money. She could exist on very little. The worst year was when they had been given the meal. After that she had learned to expect no gifts from anyone. Her sister had offered to help her with discarded clothes from the boys, but she wouldn't accept them. She hadn't been a beggar at any time during her life and she wasn't going to start now. So she knitted all Iain's clothes, jersey, trousers, stockings.

The years passed, and she almost forgot about her husband long dead in Spain.

Iain Crichton Smith, *Consider the Lilies*

Father and Son

My Lord Justice-Clerk was known to many; the man Adam Weir perhaps to none. He had nothing to explain or to conceal; he sufficed wholly and silently to himself; and that part of our nature which goes out (too often with false coin) to acquire glory or love, seemed in him to be omitted. He did not try to be loved, he did not care to be; it is probable the very thought of it was a stranger to his mind. He was an admired lawyer, a highly unpopular judge; and he looked down upon those who were his inferiors in either distinction, who were lawyers of less grasp or judges not so much detested. In all the rest of his days and doings, not one trace of vanity appeared; and he went on through life with a mechanical movement, as of the unconscious, that was almost august.

He saw little of his son. In the childish maladies with which the boy was troubled, he would make daily inquiries and daily pay him a visit, entering the sick-room with a facetious and appalling countenance, letting off a few perfunctory jests, and going again swiftly, to the patient's relief. Once, a court holiday falling opportunely, my lord had his carriage and drove the child himself to Hermiston, the customary place of convalescence. It is conceivable he had been more than usually anxious, for that journey always remained in Archie's memory as a thing apart, his father having related to him from beginning to end, and with much detail, three authentic murder cases. Archie went the usual round of other Edinburgh boys, the High School and the College; and Hermiston looked on, or rather looked away, with scarce an affectation of interest in his progress. Daily, indeed, upon a signal after dinner, he was brought in, given nuts and a glass of port, regarded sardonically, sarcastically questioned. "Well, sir, and what have you done with your book to-day?" my lord might begin, and set him posers in law Latin. To a child just stumbling into Corderius, Papinian and Paul proved quite invincible. But papa had memory of no other. He was not harsh to the little scholar, having a vast fund of patience learned upon the bench, and was at no pains whether to conceal or to express his disappointment. "Well, ye have a long jaunt before ye yet!" he might observe, yawning, and fall back on his own thoughts (as like as not) until the time came for separation, and my lord would take the decanter and the glass, and be off to the back chamber looking on the Meadows, where he toiled on his cases till the hours were small. There was no 'fuller man' on the bench; his memory was marvellous, though wholly legal; if he had to 'advise' extempore, none did it better; yet there was none who more earnestly prepared. As he thus watched in the night, or sat at table and forgot the presence of his son, no doubt but he tasted deeply of recondite pleasures. To be wholly devoted to some intellectual

exercise is to have succeeded in life; and perhaps only in law and
the higher mathematics may this devotion be maintained, suffice to
itself without reaction, and find continual rewards without excitement. This atmosphere of his father's sterling industry was the best
of Archie's education. Assuredly it did not attract him; assuredly it
rather rebutted and depressed. Yet it was still present, unobserved
like the ticking of a clock, an arid ideal, a tasteless stimulant in the
boy's life.

But Hermiston was not all of one piece. He was, besides, a
mighty toper; he could sit at wine until the day dawned, and pass
directly from the table to the bench with a steady hand and a clear
head. Beyond the third bottle, he showed the plebeian in a larger
print; the low, gross accent, the low, foul mirth, grew broader and
commoner; he became less formidable, and infinitely more disgusting. Now, the boy had inherited from Jean Rutherford a shivering
delicacy, unequally mated with potential violence. In the playing-
fields, and amongst his own companions, he repaid a coarse expression with a blow; at his father's table (when the time came for him
to join these revels) he turned pale and sickened in silence. Of all
the guests whom he there encountered, he had toleration for only
one: David Keith Carnegie, Lord Glenalmond. Lord Glenalmond
was tall and emaciated, with long features and long delicate hands.
He was often compared with the statue of Forbes of Culloden in the
Parliament House; and his blue eye, at more than sixty, preserved
some of the fire of youth. His exquisite disparity with any of his
fellow-guests, his appearance as of an artist and an aristocrat
stranded in rude company, riveted the boy's attention; and as
curiosity and interest are the things in the world that are the most
immediately and certainly rewarded, Lord Glenalmond was
attracted to the boy.

"And so this is your son, Hermiston?" he asked, laying his hand
on Archie's shoulder. "He's getting a big lad."

"Hout!" said the gracious father, "just his mother over again —
daurna say boo to a goose!"

But the stranger retained the boy, talked to him, drew him out,
found in him a taste for letters, and a fine, ardent, modest, youthful
soul; and encouraged him to be a visitor on Sunday evenings in his
bare, cold, lonely dining-room, where he sat and read in the isola-
tion of a bachelor grown old in refinement. The beautiful gentleness
and grace of the old judge, and the delicacy of his person,
thoughts, and language, spoke to Archie's heart in its own tongue.

He conceived the ambition to be such another; and, when the day came for him to choose a profession, it was in emulation of Lord Glenalmond, not of Lord Hermiston, that he chose the Bar. Hermiston looked on at this friendship with some secret pride, but openly with the intolerance of scorn. He scarce lost an opportunity to put them down with a rough jape; and, to say truth, it was not difficult, for they were neither of them quick. He had a word of contempt for the whole crowd of poets, painters, fiddlers, and their admirers, the bastard race of amateurs, which was continually on his lips. "Signor Feedle-eerie!" he would say. "O, for Goad's sake, no more of the Signor!"

"You and my father are great friends, are you not?" asked Archie once.

"There is no man that I more respect, Archie," replied Lord Glenalmond. "He is two things of price. He is a great lawyer, and he is upright as the day."

"You and he are so different," said the boy, his eyes dwelling on those of his old friend, like a lover's on his mistress's.

"Indeed so," replied the judge; "very different. And so I fear are you and he. Yet I would like it very ill if my young friend were to misjudge his father. He has all the Roman virtues: Cato and Brutus were such; I think a son's heart might well be proud of such an ancestry of one."

"And I would sooner· he were a plaided herd," cried Archie, with sudden bitterness.

"And that is neither very wise, nor I believe entirely true," returned Glenalmond. "Before you are done you will find some of these expressions rise on you like a remorse. They are merely literary and decorative; they do not aptly express your thought, nor is your thought clearly apprehended, and no doubt your father (if he were here) would say, 'Signor Feedle-eerie!'"

With the infinitely delicate sense of youth, Archie avoided the subject from that hour. It was perhaps a pity. Had he but talked — talked freely — let himself gush out in words (the way youth loves to do and should), there might have been no tale to write upon the Weirs of Hermiston. But the shadow of a threat of ridicule sufficed; in the slight tartness of these words he read a prohibition; and it is likely that Glenalmond meant it so.

Besides the veteran, the boy was without confidant or friend. Serious and eager, he came through school and college, and moved among a crowd of the indifferent, in the seclusion of his shyness.

He grew up handsome, with an open, speaking countenance, with graceful, youthful ways; he was clever, he took prizes, he shone in the Speculative Society. It should seem he must become the centre of a crowd of friends; but something that was in part the delicacy of his mother, in part the austerity of his father, held him aloof from all. It is a fact, and a strange one, that among his contemporaries Hermiston's son was thought to be a chip of the old block. "You're a friend of Archie Weir's?" said one to Frank Innes; and Innes replied, with his usual flippancy and more than his usual insight: "I know Weir, but I never met Archie." No one had met Archie, a malady most incident to only sons. He flew his private signal, and none heeded it; it seemed he was abroad in a world from which the very hope of intimacy was banished; and he looked round about him on the concourse of his fellow-students, and forward to the trivial days and acquaintances that were to come, without hope or interest.

As time went on, the tough and rough old sinner felt himself drawn to the son of his loins and sole continuator of his new family, with softnesses of sentiment that he could hardly credit and was wholly impotent to express. With a face, voice, and manner trained through forty years to terrify and repel, Rhadamanthus may be great, but he will scarce be engaging. It is a fact that he tried to propitiate Archie, but a fact that cannot be too lightly taken; the attempt was so unconspicuously made, the failure so stoically supported. Sympathy is not due to these steadfast iron natures. If he failed to gain his son's friendship, or even his son's toleration, on he went up the great, bare staircase of his duty, uncheered and undepressed. There might have been more pleasure in his relations with Archie, so much he may have recognised at moments; but pleasure was a by-product of the singular chemistry of life, which only fools expected.

An idea of Archie's attitude, since we are all grown up and have forgotten the days of our youth, it is more difficult to convey. He made no attempt whatsoever to understand the man with whom he dined and breakfasted. Parsimony of pain, glut of pleasure, these are the two alternating ends of youth; and Archie was of the parsimonious. The wind blew cold out of a certain quarter — he turned his back upon it; stayed as little as was possible in his father's presence; and when there, averted his eyes as much as was decent from his father's face. The lamp shone for many hundred days upon these two at table — my lord, ruddy, gloomy, and unreverend,

Archie with a potential brightness that was always dimmed and veil-
ed in that society; and there were not, perhaps, in Christendom two
men more radically strangers. The father, with a grand simplicity,
either spoke of what interested himself, or maintained an unaffected
silence. The son turned in his head for some topic that should be
quite safe, that would spare him fresh evidences either of my lord's
inherent grossness or of the innocence of his inhumanity; treading
gingerly the ways of intercourse, like a lady gathering up her skirts
in a by-path. If he made a mistake, and my lord began to abound in
matter of offence, Archie drew himself up, his brow grew dark, his
share of the talk expired; but my lord would faithfully and cheerfully continue to pour out the worst of himself before his silent and
offended son.

"Well, it's a poor hert that never rejoices!" he would say, at the
conclusion of such a nightmare interview. "But I must get to my
plewstilts." And he would seclude himself as usual in the back
room, and Archie go forth into the night and the city quivering with
animosity and scorn.

Robert Louis Stevenson, Weir of Hermiston

Growing

When Eddie had finally gone and the war settled down as a perma-
nent feature in our lives, a strange peace at last came over me. The
restlessness and discontent had left as mysteriously as they had
come. I no longer found fault with everything my grandmother said
or did. The longing to roam the countryside after a hard day on the
hill, left me also. And then the letter-writing began to lose its interest. I hated the idea of unknown censors and the destruction
wrought by giggling girls in Glasgow whose scissors cut out whole
passages of letters from my pen-friends in the forces.

Our experience of the war was a consciousness of it rather than
direct experience. Although by law we could no longer kill our own
lambs for home and Big House consumption and Herself disliked
old meat from the town, we nevertheless always had a good table.
During the handlings a gimmer or lamb occasionally met with an
accident. Instead of leaving the injured beasts to die my father killed them in spite of Whitehall's edicts, which made no provision
for such incidents.

With most of her visitors gone to the war and her gamekeeper unable to cover much of the hill, Florence of Arabia approved of my father helping himself to game on the understanding that half of the bag went down to the Big House. Herself preferred wildfowl to game birds because, coming from Eilean a'Cathmara, she had grown up with such food. We never lacked the poet's 'greasy victuals', especially mallard and teal.

Like the Saturday ceilidh it was a tradition in autumn and winter for Black Fergus's father and mine to go off shooting once a week. Fergus and I often hid and watched them go down the frosty shore where a flight of widgeon might be silhouetted in the moonlight, the sound of wing-strokes louder than our own heart-beats as we lay motionless trying to overhear the men's talk. We believed our fathers indulged in the same, only worse, bawdy stories as ourselves, and were disappointed when Sandy only complained about wool prices or a dirty load brought by the coal boat. My father's voice could not be easily picked up because he spoke too quietly. And in any case he would be listening to the shore cries rather than to Sandy. He had a habit of suddenly stopping whatever he might be doing in order to catch sounds, usually of birds, which his sharp ears detected and which nobody else heard until he drew attention to them.

Certain families in the township used the war as an excuse for wide-scale slaughter of gannets and puffins. Although once upon a time they had almost been Eilean a'Cathmara's staple diet, my father saw the danger of such a heavy toll and did not allow them at Blarosnich. On the other hand he was helpless to stop the gamekeeper collecting plovers' and gulls' eggs for the Big House. Alec turned his skill to fishing because he never felt comfortable with a gun.

Again no doubt because of her island childhood, Herself loved fish from local waters and scorned the wood-smoky orange kippers from the travelling grocer which were a favourite with me. In all my life I never saw anybody enjoy eating in the way that my grandmother, even as a very old lady, relished a big cock crab. With eyes bright and her mouth moist with anticipation she broke open a strong claw and set to with enviable gusto. Black Fergus's cairns never descended a fox-den full of cubs with such ado as that hoary octogenarian cleared the last scrap of white meat from the crab shell.

A dish of oysters set her singing. After such a tasty morsel Herself might break out in a spontaneous bar or two of a song used by old fishermen as they trailed their dredging nets:

> *The herring loves the merry moonlight*
> *The mackerel loves the wind.*
> *But the oyster loves the dredging song*
> *Because he comes of gentle kind.*

Besides five score or more of hens we always kept ducks and turkeys and a big gaggle of geese for ourselves and for the Big House. But the meat which appeared most frequently on our wartime table was rabbit and venison. However irritated I may have been in my adolescence with Herself when she asked me to bring in herbs from the hill, nobody appreciated them more than I did when they were sewed up with stuffing in a young rabbit deliciously roasting in the oven. And as a family we had always preferred venison to beef. Our deer herds seemed to have grown larger perhaps simply because they were joined by those escaping the wholesale slaughter further along the coast.

Since the sound of Mirren churning could still be heard at Blarosnich we had our own butter and cheese. She washed and dressed the butter, moulded on top with patterns of harebells or a blackbird. Long before drowning in the hidden skerries off Eilean a 'Cathmara, my great-grandfather made the two butter printers and the meal-ark out of driftwood. Decades of use had hardly worn the patterns away and I always admired the carver's skill in the flowers and the bird and their complicated designs round the borders. In company with a needlework picture of the twenty-third Psalm, the big wooden ark and butter moulds were the only things left from Herself's old home, except for the ruined house itself.

Although our orchard produced good apples and pears we preferred wild damsons from the far park hedge and thought these better than the plump cultivated plums. There were red and black currant bushes, gooseberries and raspberry canes whose fruit went in almost equal proportions, one half to us and the other to the birds in spite of scarecrows and Mirren's efforts at placing rattling pieces of tin to keep the pirates away. Responsibility for part of this daylight robbery could be laid at the door of our own domestic hens who concentrated their raids on the strawberry beds which my father specially cared for. What fruit remained went into jams and pickles. I cannot think of life at Blarosnich without remembering the preserving pans and spoonfuls of jam cooling on saucers so that Herself could taste them.

Old-fashioned jams like angelica and rhubarb, gooseberry and elder-flower jelly, pear marmalade, marrow and ginger were my favourites. Herself sampled the sweet jams as she made them but preferred such savouries as gooseberry relish, apple and raisin chutney, sweet pickled onions, spiced crab-apples, red cabbage, and pickled nasturtium seeds.

Many of our visitors disliked going down the garden to the 'wee house' because six hives stood among the plum and apple trees. The bees belonged to Herself's province and she loved working with them as much as we enjoyed the honey. The dark, autumn sections were best, each waxy cell full of a harvest at whose secrets we could only guess. Herself's straw hat with its long black veil hanging from the brim lived in the hall next to The Captain's yachting cap and was no less sacred, for the bee-boater had once been his too.

Never once in my boyhood years had we to buy vegetables except for planting-bundles or occasionally a new brand of seed potatoes. Often we had more than enough for our own needs and sold the surplus to the township and the Big House. And more than half the jam made was given away or converted into hot drinks during winter. Surrounded by such proof of our Maker's bounty, we had little patience with ration books except for tea and sugar.

Sugar brought the war into Herself's awareness. Her secret fear was not like Mirren's of German paratroopers jumping out at her from the blackcurrant bushes as she made her way down to the 'wee-house', but of the police coming to search her bedroom. Under the bed and under the stairs, on top of the wardrobe, in the old castle commode-chest and in a number of large biscuit tins, supplies of sugar lay concealed. A hoarder by nature, my grandmother had bought it all up before rationing began, thinking that no sugar would be obtainable at all. I think she lived with another fear that Teacher or Mirren would talk in the township about these hoards and that gossip would reach police ears. But since my grandmother never took sugar in her tea and a large part of the jam for which she saved the sugar went to the township anyway, her worry was probably groundless.

Herself did the actual preserving but Teacher and Mirren were responsible for much of the gathering. My father, in a kind of tradition, always brought the blaeberries home. Mirren could hardly be classed as a maid in our household because she principally worked out-of-doors with calves and fowl, gathering and washing eggs, and spent most of the fine weather in the hay parks. Teacher also took her turn in the meadows and on retiring from teaching she became a sort of unpaid but much loved housekeeper. We continued to call her Teacher.

Until I went to London, coffee for me meant a black syrup in a bottle whose label showed a soldier being served by an Indian servant. Camp coffee was never used at Blarosnich though we believed the township women drank nothing else. Aunt Jessie in London had superior ideas and her kitchen equipment included a coffee mill which ground up beans from Brazil. The results, I considered, did not taste so good as the coffee Herself produced from the dandelion roots she dug up in the autumn and dried at the back of the fireplace along with the rabbit skins and damp socks. But there could be no substitute in our house for real tea despite the numerous herbal brews Herself indulged in. The few ounces allowed each week were never enough and Mirren constantly engaged in bartering our homemade butter and jams to township people with large families of young children.

Except for these minor irritations, the war mostly passed us by. Its ragings seldom touched our isolated peninsula bordered on three sides by turbulent seas and rocky, inaccessible coasts. Even when billeting officers scoured the region looking at accommodation for evacuees from the bombed cities they went away without bothering to consider our desolate neighbourhood. Herself said little about this but I think she was disappointed when they ignored us. Perhaps a conflict went on inside her breast for we knew well enough the horror she expressed of everything to do with cities. She imagined our way of life being upset by gin-slogging mothers and bed-wetting, bug-ridden children. She gave my father strict instructions that at the first sign of evacuees arriving he was to take them at once to the fank for a thorough immersion in the sheep dipper. But none ever came. Our lane never saw the crocodiles of pathetic children. All the same we laughed at the stories about evacuees in other parts which entered every conversation. We liked to hear best of the outrages which took place in big castles like Balmoral or the Duke of Atholl's. We adored the plight of countesses and tweedy ladies like Florence of Arabia who were obliged to set up de-bugging stations and hang rows of mattresses to dry from their castle windows.

The war's comical inconveniences like drinking women from Glasgow and their bed-wetting offspring did not enter our lives. And even regulations such as the blackout did not bother us much. But there were moments when the war, even though far away, invaded our lives completely. Herself grew forgetful of feeding the hens. My father's hand lay on the tractor-wheel, his thoughts elsewhere. Alec became sad and never noticed that his pipe had gone out. No national tragedy affected us so much as the sinking of the *Royal Oak*. We recognised it as something profound in our lives, probably because it involved us in a personal loss.

Regularly every year my father announced that he intended going over to his cousin's farm in the Black Isle. He would take a holiday, he said, when the harvest was either finally gathered or finally abandoned and left to rot in the flooded fields. He never went. Something inevitably prevented him. I had never met the cousin's son who was only a few years my senior. When he went down on the *Royal Oak* I suddenly realized that not only had a family link been severed but what the war was meaning to lots of people every day.

When Herself came out to the barn and told my father the news she had just heard on the wireless an awful silence followed. My mother's death had not shrouded the Field of Sighing with such a sense of loss, though perhaps I had been too young to remember. Herself did not brood about her great-nephew's death only, but about all the sailors in the doomed ship. "Puir lads. Puir lads," she mumbled to herself for days afterwards. From the grave announcements on the wireless and afterwards in the papers we felt as if the great *Royal Oak* had been our only defence between the fox-like U-boats and our quiet Highland backwater. Now it had gone taking eight hundred lives with it in home waters just along the coast from where our hay still stood out in the wet parks.

We did not express our grief in words so much as in moods and in music. Although he practised on the chanter every week out in the woodshed, my father never played his pipes at a Saturday ceilidh when a pibroch master like the gamekeeper was there. But on the night we heard about the *Royal Oak* he finished work and marched slowly up and down the horse park playing laments, one after the other. The music blew sharply sad across the gathering darkness. I felt indescribably more miserable than at any other time I could remember. It seemed terrible to me that so many young men could all die at once. Our grief weighed oppressively and my father's pipes gave it voice. His laments wailed across Blarosnich for others besides the lost son of the Black Isle cousin. The reedy requiem rang out for all the hundreds of sailors, for all the shepherds and herders, young woodmen and old drovers who still had bad chests from being gassed in the First World War, the butcher boys from Plymouth and the window-cleaners from Birmingham, who had gone away to fight an enemy who, until now, had somehow seemed unreal to us. The outrages in Poland, the invasion of Russia, the fall of Paris, though terrible were distant and impersonal. But a feeling of insecurity and imminent danger came suddenly on us when we knew that a German submarine had slipped along our own Highland coast to torpedo the great battleship anchored at Scapa Flow. When the *Royal Oak* went down the war came closely home to the whitewashed walls of Blarosnich.

By the ceilidh on Saturday, Herself's melancholy had still not dispelled. She took up her harp more thoughtfully than usual. Then we heard once again the words the Lady of Clan Ranald used in the Caristone lament as she watched the homeward ship bearing a dead bride. We had heard the song so often before. But now new meaning and mournfulness imbued it. Overtones of my father's laments on the pipes ringing among the trees seemed to hover in Herself's song.

That night instead of getting straight into bed I took a pencil and paper. Somehow, I had to make my own lament for the terrible event which had cut so deeply into our peaceful round of life at Blarosnich. Without knowing how, I wrote a poem. That was the first of many and only odd lines of it come to me now out of that sad time.

Though I forgot most of my first poem, I never forgot the haunting vision in my mind of the great ship's decks crammed with faces like Black Fergus's, faces brown from hot suns and long starlit nights on watch. Pipes and harp could never be mine, and I turned to paper instead. Soon I began to write verse about Blarosnich and its changing seasons and about the long past which Alec's and Herself's tales had brought to life. I wrote about the wild animals and the birds on the hill. But none ever moved me like those first lines about the *Royal Oak*.

Donald Cameron, *The Field of Sighing*

Suggestions for Further Reading

There is a huge wealth of literature which deals with aspects of Family and Home. Some such texts are included in other sections of this book: for example, George Blake's *The Shipbuilders* and George Douglas's *The House with the Green Shutters*. There are also several other authors represented in the book who have other works which are particularly relevant: for example, George Friel — *The Boy Who Wanted Peace*; Lewis Grassic Gibbon — *Sunset Song*; Neil Gunn — *Highland River*; Cliff Hanley — *The Taste of Too Much*; Iain Crichton Smith — *The Last Summer*; Liz Lochhead — *Memo for Spring*.

Evelyn Cowan's *Spring Remembered* is a delightful book of reminiscences about a Jewish family upbringing in Scotland. A.J. Cronin's *Hatter's Castle* was an enormous public success when it first appeared in 1932, and is still worth reading. Much of Cronin's work is firmly based on his own experiences of growing up, studying medicine, and practising as a doctor, and thus there is a strongly realistic element in his work.

Two more recent novels have much of interest on this theme: Gordon Williams's *From Scenes Like These* and William McIlvanney's *Docherty*, set in Ayrshire and depicting with great accuracy the family relationships of the place and the time.

Finally, two Scottish poets may be mentioned in addition to Liz Lochhead. Stewart Conn, especially in his earlier poetry, is much concerned with family relationships. His collection *An Ear to the Ground* is particularly rich in such poems. Douglas Dunn, in his collection *Terry Street*, observes and comments on the way of life of the street's inhabitants.

3 People and Environments

'Not such a bad climate, really.' So wrote C.A. Oakley of Glasgow's weather, and he was right. Yet it remains true that Scottish people down the ages have had to convert a fairly hostile ambience into something habitable. Some parts of Scotland enjoy a pastoral luxury which is probably unexcelled in western Europe. As the old gentleman said, 'Paris is a richt, but Peebles for pleesure.' But not all Scotland is as comfortable as Peebles. Is it the struggle for life that their forebears had to put up that has made Scottish people what they are? The writers whose work now follows have given us, if they are true artists, characters who are human beings first and Scottish afterwards, yet one thing seems true — each character grows naturally out of the world he inhabits.

The first extract in this section comes from *The House with the Green Shutters* by George Douglas. Perhaps the best known feature of this novel is its cynicism; some would call it morbidity. The author himself wondered if he had put too much 'black' into the book, and it is difficult to find in it a major character who is not mutilated by some unamiable weakness or human wickedness and savagely ridiculed for it. And yet, an author who takes the trouble to know so much about cheating in cheese-making, or to picture for us the social-climbing wife tempted by the wares of the Scotch Cuddy — such an author cannot be without affection for his subject.

The second extract, from *Cloud Howe* by Lewis Grassic Gibbon, provides an example of environment used as a background to an episode. The shrewd cynicism and the recognition of human weakness occur here too, but the method is quite different from that of the author of *The House with the Green Shutters*, and so is the effect. *Cloud Howe* is the second novel in the trilogy *A Scots Quair*. Set for the most part in a semi-fictionalised Kincardineshire, it traces the effects on its characters of violent social change in the early twentieth century resulting from the First World War and other causes.

After *Cloud Howe* and its north-eastern setting comes an extract telling of an aspect of Glasgow life. It comes from *The Shipbuilders* by George Blake — one of the great Scottish novels of the 'hungry thirties'. Its atmosphere is thoroughly authentic, and its characters are firmly rooted in their surroundings.

The depression of the thirties gave way to the war years and the post-war beginnings of something like prosperity. In some parts of Scotland, however, particularly in the west, the prosperity was not immediately obvious. Liz Lochhead, a contemporary poet, reminisces here on her upbringing in industrial Lanarkshire, and in doing so recaptures for us the environment in which she and her fellow members of the post-war 'bulge' grew up. The extract is taken from a collection of autobiographical essays by various writers published under the title *Jock Tamson's Bairns*.

The change to Orkney thereafter could hardly be more dramatic, as we enter George Mackay Brown's 'world apart'. The extract, from *Greenvoe*, presents a light but understanding account written in the words of an Indian medical student peddling clothes and haberdashery from a suitcase. If his picture is unexpected, nevertheless it is illuminating — and hilarious.

As a finale to this section comes an extract — virtually a prose poem — about Edinburgh. There seems nothing of the flavour of the guide book about what Alexander Smith has to say. He gives us his picture of a character as he saw her when he wrote his book: a character with great experience of the world, bringing herself up to date when she can, but sometimes slipping into vices which she tries to hide. That character, of course, is the city of Edinburgh.

The Seeds of Conflict

Scotsmen, more than other men perhaps, have the three great essentials of commercial success — imagination to conceive schemes, common sense to correct them, and energy to push them through. Common sense, indeed, so far from being wanting, is in most cases too much in evidence, perhaps, crippling the soaring mind and robbing the idea of its early radiance; in quieter language, she makes the average Scotsman to be over-cautious. His combinations are rarely Napoleonic until he becomes an American. In his native dales he seldom ventures on a daring policy. And yet his forecasting mind is always detecting "possibeelities". So he contents himself by creeping cautiously from point to point, ignoring big reckless schemes and using the safe and small, till he arrives at a florid opulence. He has expressed his love of *festina lente* in business in a score of proverbs — "Bit-by-bit's the better horse, though big-by-big's the baulder'; "Ca' canny or ye'll cowp''; "Many a little makes a mickle'; and "Creep before ye gang." This mingling of caution and imagination is the cause of his stable prosperity. And its characteristic is a sure progressiveness. That sure progressiveness was the characteristic of Wilson's prosperity in Barbie. In him, too, imagination and caution were equally developed. He was always foreseeing "chances" and using them, gripping the good and rejecting the dangerous (had he not gripped the chance of auld Rab Jamieson's barn? — there was caution in that, for it was worth the money whatever happened, and there was imagination in the whole scheme, for he had a vision of Barbie as a populous centre and streets of houses in his holm). And every "chance" he seized led to a better one, till almost every "chance" in Barbie was engrossed by him alone. This is how he went to work. Note the "bit-by-bitness" of his great career.

When Mrs Wilson was behind the counter, Wilson was out "distributing". He was not always out, of course — his volume of trade at first was not big enough for that, but in the mornings, and the long summer dusks, he made his way to the many outlying places of which Barbie was the centre. There, in one and the same visit, he distributed goods and collected orders for the future. Though his bill had spoken of "carts", as if he had several, that was only a bit of splurge on his part; his one conveyance at the first was a stout spring cart, with a good brown cob between the shafts. But with this he did such a trade as had never been known in Barbie. The Provost said that it was "shtupendous".

When Wilson was jogging homeward in the balmy evenings of his first summer at Barbie no eye had he for the large evening star, tremulous above the woods, or for the dreaming sprays against the yellow west. It wasn't his business — he had other things to mind. Yet Wilson was a dreamer, too. His close musing eye, peering at the dusky-brown nodge of his pony's hip through the gloom, saw not that, but visions of chances, opportunities, occasions. When the lights of Barbie twinkled before him in the dusk he used to start from a pleasant dream of some commercial enterprise suggested by the country round. "Yon holm would make a fine bleaching green — pure water, fine air, labour cheap, and everything handy. Or the Lintie's Linn among the woods — water power running to waste yonder — surely something could be made of that." He would follow his idea through all its mazes and developments, oblivious of the passing miles. His delight in his visions was exactly the same as the author's delight in the figments of his brain. They were the same good company along the twilight roads. The author, happy with his thronging thoughts (when they are kind enough to throng) is no happier than Wilson was on nights like these.

He had not been a week on his rounds when he saw a "chance" waiting for development. When out "delivering" he used to visit the upland farms to buy butter and eggs for the Emporium. He got them cheaper so. But more eggs and butter could be had than were required in the neighbourhood of Barbie. Here was a chance for Wilson! He became a collector for merchants at a distance. Barbie, before it got the railway, had only a silly little market once a fortnight, which was a very poor outlet for stuff. Wilson provided a better one. Another thing played into his hands, too, in that connection. It is a cheese-making countryside about Barbie, and the less butter produced at a cheese-making place — the better for the cheese. Still, a good many pounds are often churned on the sly. What need the cheese merchant ken — it keepit the gudewife in bawbees frae week to week — and if she took a little cream frae the cheese now and then they werena a pin the waur o't, for she aye did it wi' decency and caution! Still it is as well to dispose of this kind of butter quietly, to avoid gabble among ill-speakers. Wilson, slithering up the back road with his spring cart in the gloaming, was the man to dispose of it quietly. And he got it dirt cheap, of course, seeing it was a kind of contraband. All that he made in this way was not much to be sure — threepence a dozen on the eggs, perhaps, and fourpence on the pound of butter — still, you know, every little makes a mickle, and hained gear helps weel. And more important than the immediate profit was the ultimate result. For Wilson, in this way, established with merchants, in far-off Fechars and Poltandie, a connection for the sale of country produce which meant a great deal to him in future, when he launched out as cheese-buyer in opposition to Gourlay.

It "occurred" to him also (things were always occurring to Wilson) that the "Scotch Cuddy" business had as fine a chance in "Barbie and surrounding neighbourhood" as ever it had in North and Middle England. The "Scotch Cuddy" is so called because he is a beast of burden, and not from the nature of his wits. He is a travelling packman, who infests communities of working men, and disposes of his goods on the credit system, receiving payment in instalments. You go into a working man's house (when he is away from home for preference) and, laying a swatch of cloth across his wife's knee, "What do you think of that, mistress?" you enquire, watching the effect keenly. Instantly all her covetous heart is in her eye and, thinks she to herself, "Oh, but John would look well in that, at the Kirk on Sunday!" She has no ready money, and would never have the cheek to go into a draper's and order the suit, but when she sees it lying there across her knee, she just cannot resist it. (And fine you knew that when you clinked it down before her!) Now that the goods are in the house she cannot bear to let them out the door again. But she hints a scarcity of cash. "Tut, woman!" quoth you, bounteous and kind, "there's no obstacle in *that!* — You can pay me in instalments!" How much would the instalments be, she enquires. "Oh a mere trifle — half-a-crown a week, say." She hesitates and hankers. "John's Sunday coat's getting quite shabby, so it is, and Tam Macalister has a new suit, she was noticing — the Macalisters are always flaunting in their braws! And, there's that Paisley shawl for herself, too; eh, but they would be the canty pair, cocking down the road on Sunday in *that* rig! — they would take the licht frae Meg Macalister's e'en, thae Macalisters are always so en-vy-fu'!" Love, vanity, covetousness, present opportunity, are all at work upon the poor body. She succumbs. But the half-crown weekly payments have a habit of lengthening themselves out till the packman has made fifty per cent by the business. And why not? — a man must have some interest on his money! Then there's the risk of bad debts, too — that falls to be considered. But there was little risk of bad debts when Wilson took to cloth-distributing. For success in that game depends on pertinacity in pursuit of your victim and Wilson was the man for that.

He was jogging home from Brigabee, where he had been distributing groceries at a score of wee houses, when there flashed on his mind a whole scheme for cloth-distribution on a large scale — for mining villages were clustering in about Barbie by this time, and he saw his way to a big thing.

He was thinking of Sandy Toddle, who had been a Scotch Cuddy in the Midlands and had retired to Barbie on a snug bit fortune — he was thinking of Sandy when the plan rose generous on his mind. He would soon have more horses than one on the road — why shouldn't they carry swatches of cloth as well as groceries? If he had responsible men under him, it would be their own interest, for a small commission on the profits, to see that payments were levied correctly every week. And those colliers were reckless with their cash, far readier to commit themselves to buying than the cannier country bodies round. Lord! there was money in the scheme. No sooner thought of than put in practice. Wilson gave up the cloth-peddling after five or six years — he had other fish to fry by that time — but while he was at it he made money hand over fist at the job.

But what boots it to tell of all his schemes? He had the lucky eye — and everything he looked on prospered.

Before he had been a week in Barbie he met Gourlay, just at the Bend o' the Brae, in full presence of the bodies. Remembering their first encounter the grocer tried to outstare him, but Gourlay hardened his glower and the grocer blinked. When the two passed, "I declare!" said the bodies, "did you see yon? — they're not on speaking terms!" And they hotched with glee to think that Gourlay had another enemy.

Judge of their delight when they saw one day about a month later, just as Gourlay was passing up the street, Wilson come down it with a load of coals for a customer! For he was often out Auchterwheeze road in the early morning, and what was the use of an empty journey back again, especially as he had plenty of time in the middle of the day to attend to other folk's affairs — so here he was, started as a carrier, in full opposition to Gourlay.

"Did you see Gourlay's face?" chuckled the bodies when the cart went by. "Yon was a bash in the eye to him. Ha, ha! — he's not to have it all his own way now!"

Wilson had slid into the carrying in the natural development of business. It was another of the possibilities which he saw and turned to his advantage. The two other chief grocers in the place, Cunningham the dirty, and Calderwood the drunken, having no carts or horses of their own, were dependent on Gourlay for conveyance of their goods from Skeighan. But Wilson brought his own. Naturally, he was asked by his customers to bring a parcel now and then, and naturally, being the man he was, he made them pay for the privilege. With that for a start the rest was soon accomplished. Gourlay had to pay now for his years of insolence and tyranny; all who had irked beneath his domineering ways got their carrying done by Wilson. Ere long that prosperous gentleman had three carts on the road, and two men under him to help in his various affairs.

Carting was only one of several developments in the business of J.W. When the navvies came in about the town and accommodation was ill to find, Wilson rigged up an old shed in the corner of his holm as a hostelry for ten of them — and they had to pay through the nose for their night's lodging. Their food they obtained from the Emporium, and thus the Wilsons bled them both ways. Then there was the scheme for supplying milk — another of the "possibeelities". Hitherto in winter, Barbie was dependent for its milk supply on heavy farm-carts that came lumbering down the street, about half-past seven in the morning, jangling bells to waken sleepy customers, and carrying lanterns that carved circles of hairy yellow out of the raw air. But Mrs Wilson got four cows, back-calvers who would be milking strong in December, and supplied milk to all the folk about the Cross.

She had a lass to help her in the house now, and the red-headed boy was always to be seen, jinking round corners like a weasel, running messages hot-foot, errand boy to the "bisness" in general. Yet, though everybody was busy and skelping at it, such a stress of work was accompanied with much disarray. Wilson's yard was the strangest contrast to Gourlay's. Gourlay's was a pleasure to the eye, everything of the best and everything in order, since the master's pride would not allow it to be other. But, though Wilson's Emporium was clean, his back yard was littered with dirty straw, broken boxes, old barrels, stable refuse, and the sky-pointing shafts of carts, uptilted in between. When boxes and barrels were flung out of the Emporium they were generally allowed to lie on the dung-hill, until they were converted into firewood. "Mistress, you're a trifle mixed," said the Provost in grave reproof, when he went round to the back to see Wilson on a matter of business. But "Tut," cried Mrs Wilson, as she threw down a plank, to make a path for him across a dub — "Tut," she laughed, "the clartier the cosier!" And it was as true as she said it. The thing went forward splendidly in spite of its confusion.

Though trade was brisker in Barbie than it had ever been before, Wilson had already done injury to Gourlay's business as general conveyer. But, hitherto, he had not infringed on the gurly one's other monopolies. His chance came at last.

He appeared on a market day in front of the Red Lion, a piece of pinkey-brown paper in his hand. That was the first telegram ever seen in Barbie, and it had been brought by special messenger from Skeighan. It was short and to the point. It ran: "Will buy 300 stone cheese 8 shillings stone delivery at once," and was signed by a merchant in Poltandie.

Gourlay was talking to old Tarmillan of Irrendavie, when Wilson pushed in and addressed Tarmillan, without a glance at the grain-merchant.

"Have you a kane o' cheese to sell, Irrendavie?" was his blithe salutation.

"I have," said Irrendavie, and he eyed him suspiciously. For what was Wilson speiring for? *He* wasna a cheese-merchant.

"How much the stane are you seeking for't?" said Wilson.

"I have just been asking Mr Gourlay here for seven and six," said Irrendavie, "but he winna rise a penny on the seven!"

"*I*'ll gi'e ye seven and six," said Wilson, and slapped his long thin flexible bank-book far too ostentatiously against the knuckles of his left hand.

"But — but," stammered Irrendavie, suspicious still, but melting at the offer, "*you* have no means of storing cheese."

"Oh," said Wilson, getting in a fine one at Gourlay, "there's no drawback in that! The ways o' business have changed greatly since steam came close to our doors. It's nothing but vanity nowadays when a country merchant wastes money on a ramshackle of buildings for storing — there's no need for that if he only had brains to develop quick deliveries. Some folk, no doubt, like to build monuments to their own pride, but I'm not one of that kind; there's not enough sense in that to satisfy a man like me. My offer doesna hold, you understand, unless you deliver the cheese at Skeighan Station. Do you accept the condition?"

"Oh, yes," said Irrendavie, "I'm willing to agree to that."

"C'way into the Red Lion then," said Wilson, "and we'll wet the bargain with a drink to make it hold the tighter!"

Then a strange thing happened. Gourlay had a curious stick of foreign wood (one of the trifles he fed his pride on) the crook of which curved back to the stem and inhered, leaving space only for the fingers. The wood was of wonderful toughness, and Gourlay had been known to bet that no man could break the handle of his stick by a single grip over the crook and under it. Yet now, as he saw his bargain whisked away from him and listened to Wilson's jibe, the thing snapped in his grip like a rotten twig. He stared down at the broken pieces for a while, as if wondering how they came there, then dashed them on the ground while Wilson stood smiling by. And then he strode — with a look on his face that made the folk fall away.

"He's hellish angry," they grinned to each other when their foe was gone, and laughed when they heard the cause of it. "Ha, ha, Wilson's the boy to diddle him!" And yet they looked queer when told that the famous stick had snapped in his grasp like a worm-eaten larch-twig. "Lord!" cried the baker in admiring awe, "did he break it with the ae chirt? It's been tried by scores of fellows for the last twenty years, and never a man of them was up till't! Lads, there's something splendid about Gourlay's wrath. What a man he is when the paw-sion grups him!"

"Thplendid, d'ye ca't?" said the Deacon. "He may thwing in a towe for his thplendid wrath yet."

From that day Wilson and Gourlay were a pair of gladiators for whom the people of Barbie made a ring. They pitted the protagonists against each other and hounded them on to rivalry by their comments and remarks, taking the side of the newcomer, less from partiality to him than from hatred of their ancient enemy. It was strange that a thing so impalpable as gossip should influence so strong a man as John Gourlay to his ruin. But it did. The bodies of Barbie became not only the chorus to Gourlay's tragedy, buzzing it abroad and discussing his downfall; they became also, merely by their maddening tattle, a villain of the piece and an active cause of the catastrophe. Their gossip seemed to materialize into a single entity, a something propelling, that spurred Gourlay on to the schemes that ruined him. He was not to be done, he said; he would show the dogs what he thought of them. And so he plunged headlong, while the wary Wilson watched him, smiling at the sight.

There was a pretty hell-broth brewing in the little town.

George Douglas, *The House with the Green Shutters*

Suspicion in Segget

Crossing the steep of the brae in the dark, by the winding path from the Manse to the Kaimes, Chris bent her head to the seep of the rain, the wet November drizzle of Segget. Then she minded a wall of the Kaimes still stood, and ran quick up the path to stand in its lee. That gained, she stood and panted a while, six months since she'd been up here in the Kaimes — only six months, she could hardly believe it!

It felt like years — long and long years — since she'd worked as a farmer's wife in Kinraddie. Years since she'd felt the beat of the rain in her face as she moiled at work in the parks. How much had she gained, how much had she lost? — apart from her breath, she had almost lost that!

She felt the wall and then leant against it, wrapped in her ulster, looking at Segget, in its drowse of oil-lamps under the rain. Safe anyhow to go home this time . . . And she smiled as she minded last time she had climbed to the Kaimes, and Segget had seen her go home — by the tale they told all Segget had seen her and stared astounded, a scandalled amaze —

But indeed it was only Ag Moultrie that morning, as ill-luck would have it, who saw her go home. She had gone out early to the school to redd up, she went heavy with sleep and her great mouth a-agant, as you well might believe, though she didn't tell that. Folk knew her fine, all the Moultries forbye. Rob Moultrie had once been the saddler of Segget, his shop lay down by the edge of the Square. And as coarse an old brute as you'd meet, was Rob Moultrie, though a seventy years old and nearing his grave. 'Twas only a saddler's shop in name now, the trade had clean gone this many a year. There was still a britchen or so in the shop, and a fine bit bridle Rob Moultrie had made in the days long syne when he still would work. But his trade had gone, and his sweirty had come, he was never a popular man in the toun; he couldn't abide the sight of the gentry, or the smell of the creatures either, he said, and that was why he was Radical still.

And if he went on a dander somewhere, along the road and he'd hear a car, toot-tooting behind him, would he get off the road? Not him, he'd walk on bang in the middle, dare any damn motorist try run him down. So sometimes he'd come back to Segget from a walk, step-stepping cannily along the bit road, with a two-three motorists hard at his heels, toot-tooting like mad, and the shovers red-faced. Mrs. Moultrie would be looking from the window and see, and cry as he came, *Losh, Rob, you'll be killed!* And he'd stop and glower at her with his pocked old face, and his eyes like the twinkling red eyes of a weasel, and sneer, the old creature, shameful to hear. *Ay, that would be fine – no doubt you'd get up to your old bit capers. Get out of my way!* And he'd lift his stick, maybe more than do that, syne hirple over to his armchair, and sit there and stare in the heart of the fire or turn to the reading of his old bit Bible.

For he'd never forgiven Jess Moultrie, the fact that more than a forty years before, when he'd met her and married her, she'd been with a bairn. She told how it was before she would marry, and he'd glowered at her dour: *More fool that I am. But I'm willing to take you and your shame as well.* And he took her, and the bairn was born, young Ag, no others came and maybe that was why he still kept up the sneer at his wife. But she would say nothing, she was patient and bowed, little, with a face like a brown, still pool; and she'd say not a word, getting on with her work, making ready the supper for Ag when she came.

She cleaned out the school and the hall and such places, did Ag, and in winter made the school broth, as nasty a schlorich as ever you'd taste. She looked like a horse ta'en out of a plough, and her voice was a neigh like a horse's as well, and she'd try to stand up for her mother with old Rob. *Don't speak that way to my mother!* she would cry, and he'd look at her dour, *Ay, ay no doubt she's precious in your sight. You had only one mother, though three or four fathers*; and Ag more than likely would start to greet then, she wasn't a match for the thrawn old brute, though a good enough one for most other folk. And faith! she'd a tongue for news that was awful. Ake Ogilvie called her the Segget Dispatch, she knew everything that happened in Segget, and a lot that didn't, but she liked best to tell of births and funerals and such-like things; and how the daughter of this or that corpse no sooner looked on the dead than broke down — *and fair roared and grat when she saw him there*. So folk called her the Roarer and Greeter for short.

Well, then, it was her, to get on with the tale, as she blinked her way in that morning in May, saw a woman come down the hill from the Kaimes, and stopped dumbfoundered: Who could she be?

Ag was real shocked, for the Kaimes was the place where spinners and tinks of that kind would go, of a Sabbath evening, and lie on the grass and giggle and smoke and do worse than that — Ay, things that would leave them smoking in hell, as the old minister said that they would. So no decent folk went up there at night, this creature of a woman was surely a tink. And Ag gave a sniff, but was curious forbye, and crept canny along in the lithe of the dyke that hemmed in the lassies' playground from the lads'. So she waited there till the woman went by, hurrying bare-headed, with a stride and a swing and a county-like gait. And then Ag Moultrie near fainted with joy, though she didn't tell you that when she told you the story, she saw that the woman was Mrs. Colquohoun, the wife of the new minister of Segget.

Well, afore the day was well started all Segget had heard that the wife of the new minister had been seen by Ag Moultrie up on the Kaimes, she'd been out all night with a spinner up there, Ag had seen them cuddling and sossing in the grass. Folk said, *By God, she's wasted no time; and who would the spinner have been, would you say?* Old Leslie heard the story in the smiddy and he said the thing was Infernal, just. Now, he minded when he was a loon up in Garvock — And the sweat dripped off him, pointing a coulter, and he habbered from nine until loosening-time, near, some story about some minister he'd known; but wherever that was and why it had been, and what the hell happened, if anything ever had, you couldn't make head nor tail if you listened; and you only did that if you couldn't get away.

Old Leslie was maybe a fair good smith; he was sure the biggest old claik in Segget. He'd blether from the moment you entered his smiddy, he'd ask how the wife and the bairns all were, and your brother Jock that was down in Dundon, and your sister Jean that was in a sore way, and your father that was down with the colic or the like, and your grandfather, dead this last fifty years.

And syne he'd start on your cousins, how they were, and your uncles and aunts and their stirks and their stots, their maids and all that were in their gates: till your hair would be grey and your head fair dizzy at the thought you'd so many relations at all. And his face would sweat like a dripping tap as he hammered at the iron and habbered at you and then he'd start some story of the things he'd done or seen or smelt when a loon up in Garvock, and the day would draw in, the night would come on, and the stars come out, he'd have shod all your horses and set all the coulters and you were near dead for lack of some meat; but *that* damned story wouldn't have finished, it would be going on still with no sign of an end, he'd start it the next time he saw you or heard you, though you were at the far side of a ten-acre field — as you took to your heels and run.

Well, about the only soul that couldn't do that was his son, Sim Leslie, the policeman of Segget. He had joined the police and had been sent back to Segget, and still bade with his father, he was used to the blether: and folk said if he listened with a lot of care, for a twenty years or so at a stretch, he at least might find out what really *had* happened that time when his father was a loon up on Garvock. Folk called him Feet, Sim Leslie the bobby, he'd feet so big he could hardly coup, there was once he was shoeing a horse in the smiddy, an ill-natured brute from the Meiklebogs; and the creature lashed out at him fair and square and caught him such a clout on the chest as would fair have flattened any ordinary man. But young Sim Leslie just rocked a wee bit, his feet had fair a sure grip on Scotland.

Well, Feet heard the story of Mrs. Colquhoun, from his father, as the two of them sat at dinner. And he kittled up rare, there was something in this, and maybe a chance of promotion at last. So he went and got hold of Ag Moultrie, the sumph, and pulled out his notebook with his meikle red fingers, and asked was she sure 'twas the minister's wife? And Ag said *Ay*, and Feet made a bit note; and then he seemed stuck, and he said, *You're sure?* And Ag said *Ay, I'm as sure as death*. Feet made another note, and scratched at his head, and swayed a bit in his meikle black boots. *It fair was her?* And Ag said *Ay*; and by then it seemed just about dawning on Feet it really was her and nobody else.

But Ag was real vexed, as she told to folk, she hadn't wanted to miscall a soul, *God knows I'm not a body to claik*; and she said when she'd finished with Feet and his questions she went home and sat down and just Roared and Grat, so sorry she was for the new minister. And she'd tell you some more how the woman had looked, her face red-flushed, with a springy walk; and if you were married you well could guess why all of that was — damn't man, 'twas fairly a tasty bit news!

That night Feet went up and prowled round the Manse, with his bull's-eye held in his hand and his feet like the clopping of a Clydesdale heard on the ground. He didn't know very well what he was there for, or what he would say if Mrs. Colquhoun saw him; but he was awful keen on promotion. And he said he was fine at detective-work, like, and if honest merit were given its reward they'd make him a real detective ere long. And Ake Ogilvie said in his tink-like way *A defective, you mean? God, ay, and certificated!*

Well, Feet had prowled round to the back of the Manse, and had stopped to give his head a bit scratch; when sudden the window above him opened and afore he could move there came a bit splash and a pailful of water was slung down his back. He spluttered and hoasted and his lamp went out, when he came to himself he was shaking and shivering, but the Manse was silent and still as the grave. He thought for a while of arresting the lot — ay, he would in the morning, by God; and turned and went home, running home stretches to change his bit sark, in case he might catch a cold from his wetting.

And, would you believe it, next day as he sat in his office writing up his reports, his mother said, *Here's a woman to see you*. And Feet looked up and he knew the quean, Else Queen, the maid at the Manse it was; 'twas said she'd been brought up as a lassie in Segget, though her father had moved to Fordoun since then, now she was fair a great brute of a woman, with red eyes and hair, and cheeks of like tint. And she said, *Are you Feet?* and Feet reddened a bit. *I'm Simon Leslie the policeman of Segget.* — *Well, I'm the person that half-drowned you last night; and I've come to tell you when you want the same, just prowl round the Manse at such a like hour.*

And she didn't stop only at Feet then, either. She made for Ag Moultrie and told her the same, she would have her sacked from her job at the school; and Ag broke down and just Roared and Grat, she said she'd never said an ill word of any, but what was the minister's wife doing on the Kaimes? *Looking at the hills and the sunrise, you fool. Did you never hear yet of folk that did that?* And Ag said she hadn't; and who ever had? Folk shook their heads when they heard that tale, if the woman at the Manse wasn't fair just a bitch, damn't! you could only suppose she was daft.

Lewis Grassic Gibbon, Cloud Howe

Idle in Glasgow

It was hard to bear, this knowledge that Peter had a job while he, journeyman riveter and hard grafter all his life, was on the street.

All the circumstances were bitter. Peter had qualified for nothing, but Peter could, and did, come the big man in the house on the strength of a job.

The nature of the job itself was disgusting enough — door-keeper of a small cinema in the East End beyond Bridgeton Cross. The boy was never out of his bed till ten or eleven in the morning. He quickly fell into the habit of ordering his mother about, demanding that the midday meal should be served at such and such an hour, so that he might do whatsoever he wanted to do and yet be at the picture house in good time for the afternoon session. It seemed that he had always something to do on his own — see a chap about a dog running at Carntyne in the evening, or place a bet on a sure thing for the three-thirty at Wolverhampton.

He grew in a brash, easy confidence that infuriated Danny. It became one of the father's secret grievances that Peter never came home in his uniform but went about in a flash suit, changing into braided, plum-coloured tunic and trousers in the remote obscurity of the picture palace. It was infuriating to see him yawn about the house and stretch his arms and ask again and again if the dinner was not ready yet. The bastard seemed to think he owned the place: all because he now paid his mother a lodger's rental of seven and six a week. Then he would come slamming into the house long after midnight, wakening them up all and grumbling that there was no food handy in the cupboard.

The emergence of his son as a man might have delighted Danny in other circumstances, but now it was all wrong. The boy's job he despised — one of those flash, cheap, unskilled billets that lads were tumbling into nowadays: no apprenticeship, no early hours, but just a game for any mug at a labourer's wage, and all very fancy with their jazz and chit-chat of film stars and dancing. Very soon he was to discover that Agnes was not standing for any criticism of Peter, that Agnes would even use the example of Peter to sneer at him. (Although, a strange thing, she would take no nonsense from the boy!) And the bitterest thing of all was that Peter's job was all Jim's doing. Jim had some remote interest in that seedy picture house, or some vague influence with its owner; and Jim could pose as both the powerful man of affairs and the influential and generous helper of lame dogs. While Danny knew very well that Peter, his useless son, had as the martyr of a notorious trial a commercial value shrewdly assessed by his brother-in-law.

It was enough to drive a man daft, at least to drink, but he kept himself to the strict letter of his new code. He drew the dole, handed the most of it over to Agnes, and rarely indulged himself in more than the Threepenny Roll-Up of his need. In the house he kept as quiet as he could; silent if Agnes was stirred out of her resentment to lash at him, grimly tolerant of Peter's new largeness of manner, taking only a decent pleasure in the petting of Wee Mirren or in a game on a quiet evening with Billy. Jim and Lizzie had ceased to come about the house; Agnes was often out with them, and how they amused themselves he never knew.

All he could do was walk the streets, and soon a large area of the city of Glasgow had nothing to interest him. Even the food-shops of Union Street became merely maddening in their allure. Again and again he would awaken out of a coma and find himself staring at the deft, rapid hands of a cobbler working in his window, hypnotised by the sight of a man actually at work. Or he would walk the docksides, vaguely curious as to the lives and work of the coolies from Clan and City liners, wistfully watching a vessel warped out of the Queen's Dock and setting down river for the Mediterranean ports.

He came to know all the parks within his range — Whiteinch with its bleak fossil grove, the charm of Kelvingrove, the reeking hothouses of the Botanic Gardens. On many a night he could not sleep, and sometimes he would slip out of bed and into his clothes and out of the house in the summer dawn to have the empty world of streets for his own. It was one of the big pleasures of the period to form an acquaintance and pass the time of day with an old man who led a pug into Kelvingrove every morning at six. And he also learned to nod to lamplighters and railwaymen hurrying early at regular hours to the day's work.

Life lost definition and colour and order. It came to mean nothing certain and colourful save the precious game of dominoes or halma with Billy in the evening. He knew himself to be going soft in mind and body. In Royal Terrace one evening a doctor was in trouble with his car and called him to help. He contrived to turn the engine two or three times and then gave up, his arm numb, his chest aching. The doctor glanced at him shrewdly, gave him half-a-crown, and told him to go and buy a square meal. The failure rankled.

Yet in all these weeks of idleness he made next to no attempt to find work for himself. To be sure, the sense that the search would be nearly hopeless was always at the back of his mind, but his incuriosity had deeper roots than that. There persisted in him a wholly blind faith in ship-building, in himself, and in Leslie Pagan. Battered by circumstance, he still could not believe that this stoppage, that dismal array of empty berths along the banks of the river, might last for ever. It was incredible that Pagan's would not reopen within a month or two. And since, in his ingenuous philosophy, an early resumption of work was a certainty, it was just quite impossible for him to understand that he might not be among the first to be called back to the gates and the time-clock and the old familiar darg.

The faith reposed ultimately in the Boss. The Boss would never let the Yard down. The possible defeat of his hero never haunted even his worst moments. And had not Leslie Pagan said that there was a wee job or two to be done about the house, pending the moment, the inevitable moment, the Yard would be busy again?

There were moments when Danny wondered miserably if he had been forgotten. For a long time after the trial of Peter he heard nothing from or of the man in whom rested all his beliefs. It was impossible to believe in such a terrible abandonment, but God knew the days were slow and empty.

George Blake, *The Shipbuilders*

A Protestant Girlhood

I was born at the bleak end of 1947. Stafford Cripps' Age of Austerity, I know now. I remember, can I really remember, or is it just mythology — Power Cuts and Sweetie Rationing?

There were a lot of us born then, most of us to parents just as recently demobbed, just as newly optimistic and no better housed than my father and mother were. We were the Bulge. I knew that then, as we advanced from Primary School to Secondary School to Higher Education with a lot of fanfare and rhetoric from the newspapers. The Bulge. A single frame from a comic book, this gigantic Easter Egg a spotted snake had swallowed in the Dandy Annual — this was how I pictured it as we were squeezed through the gullet of the Education System stretching everything to breaking point.

We lived, my mother, my father and I, in a single upstairs room in my grandparents' house. My father's side. A big between-the-wars council five-apartment. Roughcast. Pebbledash. Six in the block. In the shadow of all the steelworks, Colvilles, Anderson Boyes, the Lanarkshire — number thirteen, the Broadway, Craigneuk, Wishaw. Whenever I heard on the radio the Lullaby of Broadway I thought they were singing about us.

The place was full of adoring grown-ups all easily charmed and exploited by a smartypants toddler. There was my Gran, my Grandad, my father's youngest unmarried sister and brother — my Auntie Jinnet who was engaged and my Uncle George who was Restless. He was considering emigrating to Corby with half the workforce of Anderson Boyes. My Grandad spent a lump of every afternoon lying on the bed under the top knitted blanket in the back bedroom, often with me burrowed in between him and the wall, prattling and pulling his hair. He had been a miner before the steelworks and he had a touch, more than a touch of silicosis. His lungs weren't so good.

But he was good and loud in arguments. Round the tea-table I remember him, long before I could make head or tail of it, the arguing — especially on Sundays if the rest of the family were there, Bill and Jean who had two children and a prefab and Annie and John with my baby cousin. He had been a miner. He was a Unionist. He was angry at how his sons and daughters had come back from the Forces voting Labour. Said they'd sold old Churchill down the river. He blamed the war for a lot.

He had been a miner. He was a Unionist. In the early twenties, preying on fears aroused by the recent large influx of Irish Catholics to Glasgow and the industrial West of Scotland, the competition for jobs, the suspicions about cheap blackleg labour, the hard times a-coming, the Scottish Unionist Party successfully neatly split the working classes. I know that now. Divide And Rule. People have told me. Then I knew a father and his sons around a table. His white hair. My grandmother wheeshting and clucking. The words Catholic and Protestant. Raised voices.

He was not an Orangeman. He used to say he had nothing against anybody. He was a good churchgoer. Regular. He talked about Idolatry. And told me about Covenanters. There was a blue and white plate on the wall with a man-on-a-horse who was William of Orange. He was Dutch. Delft. They had brought it back from Holland when they had visited my Uncle Robert's Grave, my Gran and Grandad. After the war. He had been my father's second-youngest brother. He was dead. There was a picture of him in his uniform. I spent a lot of time looking at this photograph to see if there was anything different about a picture of somebody who was dead. It was easier with my Aunt Edith. She had died aged seven of measles ten years, fifteen years, a long time ago. It was possible to imagine, when I squinted at the family group with her in front, something slight and shifting and other-worldly about her sepia presence among her lumpier solid brothers and sisters. They said I'd her Eyes. My mother said nothing at the time, later up in the privacy of our own room said nothing of the sort. Mine were brown.

The room wasn't that big. There was my mother and father's big high bed. And my brown-varnished cot squashed in at the end of it. A green-top card table and chairs, big brown boxy rexine chairs. There was the radio, no, it was only a speaker really, it had one on-off switch, no tuner, it was attached to my Grandparents' radio downstairs. We had to listen to whatever they listened to, when they switched it off we'd had it. We listened a lot though, plays, music-nights, Take It From Here. In April 1948 over the speaker they heard Stafford Cripps' Budget increase the price of cigarettes from two-and-four pence to three-and-four pence and my forty-a-day father looked at his sleeping or squalling four-month old daughter, said well that's that and gave up just like that, never smoked again. Another piece of family mythology.

There were few ornaments. My mother and father's engagement photo, framed. Head and shoulders, printed in monochrome then hand-tinted. Cherryblossom — brown hair, pink cheeks, carmine lips. A sweet smile each and a youthful look. And the wedding photograph. Full length. My father in his army uniform, my mother in the A.T.S. She said she could stand it, the Khaki, because she'd good colouring and anyway there just weren't the coupons. She'd had nothing else to fit her because the army food blew you up. She'd consoled herself with what the teacher had told her away back when she'd had to wear the brown fairy dress in 'Fairy-Leather-Apron' in the school concert — that brown eyes like that could bring out the beauty. She said the big excitement had been seeing if my father's leave got cancelled and the whole thing was off for the time being. It had been touch and go, she said. But she'd got a lot out of the A.T.S., enjoyed it, met all sorts. She said the main thing was not to marry too young. She recommended waiting until you were twenty-four like her. It had been the ideal age.

She talked to me a lot, did my mother. All day when my father was away at work. Bits of her life became legends. Descriptions of dance dresses, what devils they'd been she and her sisters, stories of how my Auntie Elsie, fifteen and with soot on her eyelashes, had brazenly stolen someone's officer. She says now I was great company as a kid. She was that bit plumper again than in the wedding photograph. Seems that every time something my grandmother said rankled her (it was my father's side remember) every time she had to just swallow it all or just start a row over some domestic division, every time they'd had yet another disappointment over some house they'd been after — she'd walk me in my go-chair, chewing in her misery a whole quarter of newly unrationed sweets.

For a while we tried the other set of grandparents. I don't suppose things were much happier or easier for my mother and father. They kept putting in for houses here and there, getting nowhere.

They didn't seem quite so deadly respectable, my Gran and

Grandad Forrest. For instance he swore, up to the point of 'bloody' and 'wee bugger'. He had been in the Navy in the First World War, still sang songs my grandmother tutted at. He had a terrible voice. A groaner. Tone deaf. He sang me Sad Songs — 'The Drunkard's Raggit Wean' — and laughed and tickled me when I got a lump in my throat. My mother always said what a right good storyteller he was, had a way with words, embroidered things just enough.

My grandmother said poems. Long storytelling poems. At sixteen she'd been maid to one of the Misses Reid who'd been an elocutionist. And gave lessons. My grandmother had remembered by heart every word, every inflection, every arch or pointed gesture of the voice. I grew wide-eyed at Little Orphan Annie (and the goblins will get you/too/if/you/don't/watch/out), tearful at the melodrama about the little girl searching for her dead mother (And I'se looking for heaven/but I can't find the stair).

I absolutely loved them both. But it's easy to love your grandparents.

When I was four we Got A House. A brand-new council four-apartment in the small mining village of Newarthill. A couple of miners' rows, the school, the pub, the Tallies' Cafe, the Post Office and the Co-operative. Now the pits were dying and they were building two schemes around it. It was four miles from Motherwell, expanding industry.

I went with my mother to do the place up before we moved in. I could feel her excitement. Eight years married and a house at last. We approached along newly laid out paths. What would soon be careful turfed lawns and neat rose-borders were great banks and churns of clay. The rooms seemed big and empty and hollow-sounding. Full of space. Cream plasterboard walls. My mother said they could get the downstairs done but maybe if she stippled the upstairs rooms there would be no need to afford to paper right away. She measured and scrubbed and I looked out of the window at the signs of life, a parked pram, the colour of someone's curtains, elsewhere windows whitened for privacy. A girl quite a lot bigger than me was wheeling a small girl in a pushchair and dragging a small boy by the hand. My mother said I should go and make friends, that was the beauty of it, I'd have lots of boys and girls to play with. It would be great for me.

I went out warily. I suppose it was my fault really, hit the wrong note, too bluff, too braggy. I told the girl my mum and dad had a

new house and it was a Brand-New One. She said huh, who hasn't
and asked was my dad a keyworker. I said he wasn't he worked in
a big office in Glasgow and she said he *must* be because these were
Key Workers' Houses. Or else somebody must have put in a good
word for him with the Councillor.

That was what it was like, to be a child. The place, the people.
Soon you went to school. You don't want to go back there, you've
been padding it out with bits about your parents and so on. Why go
back there anyway? You know how you hate it when you find
yourself back there with no choice, in Dreams. And you're always
running along the corridors, you're late and this is always the primary school and the corridors are spiked with pegs and coats with a
damp doglike smell and you keep swinging through doors into classroom after classroom looking for your class, your empty place.
And can't find it. Or there's the dream where it's always the high
school and the history class and suddenly there you are out in the
middle of the floor wearing nothing but your vest. A too-short vest.
You pull it down in front of you, then the back of you, don't know
which way to turn. Everyone is laughing. And you don't know
which part to expose.

So why try to tell it? Not for nostalgia. Not to say ah when we
were wee. Not for all that merely. Easy, too easy to write a kind
of proletarian Molesworth compleat with French-teachers-who-
couldn't-keep-order. Yes, there were a lot of real-life cliché characters, you could without one word of a lie dredge up the Recognisable Particular. Something to have people smile to remember.
Except that would not be honest enough, to thereby imply that it
was any of it absolutely harmless. So go back, dig deep, but know
that you'll not get at any of the things you accepted most easily,
that hurt you the most. You will be the last person to know what
they are.

Newarthill Primary School. A big black stone-built place with
railings around it. Old, it had the date 1897 cut into the stone between the Boys Entrance and the entrance marked Girls. I was five.
My mother took me to enrol and on the way back she said she
hoped I'd stay on at school, go to University if I had it in me, she
and my father would make every sacrifice. It was a great shame my
father had never had the chance.

We were taught by Look and Say. Apple says ah. Miss Brown
was not particularly pleased that I knew how to recite Ay Bee See
Dee and recognise the characters, said that Parents didn't know the

damage they did. But I learned to read very quickly. Most of the class did. We learned by rote. Off by heart. Tables: nine sixes are fifty-four ten sixes are six-ty; Similes: as black as coal, as green as grass; Singulars and Plurals: hoof, hooves, sheep, sheep, fish, fish or fishes, spoonful, spoonsful. We chanted aloud like a prayer.

The school did seem to be staffed by a collection of remarkably similar mainly maiden ladies. The odd widow. Does my memory lie to me in showing me so many Miss Jean Brodies twenty years beyond their prime? Each time before you moved up a class you were afraid, had heard the shouting spill into the corridor, had heard the rumours of beltings for Nothing, knew that this was going to be the most terrifying class in the school. But it always turned out to be much the same. The teachers had their moods. The sums got harder.

Each day started off with the Lord's Prayer, half an hour or so of Bible. The Story of Joseph read verse each around the class, a chapter a day, missing out Chapter thirty-nine, being the spicy one where Potiphar's wife stages her seduction scene. But I was suspicious enough, had the sense to read it anyway. Or we had to repeat what we'd learned at home a verse a night, Isaiah 53, or the gibberish of a Scottish Paraphrase.

> 'Oh god of Be-ethel by hoosand
> thy pe-ople Still are fed
> Who through the Weary
> Wild-er-ness has stole our father's leg.'

After the Bible then Reading, your homework piece, without a stammer. Aloud. Then Spelling. Every night you had to learn one group from the little red and white Schonell's Essential Spelling Book. Every day we wrote them down.

see	six	by
tree	fix	cry
been	box	try
sky	sweet	fox

More than two wrong got the belt. Hugh Gilmour and Jeannie Nielson got the belt every day. For the Spelling and for other things. Remember his pink flush, his orange hair, his gallus grin, how cock of the walk he was when he swaggered back to his seat. He kept count of his beltings, his boast was that he could take it. Farm Jeannie Nielson was big and cow-dumb. Smelt of the byre, carried it in on her shoes. Her eyelashes were matted together with a sticky affliction called Sleep. She cried easy. Sat alone at the front to see the board. When one of us nice girls or clever boys was Bad we were moved down to sit beside her as punishment. She cried easy. Still she was belted for her Spelling Errors.

Can that be true? Can they have been so cruel, those dedicated ladies with their flowery smocks to keep the chalk-dust from their good-wool dresses, with their churchy peppermint mothball breaths. They all played a club-footed piano, taught songs. Flow gently Sweet Afton. On their autumn window-sills bulbs split their sides in purple crocks, in spring milky frogspawn quickened into wriggling punctuation marks. The weather chart was filled in up to date. They taught us to tell a tree by its leaves. Once, thanks to my teachers, I knew the difference between the Mute and the Bewick's Swan. Nature Study was the gentle ladies' favourite subject. Once for weeks we had a snuffling hedgehog in a cardboard box. They loved animals.

Everything was a competition.

Every Friday there was a reshuffle, you were moved in descending order from the back row to the front, according to your marks, according to your stars.

Every summer there was a week of Tests. From this was decided the list of prizewinners. *Black Beauty* — for General Excellence Elsie Lochhead has been awarded Third Prize (Equal) in Class Primary V says this florid label, laurel leaves, a garland. My mother thought this poor and to be honest I had not thought to sink so low. One place lower next year and it would be a mere Certificate of Merit. No book.

And there was the Gala Day to consider too. Newarthill Miners Welfare Association organised it. There was a marquee, the sweet smell of cut grass under canvas, a tombola, a ride around the village on the back of a crêpe-paper-decorated lorry, milk and a bag of buns. And every year from the Top Class of the Primary School there was the Gala Queen, the cleverest girl in all the school, not the prettiest, the most popular, not the voted-for. The miners respected education above all. Like everything else this was a glittering prize for cleverness, the true worth. No one questioned it. The Girl Dux, the Queen, and the Boy Dux her Champion. Led around on a white horse. Made to wear brown velvet doublet and hose, usually wrinkled. And the Queen in a white dress in a car like a wedding car.

Even the colour of your sewing was a prize. Twice a week at the end of the afternoon for an hour we were Split Up. The boys from the girls. The boys got handwork, raffia mats, the girls sewing. We made lap bags of linen to keep our knitting in. Learned in theory to turn a heel. The linen was in three colours. Miss Ferguson gave the cleverest — according to last weeks Test Marks — first choice. Pink, blue or helio. No one liked helio. Miss Ferguson said the stupid did not deserve a choice in anything. Had to take what they got.

History and Geography. The Tulipfields of Holland. Bruce and the Spider. Or Composition. A Day In the Life of a Penny, A Walk In the Rain. Never use the word got or a preposition to end a sentence with. Mine were usually best, sometimes they even got Read Out and I'd be extra proud, go home with something good to tell. To maybe make up for the six out of ten for sums. I loved Composition. I knew what they wanted you to write. I knew to be one of the Winners, the Clever Ones, you had to be clean and neat and quiet and eager and just anxious enough under the tense time-counting pressure of Mental Arithmetic or Dictation. I loved school.

Except for that Worst Day. Remember it. Go back. Before your bath on Friday nights your mother combed your hair in her lap with a fine-tooth comb, carefully checking. There was once she found Something, said who had you been playing with, never never to try on anyone else's pixie. Next day she bought a bottle from the Chemists called Suleo Emulsion. Smelt horrible. A sticky pomade. You had to keep it on for at least forty-eight hours, so on Monday you had to go to school slicked with it, your hair in ratstails. You prayed the nit-nurse would not come that day. She did not come often, five times, six times in the seven years of Primary School. But that day she came. You could not believe it, you wanted to die, you wished you'd wake up and it wasn't true. Your class went to the hall. You queued up. Girls first. She lifted all your skirts quickly, tested your eyes, made you read a row of letters, looked in your ears, looked at your hair. You felt sick and dumb. She said Hmm, and stay behind please. The rest of the class went back to the classroom, looking back. Your best friend waved. You were left there with Jeannie Nielson and Hugh Gilmour. The Nurse said did you realise you had a Dirty Head. You explained about your mother checking, the stuff she'd put on, on Saturday. She said Ah yes but this should have been noticed Before. But there was prob-

ably no need to notify the parents as it was being dealt with. She
gave Jeannie Nielson and Hugh Gilmour a Letter to Take Home.
You went back to the classroom, burning, heard whispers, kept
your head down over your sums, tried to concentrate. You were in
the Very Back Seat, were Top that week, all the morning heads
kept turning round, the people who had been your friends hissing
Did You Get A Note. You did not answer. Later you said you had
really been kept back because you might need glasses.

My mother was angry when I told her at lunchtime. Said what
had the nurse meant should have been noticed before, she checked
every week in life. My grandmother was there on a visit, said it
was a disgrace and if my mother did not go and see the headmaster
then she would. I said please granny don't come, just leave it. It
was a whisper.

All afternoon you dreaded it. Kept looking at the glass above the
door waiting for her smart felt hat to show, for the rap of her
knuckles. Eventually the headmaster came, asked to see you, took
you to his office. Asked for the whole story. Your grandmother was
on her high horse, saying it was a well-known fact they'd rather
leave a Dirty Head for a clean one. The Nurse was there, flustered.
The headmaster was saying the whole thing was Very Regrettable.
You felt terrible.

It was a much worse day even than the Qualifying, which kept
you awake for nights. We were the Bulge. There was a shortage of
places. Competition would be that much greater.

You passed for Dalziel High, and a five-year Academic Course.
The best. Your mother and father said they had always known you
would.

We went for the uniform early on in the school holidays. A
royal, black and white striped tie, two pale blue shirt blouses, a
grey permaprest pleated skirt and a royal blue blazer with a school
crest and a Latin motto. *Summa Petenda*. Seek the Highest. Almost
every night for two months I tried on my uniform, admired it. I
read school story after school story that summer, *The Chalet
School, Mallory Towers*.

To be at Dalziel High is to realise that you are part of a tradition.
So goes my schoolgirl round hand English Ink Exercise. Thoughts
After One Week As a New Dalzielian. An Essay. I get (scored out,
replaced by *obtain*) a feeling of History although I do not under-
stand it from the Greek writing around the Entrance hall outside
Room One, and greatness from the gold names on boards that line

the Assembly Hall. The School Duxes, The Intermediate Duxes, The School Captains, The Roll of Honour showing those who died in the war that we might be free. My ambition is to be worthy of this tradition.

I got a good mark. The English teacher said the best of them had been very good, very little to choose between them. But in my second Essay was the chance to shine. Was Top. My Favourite Season. Autumn. Compare the falling leaves to ballerinas pirouetting to the ground. Get in the words golden-ochre and russet. And not least of my pleasures when autumn spreads its golden wings around us is a good book and tea by the fire and toasted muffins and jam while the wind and rain blusters on the window pane: I don't think I'd ever tasted toasted muffins and jam in my life but they sounded right, English enough, almost Enid Blytonish. It was not a lie, exactly. Just that it had never occurred to me, nothing in my Education had ever led me to believe that anything among my own real life ordinary things had the right to be written down. What you wrote could not be the truth. It did not have the authority of the English things, the things in books. Muffins and jam. I knew what they wanted you to write. My grown-up writer's fear is that this might still be so.

It was a good school. They kept telling you so. It had wonderful playing fields, old traditions, an excellent academic record which it was up to you as One of the Lucky Ones to maintain. Perhaps to its credit it practised no discrimination between the sexes, rather we girls in our school ties were only slightly inferior boys. Its teachers were of the old school, tweedy old suits, chalky gowns, kept order mainly by a pedantic weary sarcasm, the occasional tawse. The school had a Debating Society, A Junior Choir, A Chess Club, A Christian Union. I wanted to be in everything. There was an annual Drama Festival with a play from every class in the school. (I can still remember my debut in 1.A.'s play, a fantasy by A.A. Milne: 'Oh, Oliver! Isn't it a *lovely* island.') And all the time around us sprawled gritty old Motherwell, its steelworks, smoke, pubs, Orange Halls, Gospel Halls, Chapels, Churches, social clubs, shops and factories.

We did Latin. Learned Grammar. Learned up pages of French vocabulary, never spoke a word, translated in writing of course from French to English. History was a mish-mash of dates, the exam was a series of sentences from your history book with key words missing and, to show you'd learned it, you filled in the blanks. The History teacher had No Discipline. We played an elaborate game where you changed shoes with your neighbour, they changed them with the next person and so on round the class. When the bell rang there was a scramble of swapping back. Geography was marvellous. Logical. A Revelation. Position, Climate, Natural Vegetation. It seemed that maybe people were different because their conditions were different. Something which had never occurred to me in twelve years. I had thought God made everybody different and people were born that way.

Art was doing washes. Chrome yellow to palest lemon, crimson to blush rose. But I loved it. And yet English was my favourite. Shakespeare. The Merchant of Venice. His Jewish Gaberdine, the Quality of Mercy. Put it into your own words. And Poetry. Horatio On the Bridge. And how can man die better than facing fearful odds/for the ashes of his temple and the something of his gods.

Maths was the Hated Thing. Algebra was awful. I decided I could never understand it. Every evening my father tried to help me with it, it became our battleground for about two or three years until he gave up. I could not possibly be so stupid. I was determined I could.

Ungrateful, unfair to say only this of your father. Didn't he always encourage you? Yes. Took you to a planetarium, tried to get you interested. Brought home special paper glue when you wanted to make up that cut-out cardboard puppet theatre, never complained when you didn't use it, just left the top off, let it dry up. Took you to the baths. Bought you Bumpers once because you liked them so much, although your mother had said to get Clarks Sandals. Once when your wee sister was just a tiny baby, you must have been ten, he took you to Edinburgh for the day all by yourself. He took you to Art Galleries, remember the thrill of a *trompe l'oeil* picture of Mary Queen of Scots with a skull, a deathshead replacing her when you walked past at a slant. And a picture of a Minister on Skates, a black sober man on thin ice. You went to John Knox's house, up Scott Monument, into the Camera Obscura. And he took you out for lunch and let you choose what you wanted from the menu. You asked him what were rissoles and he said something sort of Italian and he didn't fancy them but it was absolutely up to you. They were delicious.

All your childhood they told you this, at school, at home. Freedom. The Protestant Ethic and etcetera. One's own conscience face to face with god. Free will. Why then the guilt when what you have wanted has seemed to be different from what they wanted you to want?

That is how it was with Art. It was Art which caused the rift between you and your schooling. Before that the report cards glowed.

I was fifteen. I had chosen my course for the Highers, English and French, Geography, Latin and Greek. I had only just begun Greek. There were three of us in the class only, two of the cleverest pupils of the year, a pair who would go on and get in the First Hundred of the Bursary Comp. no bother. And me. I did not like to be bottom, even of three. I did not find Greek so congenial as Latin. One day from the bus I saw Jim Lindsay who had left school the year before. He was walking down Newarthill main street, he had a huge piece of hardboard under his arm. He looked free. He was at Art School.

I decided I wanted to go to Art School. I would drop this stupid Greek, do Higher Art.

It wasn't that easy. The Art teacher said yes if you've got permission from your parents and the Rector. My parents were not keen. But if that was what I wanted. The Rector said no, it would be a waste, said Higher Art was given absolutely no credit for University Entrance. I said I wanted to go to Art School, was sure, decided absolutely. He said I ought to do English at University and besides some of the people who had gone on to Art School had been awkward types, caused trouble, worn white socks, been lax about the uniform, thought they were somebody special.

After my third visit to his office he said all right, washed his hands of me, said it was my own look out.

In the Art class we got absolutely no instruction. But perfect peace to do what we wanted. My friend Irene and I spent our spare time in Motherwell Public Library borrowing books on Impressionism, Post Impressionism, German Expressionism. By the time we were filling in our last months at school we had flirted with Surrealism, even Dada. We thought Cubism too cold, too formal, too mathematical, altogether felt more of an emotional empathy with the line which followed Matisse out of Impressionism, rather than the one which sprang from Cezanne. But we hated the mess of American Abstract Expressionism — what had Jackson Pollock been playing at? Scribbles. Dribbles. And yet to think that only a year ago we'd thought gooey pink Renoirs were the greatest thing ever painted, so who knew we might end up Pollock fans yet. Friday nights we listened to the Record Library Recording of *Under Milk Wood* with Richard Burton, we tried in vain to develop a taste for Jazz, we talked about Art School, what we'd wear, we looked at *Honey* magazines and imagined ourselves with asymmetrical haircuts and kinky boots. It was the mid sixties and things were just about to swing. Especially for us. We dreamed of beautiful bearded men who'd rescue us from the boredom and humiliation of staying in on Saturday nights. I gazed into the mirror and made self-portrait after self-portrait of myself in my version of the style of Modigliani, whom I was keen on at the time.

I dyed my hair a startling blonde with some spray on concoction that lightened as it brightened as it set, grew my fringe to nosetip level, peered through it with eyes fashionably ringed with the burnt cork effect of black eye pencil and lashbuilder mascara, asked my mother did she think I looked like Marianne Faithful at all? Irene and I took to black stockings and elastic-sided suede bootees, were engaged in a lot of tiresome arguments with the lady adviser about uniform and maintaining standards. It was grey skirts only and if that was supposed to be charcoal then it was so dark a charcoal as to be practically black. We were going downhill fast. We got into trouble for laughing while a lady from Army Recruiting was giving us a Careers Talk. We couldn't wait to leave.

It dragged itself on and on, that last year. Until finally the last day, the day I'd been longing for when I could tell all those teachers exactly what I thought of them. But of course it was easy in the relief to let half-maudlin nostalgia take over before you'd even left the place, sitting in Motherwell Town Hall at the last Prizegiving Day looking at the rows of teachers in Academic gowns and the rows of parents in flowery hats; singing 'Who would true valour see'; sniggering for the last time up the sleeves of our Banner blue-blouses at the bad grammar of the local councillor convenor. (Seventeen and snobbish, we could swallow a platitude any time and not bat an eyelid — but one thing our education had done was provide us, we thought, with a litmus for the glaringly ungrammatical, and without any sympathy for the feelings of those we regarded as less fortunate than ourselves either.)

So I shook hands with my teachers on the way out, thanked them even if I mumbled it and contented myself with throwing away my school tie under the cars at Motherwell Cross.

Freedom. And if I'd any complaints about the next bit, the Art School, then I'd only myself to blame. It was my own choice.

Liz Lochhead

A Letter to Uncle Pannadas

Mrs Learmonth's hotel,
HAMNAVOE

My Dear Uncle Pannadas,

As you have commanded me, so I have obeyed: namely, the day before yesterday (Wednesday) by crossing over by ferry-boat to the island of Hellya with a full bag of assorted draperies and fancy goods, of a gaudiness and general shining quality to take the eye of the ladies. As you further commanded me, dear Uncle, so now I write. 'Be brief, succinct,' you said. This I will attempt, though it may prove difficult in one whom you have so often rebuked for discursiveness.

At the wheel of the boat, as last year, was the ferryman Westray, the silent bright-headed one. You remember how last year I called him in joke 'the bringer of warriors and heroes to Valhalla'. At once he set a black look on us, but proved subsequently to be friendly in a brusque laconic way, and charged twelve shillings and sixpence for each crossing.

Just so it turned out today, one year later, with one serious exception, that is, that the fare was higher.

— Please, how much? I enquire on the slipway at Greenvoe.

— Fifteen bob, he replies.

— Fifteen shillings! I state. This is most expensive.

— And fifteen bob return. One pound ten shillings. What time are you wanting to go back? he said, unmoved.

— I cannot pay such ransom money, I exclaim. O no.

— I'll tell you what I'm going to do then, says this Westray. I'm going into that phone box up there and I'm going to ring the police station in Kirkwall and the sergeant will be meeting you at Kirkwall pier with handcuffs.

All the while he is coiling a rope.

— Let us please be reasonable people, I say.

— Your move, Johnny, he says.

— The perfect solution has occurred to me, I say. Wait. Is not this good?

Thereupon I kneel down and remove the leather strap from my case and open it and lift out an art silk scarf or cravat, black and white dots upon a scarlet ground, and make a heavenly bridge with it over my two extended arms.

 — This silk scarf, I say, is value two pounds. I will give you this. This pays for the ferry, eh?

 — No, he says.

 — But surely, I say. Such a bargain.

 — I never wear a scarf, he says.

Whereupon I make deeper delvings into the case.

 — Here are socks, I say, black silk. Box of handkerchiefs, initial-led. A necktie. One suit pyjamas, Paisley pattern, so lovely.

 — I sleep naked, he says. What's that?

 — That is headsquare, I say, silken, for ladies, twelve shillings.

 — That will do, he says.

 — Is for ladies, I say.

 — I'll take it, he makes swift answer. That's you and me square, Johnny.

So, my dear uncle, this turned out most satisfactory. I trust you will approve my acumen.

I fasten my case. The ferryman is attaching his boat by a rope to an iron bolt in the face of the pier.

 — We are good friends, no? I say.

 — Same as always, he answers.

Whereupon we shake hands.

 — Where is old Abdul the Damned this year? he says. (My dear uncle, I trust you will not take it amiss, he was referring, in joke, to you. I explain that you are incapacitated temporarily by reason of very painful arthritis in your knee.)

 — Poor old bastard, he answers. (Please, Uncle, not to take this amiss; it came out of a rough kindliness.)

 — These bargainings between us at the pier of Greenvoe, pedlar and boatman, I say, are always so very keen. I laugh to remember them afterwards.

We part most good friends.

Thereupon I made a circuit of village and island with my merchandise. The bag was very heavy. I fear, by the time this summer is over, my right shoulder will be nearer Leith Street by six inches than my left.

I came first to the burnt house whose door was of undulating iron, as last year, only more rusted. No steps had been attempted towards repair.

— Ah, my good friend, I call in at the window, are you in there? Are you at home?

— Timmy is in residence, comes the answer.

— Here I have many silken articles for you, I say.

— Timmy is impecunious.

I heave my bag in through the window and climb in after it. Such is the only mode of entry into this house. This Timmy is lying on his bed, if such it can be called by western standards, being the floor, and he is covered with a drift of ancient coats. It is a house of the utmost gloom. I perceive a table with a tin of cat-food on it, and a half loaf of bread, and a sculpted slab of margarine. Dominant upon the table, like a king in an evil purple robe, is an almost full bottle of meth. There is a spirit stove under the table. No brush has kissed that floor for many a month past. There is an odour of ancient rot everywhere. It is a kingdom for spiders. Beside Timmy's bed is a zinc pail with a quantity of stale urine in it. The curtains are as they were last year, abbreviated and scorched.

Yet Timmy from his litter of coats gives me a cheerful welcome.

— Timmy is pleased to see you again. Timmy has no colour prejudice. All men are equal to Timmy.

George Mackay Brown, *Greenvoe*

The Old Town of Edinburgh

From a historical and picturesque point of view, the Old Town is the most interesting part of Edinburgh; and the great street running from Holyrood to the Castle — in various portions of its length called the Lawnmarket, the High Street, and the Canongate — is the most interesting part of the Old Town. In that street the houses preserve their ancient appearance; they climb up heavenward, story upon story, with outside stairs and wooden panellings, all strangely peaked and gabled. With the exception of the inhabitants, who exist amidst squalor, and filth, and evil smells undeniably modern, everything in this long street breathes of the antique world. If you penetrate the narrow wynds that run at right angles from it, you see traces of ancient gardens. Occasionally the original names are retained, and they touch the visitor pathetically, like the scent of long-withered flowers. Old armorial bearings may yet be traced above the doorways. Two centuries ago fair eyes looked down from yonder window, now in possession of a drunken Irishwoman. If we but knew it, every crazy tenement has its tragic story; every crumbling wall could its tale unfold. The Canongate is Scottish history fossilised. What ghosts of kings and queens walk there! What strifes of steel-clad nobles! What wretches borne along, in the sight of peopled windows, to the grim embrace of the "maiden"! What hurrying of burgesses to man the city walls at the approach of the Southron! What lamentations over disastrous battle days! James rode up this street on his way to Flodden. Montrose was dragged up hither on a hurdle, and smote, with disdainful glance, his foes gathered together on the balcony. Jenny Geddes flung her stool at the priest in the church yonder. John Knox came up here to his house after his interview with Mary at Holyrood — grim and stern, and unmelted by the tears of a queen. In later days the Pretender rode down the Canongate, his eyes dazzled by the glitter of his father's crown, while bagpipes skirled around, and Jacobite ladies, with white knots in their bosoms, looked down from lofty windows, admiring the beauty of the "Young Ascanius", and his long yellow hair. Down here of an evening rode Dr Johnson and Boswell, and turned in to the White Horse. David Hume had his dwelling in this street, and trod its pavements, much meditating the wars of the Roses and the Parliament, and the fates of English sovereigns. One day a burly ploughman from Ayrshire, with swarthy features and wonderful black eyes, came down here and turned into yonder churchyard to stand, with cloudy lids and forehead reverently bared, beside the grave of poor Fergusson. Down the street, too, often limped a little boy, Walter Scott by name, destined in after years to write its "Chronicles". The Canongate once seen is never to be forgotten. The visitor starts a ghost at every step. Nobles, grave senators, jovial lawyers, had once their abodes here. In the old, low-roofed rooms, half-way to the stars, philosophers talked, wits coruscated, and gallant young fellows, sowing wild oats in the middle of last century, wore rapiers and lace ruffles, and drank claret jovially out of silver stoups. In every room a minuet has been walked, while chairmen and linkmen clustered on the pavement beneath. But the Canongate has fallen from its high estate. Quite another race of people are its present inhabitants. The vices to be seen are not genteel. Whisky has supplanted claret. Nobility has fled, and squalor taken possession. Wild, half-naked children swarm around every door-step. Ruffians lounge about the mouths of the wynds. Female faces, worthy of the

"Inferno", look down from broken windows. Riots are frequent; and drunken mothers reel past scolding white atomies of children that nestle wailing in their bosoms — little wretches to whom Death were the greatest benefactor. The Canongate is avoided by respectable people, and yet it has many visitors. The tourist is anxious to make acquaintance with it. Gentlemen of obtuse olfactory nerve, and of an antiquarian turn of mind, go down its closes and climb its spiral stairs. Deep down these wynds the artist pitches his stool, and spends the day sketching some picturesque gable or doorway. The fever-van comes frequently here to convey some poor sufferer to the hospital. Hither comes the detective in plain clothes on the scent of a burglar. And when evening falls, and the lamps are lit, there is a sudden hubbub and crowd of people, and presently from its midst emerge a couple of policemen and a barrow with a poor, half-clad, tipsy woman from the sister island crouching upon it, her hair hanging loose about her face, her hands quivering with impotent rage, and her tongue wild with curses. Attended by small boys, who bait her with taunts and nicknames, and who appreciate the comic element which so strangely underlies the horrible sight, she is conveyed to the police cell, and will be brought before the magistrate tomorrow — for the twentieth time perhaps — as a "drunk and disorderly", and dealt with accordingly. This is the kind of life the Canongate presents to-day — a contrast with the time when the tall buildings enclosed the high birth and beauty of a kingdom, and when the street beneath rang to the horse-hoofs of a king.

The New Town is divided from the Old by a gorge or valley, now occupied by a railway station; and the means of communication are the Mound, Waverley Bridge, and the North Bridge. With the exception of the Canongate, the more filthy and tumble-down portions of the city are well kept out of sight. You stand on the South Bridge, and looking down, instead of a stream, you see the Cowgate, the dirtiest, narrowest, most densely peopled of Edinburgh streets. Admired once by a French ambassador at the court of one of the Jameses, and yet with certain traces of departed splendour, the Cowgate has fallen into the sere and yellow leaf of furniture brokers, second-hand jewellers, and vendors of deleterious alcohol. These second-hand jewellers' shops, the trinkets seen by bleared gaslight, are the most melancholy sights I know. Watches hang there that once ticked comfortably in the fobs of prosperous men, rings that were once placed by happy bridegrooms on the fingers of happy brides, jewels in which lives the sacredness of death-beds. What tragedies, what disruptions of households, what fell pressure of poverty brought them here! Looking in through the foul windows, the trinkets remind one of shipwrecked gold embedded in the ooze of ocean — gold that speaks of unknown, yet certain, storm and disaster, of the yielding of planks, of the cry of drowning men. Who has the heart to buy them, I wonder? The Cowgate is the Irish portion of the city. Edinburgh leaps over it with bridges; its inhabitants are morally and geographically the lower orders. They keep to their own quarters, and seldom come up to the light of day. Many an Edinburgh man has never set his foot in the street; the condition of the inhabitants is as little known to respectable Edinburgh as are the habits of moles, earth-worms, and the mining population. The people of the Cowgate seldom visit the upper streets. You may walk about the New Town for a twelvemonth before one of these Cowgate pariahs comes between the wind and your gentility. Should you wish to see that strange people "at home", you must visit them. The Cowgate will not come to you: you must go to the Cowgate. The Cowgate holds high drunken carnival every Saturday night; and to walk along it then, from the West Port, through the noble open space of the Grassmarket — where the Covenanters and Captain Porteous suffered — on to Holyrood, is one of the world's sights, and one that does not particularly raise your estimate of human nature. For nights after your dreams will pass from brawl to brawl, shoals of hideous faces will oppress you, sodden countenances of brutal men, women with loud voices and frantic gesticulations, children who have never known innocence. It is amazing of what ugliness the human face is capable. The devil marks his children as a shepherd marks his sheep — that he may know them and claim them again. Many a face flits past here bearing the sign-manual of the fiend.

But Edinburgh keeps all these evil things out of sight, and smiles, with Castle, tower, church-spire, and pyramid rising into sunlight out of garden spaces and belts of foliage. The Cowgate has no power to mar her beauty. There may be a canker at the heart of the peach — there is neither pit nor stain on its dusty velvet. Throned on crags, Edinburgh takes every eye; and, not content with supremacy in beauty, she claims an intellectual supremacy also. She is a patrician amongst British cities, "A penniless lass wi' a lang pedigree".

Alexander Smith, *A Summer in Skye*

Suggestions for Further Reading

Hatter's Castle by A.J. Cronin (already referred to in the previous section) describes a character of just the same brutal type as Gourlay in *The House with the Green Shutters*.

The Goat-Wife by Alasdair Alpin MacGregor is a good example of the host of books about crofting life in the north, many of them excellent; this one is a combination of anecdote and continuous narrative, and has, incidentally, evocative passages about the author's early life in Edinburgh and superb photographs.

No Mean City by Alexander McArthur is perhaps a work of limited literary merit, but it does give a vivid picture of the famous Glasgow gangs of the thirties.

In *King Billy* Edwin Morgan, one of the most considerable poets at present writing in Scotland, looks back from the standpoint of the sixties on the life of a gang leader.

Wax Fruit by Guy McCrone is a family saga showing some other aspects of Glasgow life.

The poems and short stories of George Mackay Brown tell us much about Orkney. The poetry of Edwin Muir, too, owes much to the author's Orcadian origins.

The work of the Edinburgh poet Robert Fergusson, a senior contemporary of Burns, is full of the writer's native city. *The Heart of Midlothian* by Sir Walter Scott and *Weir of Hermiston* also give pictures of Edinburgh at different times in history. *The Prime of Miss Jean Brodie* by Muriel Spark mischievously portrays Edinburgh in the earlier part of this century.

Other modern pictures of Edinburgh can be found in poetry: among others, the work of Norman MacCaig and Robert Garioch's *Embro to the Ploy*.

Liz Lochhead's essay, despite its title, merely touches on the religious rivalry that has so disfigured life in the west of Scotland in the past. This subject is more fully dealt with in Alan Spence's story *Its Colours They Were Fine* and in Hector MacMillan's play *The Sash*.

4 Work and the Economy

The first three passages in this section explore the philosophy of work and its place in the economy of a nation. *Labour* comes from a collection of essays by Thomas Carlyle (1795–1881), essayist and historian, who through his repute as a character in Chelsea, and his influential writings, became the best known literary Scot of his day. Here he sets out a flamboyant radical case for 'Know thy work and do it.' Sir Compton Mackenzie in his *Rectorial Address* of 1932 discusses the value of a sense of vocation in a world of increasing material and technological progress. The idea of the contribution that a trained citizen makes to his community is linked by Mackenzie with the awakening interest of his time in common national aims and identity, and invites comparison with similar themes in James Reid's 1972 Address, *Alienation*, which discusses the attitude of those who control industry. (See also George Blake's presentation of a manager's point of view in the next group of passages in this section.)

The next three passages look at specific groups of people whose way of life is seen to be influenced and controlled by what happens to their work. Henry Thomas, Lord Cockburn (1779–1854) was a Scottish judge who left on record a vivid and penetrating picture of Edinburgh life and society of the early nineteenth century. Here, he writes in 1843 about unemployment in Scotland as a whole. Hugh Miller (1802–1856), who worked as a stone-mason from the ages of sixteen to thirty-three, devoting the winter months to writing and natural history, continues the protest against the careless manipulation of the work-force. (Compare the mole-catcher's satisfaction with his job in Neil Gunn's essay.) George Blake (1893–1961), novelist and journalist in London (where he edited *John o' London's Weekly* and the *Strand Magazine*) and Glasgow, sees the passing of work for many skilled and unskilled workmen through the eyes of a sensitive and deeply interested employer.

In the final two passages in this section we come from discussion of labour in general and the economics of specific trades to people observed while *at* work. Two twentieth-century novelists, Archie Hind from Glasgow and Neil Gunn from Caithness, show something of the difference between working on one's own and being a member of a team — Matthew Craig, indeed, having the added complication of being a temporary member of a team.

Labour

For there is a perennial nobleness, and even sacredness, in Work. Were he never so benighted, forgetful of his high calling, there is always hope in a man that actually and earnestly works: in Idleness alone is there perpetual despair. Work, never so Mammonish, mean, *is* in communication with Nature; the real desire to get Work done will itself lead one more and more to truth, to Nature's appointments and regulations which are truth.

The latest Gospel in this world is, Know thy work and do it. 'Know thyself': long enough has that poor 'self' of thine tormented thee; thou wilt never get to 'know' it, I believe! Think it not thy business, this of knowing thyself; thou art an unknowable individual: know what thou canst work at; and work at it, like a Hercules! That will be thy better plan.

It has been written, 'an endless significance lies in Work'; a man perfects himself by working. Foul jungles are cleared away, fair seedfields rise instead, and stately cities; and withal the man himself first ceases to be a jungle and foul unwholesome desert thereby. Consider how, even in the meanest sorts of Labour, the whole soul of a man is composed into a kind of real harmony, the instant he sets himself to work! Doubt, Desire, Sorrow, Remorse, Indignation, Despair itself, all these like hell-dogs lie beleaguering the soul of the poor dayworker, as of every man, but he bends himself with free valour against his task, and all these are stilled all these shrink murmuring far off into their caves. The man is now a man. The blessed glow of Labour in him, is it not as purifying fire, wherein all poison is burnt up, and of sour smoke itself there is made bright blessed flame!

Destiny, on the whole, has no other way of cultivating us. A formless Chaos, once set it *revolving*, grows round and ever rounder; ranges itself, by mere force of gravity, into strata, spherical courses; is no longer a Chaos, but a round compacted World. What would become of the Earth, did she cease to revolve? In the poor old Earth, so long as she revolves, all inequalities, irregularities disperse themselves; all irregularities are incessantly becoming regular. Hast thou looked on the Potter's wheel, — one of the venerablest objects; old as the Prophet Ezekiel and far older? Rude lumps of clay, how they spin themselves up, by mere quick whirling, into beautiful circular dishes. And fancy the most assiduous Potter, but without his wheel; reduced to make dishes, or rather amorphous

botches, by mere kneading and baking! Even such a Potter were
Destiny, with a human soul that would rest and lie at ease, that
would not work and spin! Of an idle unrevolving man the kindest
Destiny, like the most assiduous Potter without wheel, can bake
and knead nothing other than a botch; let her spend on him what
expensive colouring, what gilding and enamelling she will, he is
but a botch. Not a dish; no, a bulging, kneaded, crooked, shambl-
ing, squint-cornered, amorphous botch, — a mere enamelled vessel
of dishonour! Let the idle think of this.

Thomas Carlyle, *Past and Present*

The New Humanitarian World

But set on one side the problem of your livelihood and contemplate
the world you will presently enter, not as competitors in the struggle for existence, but as cool observers. As each year goes by that
world becomes a little smaller. New achievements in rapid flight
make it possible to suppose that before you die you may go round
the world in eighty hours with more ease than Jules Verne's hero
went round it in eighty days. Long before that, however, wireless
and television will have made even such a brief voyage tiresome,
for you will have already heard and seen the whole world from
your own armchairs. There will be so much to titillate your attention when you are not slaving at a desk in the service of some
machine invented to serve mankind that you may lose the habit of
reading, and perhaps the ability to read anything except the jargon
of commercial exchange. Even illustrated newspapers with a few
headlines may be extinct before any of you have reached the century of years which with the perfection of hygiene most of you may
reasonably expect to reach. Art in any sense in which we use the
word to-day will be confined to the efforts of architects to pack
people into their huge concrete hives, of dramatists to stimulate
with coloured stereoscopic films the appetites of a satiated and
incurious public, and of musicians to translate industry into rhythm
by volumes of electrical sound.

The task of education will be to create various group-minds and
to take care that the group-mind thus created shall never advance
beyond a fixed condition, so that it may not interfere with other

group-minds. Recreation will still be provided by various forms of ball games, and as members of the British group of commercial interests you will recall, not without pride, that Britons taught the rest of the world to play association football. The relentless onset of knowledge will have finally disposed of the myth of immortality; but by offering artificial rejuvenation together with a normal expectancy of a century of life, or even longer, it will justify the old proverb that a bird in the hand is worth two in the bush. I might add that there will be few actual birds left in the air, few fish left in the sea, and though by the enclosure of municipal parks a certain amount of wild life will be preserved for the amusement of those who on holidays cannot find room at the football matches, there will be few animals elsewhere except rats.

Perhaps in offering to you the prospect of attaining such an earthly paradise I am being optimistic; but be not down-hearted, your children will live to enjoy it. And if some of you cherishing a few shreds of what is scornfully known as romance resent such a future for posterity, if some of you still believe that after death you will wake to the truth of life's object on this mathematically insignificant green planet, you must weigh your private regrets against the benefits of material progress. There will be no poverty. There will be no disease. Physical pain will not be allowed. Mental agony will not be able to exist in that rich ennui. The commodities of the world will be equitably distributed; and there will be hot and cold water laid on in every room. To be sure, nobody in posterity will be able to call his soul his own; but that will not greatly matter, because by then it will have been definitely established that nobody possesses such an exclusively personal piece of property.

This picture of a new humanitarian world freed from the shackles of nationalism and individualism may seem a caricature of the ideals of those who now in an intellectual majority condemn people like myself as the romantic exponents of discredited social, political and religious theories; but it is not more unkindly distorted than the picture of a parochial nationalism which it amuses the fancy of international idealists to draw. If nationalism be something more than a sentimental emotion it must be able to fight for itself in the arena of mundane tendencies. I have too infrangible a faith in the spiritual destiny of man to propose that Scotland should retire from the struggle in order to preserve an ignominious unimportance as a small nation on the edge of the great Eurasian continent. If I suggest that she should step back, it is because I believe that by step-

ping back and living upon herself she can leap forward to the
spiritual and intellectual leadership of mankind. It is not because I
believe that Scotland is dying, but because I believe that Scotland is
about to live with a fullness of life undreamed of yet, that I count it
the proudest moment of my career to be standing here to-day.

Compton Mackenzie, *Rectorial Address*,
University of Glasgow, 1932

Profit

Recently on television I saw an advertisement. The scene is a banquet. A gentleman is on his feet proposing a toast. His speech is
full of phrases like "this full-bodied specimen". Sitting beside him
is a young, buxom woman. The image she projects is not pompous
but foolish. She is visibly preening herself, believing that she is the
object of this bloke's eulogy. Then he concludes — "and now I
give..." then a brand name of what used to be described as
Empire sherry. The woman is shattered, hurt and embarrassed.
Then the laughter. Derisive and cruel laughter. The real point, of
course, is this: in this charade the viewers were obviously expected
to identify not with the victim but with her tormentors.

The other illustration is the widespread, implicit acceptance of
the concept and term, "the rat race". The picture it conjures up is
one where we are scurrying around scrambling for position, tramp-
ling on others, back-stabbing, all in pursuit of personal success.
Even genuinely intended friendly advice can sometimes take the
form of someone saying to you, "Listen, you look after number
one." Or as they say in London, "Bang the bell, Jack, I'm on the
bus."

To the students I address this appeal. Reject these attitudes.
Reject the values and false morality that underlie these attitudes. A
rat race is for rats. We're not rats. We're human beings. Reject the
insidious pressures in society that would blunt your critical faculties
to all that is happening around you, that would caution silence in
the face of injustice lest you jeopardise your chances of promotion
and self-advancement. This is how it starts and before you know
where you are, you're a fully paid-up member of the rat-pack. The
price is too high. It entails the loss of your dignity and human
spirit. Or as Christ put it, "What doth it profit a man if he gain the

whole world and suffer the loss of his soul?''

Profit is the sole criterion used by the establishment to evaluate economic activity. From the rat race to lame ducks. The vocabulary in vogue is a give-away. It is more reminiscent of a human menagerie than human society. The power structures that have inevitably emerged from this approach threaten and undermine our hard won democratic rights. The whole process is towards the centralisation and concentration of power in fewer and fewer hands. The facts are there for all who want to see. Giant monopoly companies and consortia dominate almost every branch of our economy. The men who wield effective control within these giants exercise a power over their fellow men which is frightening and is a negation of democracy.

Government by the people for the people becomes meaningless unless it includes major economic decision-making by the people for the people. This is not simply an economic matter. In essence it is an ethical and moral question, for whoever takes the important economic decisions in society *ipso facto* determines the social priorities of that society.

From the Olympian heights of an executive suite, in an atmosphere where your success is judged by the extent to which you can maximise profits, the overwhelming tendency must be to see people as units of production, as indices in your accountants' books. To appreciate fully the inhumanity of this situation, you have to see the hurt and despair in the eyes of a man suddenly told he is redundant without provision made for suitable alternative employment, with the prospect in the West of Scotland, if he is in his late forties or fifties, of spending the rest of his life in the Labour Exchange. Someone, somewhere has decided he is unwanted, unneeded, and is to be thrown on the industrial scrap heap. From the very depth of my being, I challenge the right of any man or any group of men, in business or in government, to tell a fellow human being that he or she is expendable.

The concentration of power in the economic field is matched by the centralisation of decision-making in the political institutions of society. The power of Parliament has undoubtedly been eroded over past decades with more and more authority being invested in the Executive. The power of local authorities has been and is being systematically undermined. The only justification I can see for local government is as a counter-balance to the centralised character of national government.

Local government is to be re-structured. What an opportunity, one would think, for de-centralising as much power as possible back to local communities. Instead the proposals are for centralising local government. It is once again a blue-print for bureaucracy, not democracy. If these proposals are implemented, in a few years when asked "Where do you come from?" I can reply: "The Western Region." It even sounds like a hospital board.

It stretches from Oban to Girvan and eastwards to include most of the Glasgow conurbation. As in other matters, I must ask the politicians who favour these proposals — where and how in your calculations did you quantify the value of a community? Of community life? Of a sense of belonging? Of the feeling of identification? These are rhetorical questions. I know the answers. Such human considerations do not feature in their thought processes.

Everything that is proposed from the establishment seems almost calculated to minimise the role of the people, to miniaturise man. I can understand how attractive this prospect must be to those at the top. Those of us who refuse to be pawns in their power game can be picked up by their bureaucratic tweezers and dropped in a filing cabinet under "M" for malcontent or maladjusted. When you think of some of the high flats around us, it can hardly be an accident that they are as near as one could get to an architectural representation of a filing cabinet.

If modern technology requires greater and larger productive units, let us make our wealth-producing resources and potential subject to public control and to social accountability. Let us gear our society to social need, not personal greed. Given such creative reorientation of society, there is no doubt in my mind that in a few years we could eradicate in our country the scourge of poverty, the underprivileged, slums, and insecurity.

Even this is not enough. To measure social progress purely by material advance is not enough. Our aim must be the enrichment of the whole quality of life. It requires a social and cultural or, if you wish, a spiritual transformation of our country. A necessary part of this must be the restructuring of the institutions of government and, where necessary, the evolution of additional structures so as to involve the people in the decision-making processes of our society. The so-called experts will tell you that this would be cumbersome or marginally inefficient. I am prepared to sacrifice a margin of efficiency for the value of the people's participation. Anyway, in the longer term, I reject this argument.

To unleash the latent potential of our people requires that we give them responsibility. The untapped resources of the North Sea are as nothing compared to the untapped resources of our people. I am convinced that the great mass of our people go through life without even a glimmer of what they could have contributed to their fellow human beings. This is a personal tragedy. It is a social crime. The flowering of each individual's personality and talents is the pre-condition for everyone's development.

James Reid, *Rectorial Address*,
University of Glasgow, 1972

The Unemployed Poor

Of all the new features of modern society in Britain, none is so peculiar or frightful as the hordes of strong poor, always liable to be thrown out of employment by stagnation of trade. There have been above 10 000 of them in Paisley for more than a year; and a similar cloud darkens every considerable town in Scotland. In Edinburgh, besides its fullest complement of ordinary distress, we have a battalion of at least 1 200 of what are now known by the almost technical term of "Unemployed Poor". Work (generally useless and often mischievous) is invented for these men (for the whole 12 000 are males, many of them with families); but as there is really nothing for them to do, they work languidly and idly, knowing perfectly well that it is not for their labour but for their poverty that they are paid. And, being congregated in numbers, and distinguished by a title, they form a separate class, a new state. No doubt there are many good people among them, but their position does not tend to improve them. They are more lazy, more unreasonable, more reckless, than when they had nothing to depend upon but their own exertions. The alarming circumstance in their condition is, that they have discovered that their number is their force. Instead of resorting to places less distressed, and there getting themselves absorbed obscurely into the ordinary population, they prefer towns, where the magnitude of the evil has terrified the authorities, and produced compulsory subscriptions and earnest applications to Government. Paisley, from the precarious nature of its fancy manufactures and the character of its people the worst town in Scotland, is their favourite resort; while they shudder at the word Aberdeen, where, though much better attended to, they are not acknowledged as a distinct class. They are gratified by appearing in their corporate character, not merely from pride, but because they see that number and unity best secure relief, and, if carried far enough, make them irresistible. Indeed, what answer can be made to 10 000 people who violate no law, but simply stand on the street and say truly — We have no work. They know that they won't be allowed to die there, and provided they live, the difficulty, the sacrifices, the discussion, the terror, and the apparatus by which they are supplied, only increase their importance in their own eyes. Scarcely one of them enlists — I believe in Paisley almost literally not one; and their aversion to undertake ordinary labour at higher wages makes it certain that they prefer lounging, as public characters, on sixpence a day, to toiling privately on a shilling. Hitherto they have behaved peaceably, but they are excellent materials for the demagogue. The sufferings of the class just above them — of those who are struggling to avoid falling down to public destitution, have been very severe, and have been endured with the most honourable patience. The silent misery, the ungrudged sacrifices, and the unnoticed exertions of this whole layer of the community ought to raise our estimate of its virtue.

This is an entirely new element in the population, and the prospects it conjures up are terrible. Are we *ever* to get the better of it? We may possibly get the better of this as of any other individual crisis; but can we or any highly manufacturing community expect to be ever free of the risk of the constant recurrence of such scenes? Until machinery shall be so perfect as that it can dispense with human limbs almost entirely, and until the generation which shall witness its perfection shall have passed away, are not millions of starving people the necessary occasional sloughs of a very manufacturing nation? Whatever political economy may predict for distant futurity, I see no visible prospect of this country being unafflicted by this scourge. It was only about the end of the American war that the spring-tide of our commercial prosperity began to flow. After this, twenty years of a war, which closed every port in Europe to every vessel except our own, gave us the almost exclusive trade of the world, and for about ten years after the war ceased there was no such competition, though it was rapidly rising, as could shake our supremacy. During all this period, extending from 1785 to 1825, it was our monopoly of the steam-engine that made us. There were then probably more of these wealth-producers in Glasgow than in all the continent of Europe. That monopoly is now gone for ever. A richer world may make us a richer people, but still we must feel its vicissitudes, which, if it be a world whose wealth depends mainly on manufactures, must be as periodical as our own; and therefore I see no ground for expecting that, so long as we are a nation of manufacturers, we can ever be uncursed by these heartrending visitations — visitations which are bad enough as productive of misery, but far worse when viewed as instruments of political danger.

Henry Cockburn, *Memorials of his Time*

The North-Country Mason

The professional character of the mason varies a good deal in the several provinces of Scotland, according to the various circumstances in which he is placed. He is in general a blunt, manly, taciturn fellow, who, without much of the Radical or Chartist about him, especially if wages be good and employment abundant, rarely touches his hat to a gentleman. His employment is less purely mechanical than many others: he is not like a man ceaselessly engaged in pointing needles or fashioning pin-heads. On the contrary, every stone he lays or hews demands the exercise of a certain amount of judgment for itself; and so he cannot wholly suffer his mind to fall asleep over his work. When engaged, too, in erecting some fine building, he always experiences a degree of interest in marking the effect of the design developing itself piecemeal, and growing up under his hands; and so he rarely wearies of what he is doing. Further, his profession has this advantage, that it educates his sense of sight. Accustomed to ascertain the straightness of lines at a glance, and to cast his eye along plane walls, or the mouldings of entablatures or architraves, in order to determine the rectitude of the masonry, he acquires a sort of mathematical precision in determining the true bearings and position of objects, and is usually found, when admitted into a rifle club, to equal without previous practice its second-rate shots. He only falls short of its first-rate ones, because, uninitiated by the experience of his profession in the mystery of the parabolic curve, he fails, in taking aim, to make the proper allowance for it. The mason is almost always a silent man:

the strain on his respiration is too great, when he is actively employed, to leave the necessary freedom to the organs of speech; and so at least the provincial builder or stone-cutter rarely or never becomes a democratic orator. I have met with exceptional cases in the larger towns; but they were the result of individual idiosyncrasies, developed in clubs and taverns, and were not professional.

It is, however, with the character of our north-country masons that I have at present chiefly to do. Living in small villages, or in cottages in the country, they can very rarely procure employment in the neighbourhood of their dwellings, and so they are usually content to regard these as simply their homes for the winter and earlier spring months, when they have nothing to do, and to remove for work to other parts of the country, where bridges, or harbours, or farm-steadings are in the course of building — to be subjected there to the influences of what is known as the barrack or rather bothy life. These barracks or bothies are almost always of the most miserable description. I have lived in hovels that were invariably flooded in wet weather by the overflowings of neighbouring swamps, and through whose roofs I could tell the hour at night, by marking from my bed the stars that were passing over the openings along the ridge: I have resided in other dwellings of rather higher pretensions, in which I have been awakened during every heavier night-shower by the rain-drops splashing upon my face where I lay a-bed. I remember that Uncle James, in urging me not to become a mason, told me that a neighbouring laird, when asked why he left a crazy old building standing behind a group of neat modern offices, informed the querist that it was not altogether through bad taste the hovel was spared, but from the circumstance that he found it of great convenience every time his speculations brought *a drove of pigs* or *a squad of masons* the way. And my after experience showed me that the story might not be in the least apocryphal, and that masons had reasons at times for not touching their hats to gentlemen.

In these barracks the food is of the plainest and coarsest description: oatmeal forms its staple, with milk, when milk can be had, which is not always; and as the men have to cook by turns, with only half an hour or so given them in which to light a fire, and prepare the meal for a dozen or twenty associates, the cooking is invariably an exceedingly rough and simple affair. I have known mason-parties engaged in the central Highlands in building bridges, not unfrequently reduced, by a tract of wet weather, that soaked

their only fuel the turf, and rendered it incombustible, to the
extremity of eating their oatmeal raw, and merely moistened by a
little water, scooped by the hand from a neighbouring brook. I have
oftener than once seen our own supply of salt fail us; and after
relief had been afforded by a Highland smuggler — for there was
much smuggling in salt in those days, ere the repeal of the duties
— I have heard a complaint from a young fellow regarding the
hardness of our fare, at once checked by a comrade's asking him
whether he was not an ungrateful dog to grumble in that way,
seeing that, after living on fresh poultices for a week, we had actually that morning got porridge with salt in it. One marked effect of
the annual change which the north-country mason has to undergo,
from a life of domestic comfort to a life of hardship in the bothy, if
he has not passed middle life, is a great apparent increase in his
animal spirits. At home he is in all probability a quiet, rather dull-
looking personage, not much given to laugh or joke; whereas in the
bothy, if the squad be a large one, he becomes wild, and a humor-
ist — laughs much, and grows ingenious in playing off pranks on
his fellows. As in all other communities there are certain laws recognised in the barrack as useful for controlling at least its younger
members, the apprentices; but in the general tone of merriment,
even these lose their character, and, ceasing to be a terror to evil-
doers, become in the execution mere occasions of mirth. I never, in
all my experience, saw a serious punishment inflicted. Shortly after
our arrival at Conon-side, my master, chancing to remark that he
had not wrought as a journeyman for twenty-five years before, was
voted a "ramming" for taking, as was said, such high ground with
his brother workmen; but, though sentence was immediately
executed, they dealt gently with the old man, who had good sense
enough to acquiesce in the whole as a joke. And yet, amid all this
wild merriment and license, there was not a workman who did not
regret the comforts of his quiet home, and long for the happiness
which was, he felt, to be enjoyed only there. It has been long
known that gaiety is not solid enjoyment; but that the gaiety should
indicate little else than the want of solid enjoyment, is a circumstance not always suspected. My experience of barrack-life has
enabled me to receive without hesitation what has been said of the
occasional merriment of slaves in America and elsewhere, and fully
to credit the often-repeated statement, that the abject serfs of despo-
tic governments laugh more than the subjects of a free country.
Poor fellows! If the British people were as unhappy as slaves or

serfs, they would, I daresay, learn in time to be quite as merry. There are, however, two circumstances that serve to prevent the bothy life of the north-country mason from essentially injuring his character in the way it almost never fails to injure that of the farm-servant. As he has to calculate on being part of every winter, and almost every spring, unemployed, he is compelled to practise a self-denying economy, the effect of which, when not carried to the extreme of a miserly narrowness, is always good; and Hallow-day returns him every season to the humanizing influences of his home.

Hugh Miller, *My Schools and Schoolmasters*

The Clyde — 'For Sale'

The *Estramadura* went down the river on the Wednesday afternoon, and Leslie Pagan travelled with her.

He was busy and preoccupied while the tugs moved her from the basin in their fussily efficient way. She was still his own, and the more precious for being the last he had in that kind. His heart was in his mouth when her cruiser-stern cleared the pierhead with only a foot to spare. He was haunted by daft fears that this winch would not function and that bollard fail to hold the pull of the tow-ropes. The extinction of a series of lights on the promenade deck at one moment gave him the panic notion that the dynamos had broken down. Knowing well that the apprehension was excessive, he was haunted by a sense of the fallibility of the intricate and interdependent mechanisms of the ship; her security, the thousands of pounds of value she represented, resting perhaps on an abraded inch of insulation on a mile or so of electric cable.

As soon, however, as she was fair in mid-channel, her head downstream and her beautiful light hull towering over the riverside buildings, he suddenly resigned his creation to chance and the skill of the pilot. At another time he would have been fretfully active until her anchor-chain rattled over the Tail of the Bank, dodging now into the engine-room, now up steel ladders to where the steering-gear churned forward and back again with its own queer air of independence, and then hurrying to the bridge and the battery of telltale lights up there. But now he did nothing, keeping in a mood of uneasy detachment out of the way of busy men in overalls. He found a corner for himself on A deck, well forward below the navigating bridge, and in that retired position stood for a long time — watching, as it were, the last creation of his own hands pass forever beyond him.

It was in a sense a procession that he witnessed, the high, tragic pageant of the Clyde. Yard after yard passed by, the berths empty, the grass growing about the sinking keel-blocks. He remembered how, in the brave days, there would be scores of ships ready for the launching along this reach, their sterns hanging over the tide, and how the men at work on them on high stagings would turn from the job and tug off their caps and cheer the new ship setting out to sea. And now only the gaunt, dumb poles and groups of men, workless, watching in silence the mocking passage of the vessel. It was bitter to know that they knew — that almost every man among them was an artist in one of the arts that go to the building of a ship; that every feature of the *Estramadura* would come under an expert and loving scrutiny, that her passing would remind them of the joy of work and tell them how many among them would never work again. It appalled Leslie Pagan that not a cheer came from those watching groups.

It was a tragedy beyond economics. It was not that so many thousands of homes lacked bread and butter. It was that a tradition, a skill, a glory, a passion, was visibly in decay and all the acquired and inherited loveliness of artistry rotting along the banks of the stream.

Into himself he counted and named the yards they passed. The number and variety stirred him to wonder, now that he had ceased to take them for granted. His mental eye moving backwards up the river, he saw the historic place at Govan, Henderson's of Meadowside at the mouth of the Kelvin, and the long stretch of Fairfield on the southern bank opposite. There came Stephens' of Linthouse next, and Clydeholm facing it across the narrow, yellow ditch of the ship-channel. From thence down river the range along the northern bank was almost continuous for miles — Connell, Inglis, Blythswood, and the rest: so many that he could hardly remember their order. He was distracted for a moment to professionalism by the lean grey forms of destroyers building for a foreign Power in the sheds of a yard that had dramatically deserted Thames for Clyde. Then he lost himself again in the grim majesty of the parade. There came John Brown's, stretching along half a mile of waterfront at Clydebank, the monstrous red hull of Number 534 looming in its abandonment like a monument of the glory departed; as if shipbuilding man had tried to do too much and had been defeated by the mightiness of his own conception. Then came, seeming to point the moral, the vast desolation of Beardmore's at Dalmuir, cradle of the mightiest battleships and now a scrapheap, empty and silent forever, the great gantry over the basin proclaiming stagnation and an end.

Even where the Clyde opened out above Erskine, with the Kilpatricks green and sweet above the river on the one hand and the wooded, fat lands of Renfrewshire stretching to the escarpment of Misty Law on the other, the sight of a legend — FOR SALE — painted large on the walls of an empty shed reminded him with the effect of a blow that Napier and Miller's were gone, shut down, finished, the name never to appear again on a brass plate below the bridge of a good ship. And he suddenly remembered that there lay on his desk at the office a notice of sale of the plant at Bow, Maclachlan's on the Cart by Paisley. His world seemed visibly to be crumbling. Already he had been appalled by the emptiness of Lobnitz's and Simons's at Renfrew, and the sense of desolation, of present catastrophe, closed the more oppressively upon him.

As they rounded the bend by Bowling, passing close under the wooded crags of Auchentorlie on the one hand and, as on a Dutch canal, past the flats of Erskine on the other, his eye was taken by the scene ahead. The jagged, noble range of the Cowal hills made a purple barrier against the glow of the westering winter sun. Now he was lost for a space in wonder that this cradle and home of ships enjoyed a setting so lovely. Through the gap of the Vale of Leven he could see the high peak of Ben Lomond, and his fancy ranged up those desolate, distant slopes. But then the dome of Dumbarton Rock, the westernmost of the chain strung across the neck of Scotland, brought him to think of the mean town at its base, and of Denny's yard in the crook of the Leven behind it, and of the lovely, fast, small ships they could build, and of the coming of the turbine. And another yard, there, Macmillan's, derelict.

Past Dumbarton, the river opening to the Firth, the scene took on an even more immediate grandeur. The sands of the Pillar Bank were showing in golden streaks through the falling tide. The peninsula of Ardmore was a pretty tuft of greenery thrust out towards the channel. Dead ahead lay the mouth of the Gareloch, backed by the jagged peaks on the western side of Loch Long. A man could almost feel the freshness of the open sea coming to meet him over the miles of island, hill and loch; and Leslie Pagan marked how the fresher and larger waves slapped against the sides of the *Estramadura* and could almost imagine that the ship responded with quiver and curtsey to their invitation.

That openness of the river below the derelict timber ponds of Langbank, however, is deceptive; for still the channel must run round the end of the bank and close into the Renfrewshire shore. There are miles of waste space there over the shallows, and Glasgow is more than twenty miles away before a ship of size has more than a few feet of water between her keel and the bottom. Port Glasgow and Greenock look across miles of sand and sea to the Highland hills, but the yards there must launch their ships into narrow waters; so that the man who had built the *Estramadura*, scanning the shores, saw thereabouts an even thicker crowding of berths than he had marked on the upper reaches.

It was another roster of great names, older, more redolent even than those that had become namely about Glasgow with the deepening of the Clyde. Ferguson's, Duncan's, Murdoch's, Russell's, Hamilton's ... Even he could not be sure that he had them right; there had been so many changes. Out on Garvel Point, under the old marooned Scots mansion-house, stood Brown's — the "Siberia" of the artisan's lingo. There came Scott's East Yard — was it not once Steele's, where the clippers were built? There came the Greenock and Grangemouth, once the artisan's "Klondike". Then Scott's Mid Yard, then Caird's, the last of the lot — closed down. It was queer to see how Newark Castle survived in its pink grace and antiquity among the stocks and gantries.

George Blake, *The Shipbuilders*

Killers and Skinner

After the morning halt for breakfast Mat was working in a room beside two killers with whom he didn't usually work. The benefit man who usually did their room had cut himself and as Mat's own rooms weren't too busy he took his place. One of the killers in the room was a big, coarse-built man with a slow sarcastic manner who was in the habit of baiting any benefit man who came into the room to work. He would take a gratuitous dislike to somebody and then he'd try to make their lives miserable with his malicious sadistic remarks. He had the knack of finding out the sore spots in people and the gift of probing them with his wheedling jocular manner. He started on Mat.

"I see you had a day off yesterday."

Mat had lost a day's wages and the boss had bawled him out, so he didn't want to talk about it. "Aye, Wullie."

"You'll have lost a day's wages. You'll be feeling that on Friday wull ye not?"

"Ach, not so bad," Mat said.

"Whit? Are you rich then?"

"I'm no' rich. Just nut worried. There's other things than money."

"Of course," Wullie said, "I forgot you don't worry about money. You just worry about higher things." He gloated to people often about money because he himself was invulnerable on that point. Apart from his work as a killer he also dealt in cattle, buying beef on the hoof and selling it in the market to the butchers. "You wait till the bairnies start coming. Then you'll worry all right."

"Right, Wullie," Mat said. "*I'll* do the worrying." Mat didn't want to needle with Wullie. In spite of the fact that he could be so aggravating Mat felt sympathy towards him. There was a feeling of intelligence which came from the man and Mat guessed that his awareness of other people's vulnerability came from a genuine sensitivity towards them. Also there was this contradiction in the man's make-up in that his bigness, his bulky powerfulness, exuded that kind of gentleness which is so often found in physically strong men and gave a feeling from him that belied his maliciousness.

Mat started to skin the head on Wullie's beast. He cleared the thrapple up to the breast, cut the hide away from the cheeks, slit the nostrils and was about to skin down the last strip of hide from the nose to between the horns. He was bending down over the head when Wullie, who was clearing the hide from the breast, backed into him.

"Oops! Sorry!" Wullie said, and he stood up straight, stroking his knife and looking over his shoulder at Mat. "Are you nut finished that heid yet?"

Mat muttered at him. "How in the hell can I skin the heid when your big fat arse is in the road!" He was sure that Wullie had backed into him to annoy him.

Wullie just grinned. "Temper, temper."

"Oot the road," Mat said, and he bent down and skinned the head.

Wullie stood back, ostentatiously giving Mat room. Mat's knife had just been set and he had a good edge to it so that he cleared the last strip of hide in one stroke.

"My, my!" Wullie said. "Look at the knife flying. It's a pity ye cannae keep up wi' it."

Mat felt his temper going, but he suppressed it and went on working. He looked at Wullie while he was working and began to think that his dryness and dourness was an affectation in the man — and Mat guessed that he held an image of himself as being like this — slow, indifferent, invulnerable, contained. There was a period of silence while the beasts were being hung on the cambrels. As the carcases started to lift from the ground Mat slit the belly in Wullie's beast, cleared the fat, removed the intestine, punched down the swelling paunch to expose the gullet, deftly slitting the little pink tube and pulling the stomachs on to the floor. Then he went over to the other killer's beast and did the same, working fast in order to keep himself ahead of the killer. Wullie had started to make a running commentary on Mat's work. He was standing grinning behind the beast, clearing the vent and shouting in mock admiration. "Oh, look at him go. Mind yersel. Watch his knife." When Mat ran out of the room with the intestines draped over his arm he had to use that characteristic mincing gait as his feet slid over the greasy floor and among the piled up hooves. Wullie shouted. "Oh! You'll heat your watter."

When Mat came into the room again he moved ponderously and slowly, keeping his face dour and in fact half-mimicking all Wullie's mannerisms. He stroked his knife slowly on the steel, put it into its wooden sheath, then stuck his arms akimbo. He spoke in a friendly tone of voice.

"Wullie, lad. You're nattering away there like some auld sweetie wife." The other killer in the room looked up and grinned as Mat addressed him. "Tut, tut. What a chatterbox. His tongue's goin' like the clapper of a bell." He turned his back on Wullie and started to separate the stomachs on the floor. He affected an air of indifference. Wullie didn't like the garrulous role which Mat had cast him in and his face only half hid his annoyance as he pulled viciously at the hide under the tail.

Wullie didn't speak again until the next two beasts had been felled and he had just about finished. Mat had cleared the room, hung up the offals and was standing watching Wullie splitting the beast's back bone. Both Wullie and the other killer were taking great care with the splitting as both the beasts belonged to Wullie himself. The carcases were from young bullocks and the bones were soft and easy to split. Wullie got back into his jocular mood again for he turned and smiled sarcastically at Mat.

"You've got time to go down and get a haircut before the next felling."

"Go and get stuffed," Mat said. He turned and walked away to the door of the room and Wullie shouted after him. "Look at the intellectual cheating the barber." Mat stood at the door of the room looking into the pass. He wished that the next felling was past so that he could get away from Wullie to another room. Wullie was still shouting at him. "He's saving up for a fiddle. He cannae get his hair cut till he gets an estimate from the barber."

"I thought," Mat asked, "that you had enough big deals of your own without worrying about other people's business."

"It is my business." Wullie spoke with his voice full of moralistic viciousness. "You shouldnae be allowed to work wi' food wi' your hair that length." Wullie had stopped splitting the beast and was now stripping the pleural membrane from the inside of the ribs. Mat watched. There were two diffuse pink spots on the inner side of each rib cage and as Wullie removed the pleural membrane he was also removing these pink spots along with some little brown oval-shaped tubers. Adhesions and tubers.

"Why?" Mat asked.

"Because people have to eat the beef," Wullie said, still moralising.

Mat looked at Wullie incredulously. He felt goose pimples crawl all over him as he realised that as Wullie was reproving him with all the fervour of his moral indignation he could also remove this slight trace of tuberculosis from the carcase so that the meat inspector wouldn't see it, and so that he wouldn't lose the price of the carcase.

"So they have, Wullie," Mat said and went over to where the lungs were hanging. He trimmed some fat away and cut through the lymph nodes attached to the trachea. In the centre of each gland there was a focus of yellow pus. Mat started to shout. "Inspector! IN-SPEC-TOR!"

"Shurrup," Wullie said.

Mat went on shouting. When you are used to working amongst

the clatter of bogey wheels, the crack of pistols, the grinding of gears, the bawling of cattle, you have to learn to make yourself heard and Mat had cultivated a clear mountaineer's yell which pierced through the other sounds and could be heard in every part of the slaughter-house. Wullie came out from behind the hanging carcase with an expression of pain and disgust on his face. Mat started to shout again using his hands against his mouth like a trumpet.

"Inspector! Inspector!"

When the meat inspector came in his white coat he glanced casually at the suppurating glands and gestured towards the door and Mat took the offals and dumped them on the floor outside. The rest of the carcase as well was condemned as unfit for human consumption. Wullie was furious and when the inspector had left the room he turned on Mat. He spoke slowly, and he seemed genuinely hurt. "Whit did you dae that for?"

"People have to eat that beef," Mat said, deliberately repeating Wullie's phrase.

"That carcase would maybe have been cleared if you had kept your mouth shut," Wullie said.

"You're a big firm. You can stand it."

Wullie shrugged. He wouldn't admit that he could be touched by any financial loss. In fact the loss of the carcase would make no real difference to him. Much less than the loss of a day's wages to Mat. Wullie wouldn't have to do without anything, yet Mat knew that he'd brood and concentrate on his loss, that it really hurt him. He showed his anger at Mat with a huffy silence.

After the next felling Mat was finished in Wullie's room. By this time it had spread around the slaughter-house what had happened and several benefit men had come into the room to gloat at Wullie and give Mat the thumbs up sign. When the two carcases were hung up and the offals cleared, Mat cleaned the fat from his knife under the hot water tap. Wullie was standing at the top of the rooms steeling his knives and putting on a sad reproachful look. He shook his head and clicked his tongue. "I didn't think you'd do a thing like that."

Mat felt the hilarity bubbling up inside him, he put his hands to his mouth and bawled at Wullie. "You're nothing but an effing big hypocrite."

Wullie picked up a foot and slung it viciously at Mat who ducked giggling behind the wall of the room. Mat heard the thud of the foot against the wall, then poked his head round the corner of the room and made an obscene gesture at Wullie but Wullie had turned and was poking away at the carcase with his knife.

In the next room where Mat had to work there was only a single killer and Mat gave him a hand to get the cattle out of the pen and tied up in the room. These were the last two beasts to be killed that day as far as concerned Mat. The killer with whom he was working now, Jimmy McGuire, was a slightly built elderly man, a very good tradesman whom Mat liked. He was the kind of man who'd look up from his work and say, "Gie's a song," or when he was standing steeling his knives he'd grin at everyone and say, "Are you all right?" Otherwise he didn't talk much but just whistled and sang all the time. After they had got the beasts tied to the stunning posts Jimmy waved to Mat. "Don't shout on the gunner. We'll have a smoke first." They stood facing one another across the room, leaning against the haunches of the beasts and smoking their cigarettes. Mat felt relieved to be away from Wullie's room but the depressing thought came to him that everyone's approval of the trick he'd played on Wullie came from the fact that Wullie was so unpopular and not from the fact that he was right to point out a diseased beast to the inspector. Also he thought of Wullie's remark. "He's saving up for a fiddle." This was part of a general feeling of aggressive philistinism that he was always having to put up with. He felt so disgusted with this attitude that it was worse to have the taint of fiddler than it was to try and hide a diseased beast. He had sometimes found himself at the receiving end of contemptuous remarks from people other than Wullie, sometimes from the very ones who were laughing at Wullie now. If he didn't know how to defend himself it would be worse. He thought of the invitation he had received from George Duncan, to visit him the following Sunday. It would be a pleasant change from people like Wullie.

They finished their cigarettes and brought the gunner into the room. Both beasts were dropped to the floor. On one side there was an Aberdeen Angus bullock and on the other a bull. Mat took the rope from the bullock's neck and hung it up, then took the cane down from its hook, pithed the bullock and went over to where Jimmy was loosening the rope from the stunning post next to the bull. It had fallen badly and was lying, its forequarters slumped against the wall, its feet tucked beneath it and its haunches pointing out into the room at an angle. Jimmy was standing inside this angle between the bull and the wall trying to get a purchase with his feet on its shoulders and pushing with his back to the wall. Mat was busy thinking of the violence of the humane killer, the bolt gun with its tiny brass cartridges which could slap the big bulls on to the floor so easily and he was searching in his mind for words that would express the locked spasmodic pose of the bull as it lay shuddering against the wall. He took the bull by the horns and started to pull, trying to help Jimmy roll the beast over on to its other side and away from the wall. It came half way over until its feet were tucked directly under it.

Mat still had a grip of the horns and was still searching in his mind for words. He was tugging hard and only half aware of the bull's growing resistance when he heard Jimmy give a sudden exclamation, three short rising expirations of the breath, "Ha, huh, *huh*!" and Mat realised that the bull's hindquarters were up and that its forelegs were scrabbling for purchase on the floor. He gripped the horns tighter, tugged violently at the head and tried to kick the forelegs away from under the beast, but the laxness had gone from its neck and Mat might as well have tugging at a wall. There was a blur of impressions, the bull's glaucous rolling eye, Jimmy's surprised face, the vicious lowering of the bull's head.

Mat threw himself on to the bull's head right between the horns just as it hooked at him, then was surprised by the soft ease with which his body flew through the air. He went flying backwards out through the door of the room just missing the wall. His steel described an arc in the air and hit him on the shoulder and he heard the slither of his razor-edged knives as they fell out of the wooden box. The thing happened so quickly that Mat's reflexes took over and he twisted in the air to land crouched among a pile of feet and manyplies. He rolled over to break his fall and was up on his feet to face the bull all in one movement. His knives had fallen safely away from him and the bull had fallen again on to its side. It was lying further away from the wall now and thrashing its head up and down. The tip of its right horn had impaled Jimmy's foot and he was standing on one leg holding on to the stunning post and working his impaled foot up and down with the thrashing of the bull's head. His face was twisted in pain.

Mat threw himself again at the bull, grabbing a horn as the head came up. He put as much strength as he could into taking the weight of the head and for a second or two held it twisted away from the floor. Jimmy jerked his caught foot from the horn and hopped away. Mat grabbed the pithing cane from the floor and jumped on the head kneeling on the animal's face. He was shocked by the animal's distress for he could see the little round hole edged with pink froth where it had been shot. As he went up and down with the motion of the bull's head, he held on to a horn with one hand and felt for the little round hole with the other. He went up and down a couple of times before he felt the cane slip in and the head jerk throwing Mat off again. As the animal's head went down again both Mat and Jimmy threw themselves on to it and Jimmy pushed the cane right in for its full length. The legs thrashed while Jimmy worked the cane in and out, then suddenly the animal went lax.

Jimmy hopped over to the wall, propped his back against it and pulled off his boot and sock. The horn had gone in through the upper of his boot, scraped the side of his foot then stuck into the sole. There was a pink splotch on the side of his foot where a bruise was starting and he had lost some skin. Mat picked up the wellington boot and examined it. Jimmy was rueful.

"A brand new pair of wellingtons"

Mat stood silent for a moment with his finger poked through the tear in the wellington, then said, "How the hell did that happen?"

Jimmy looked down at the bull, pursed his lips and blew, "God knows. I thought you were away for it. *You're* going to be sore wi' that bump you took."

Mat laughed. He pulled his shirt away from his ribs and they both looked down. Over a large part of the front of his chest the skin had all flaked away and underneath the flakes of skin were tiny little spots of blood. He laughed again. "I never even felt that." Then he felt shaky and he went away to look for his knives. Usually when an animal is shot it is dead. He supposed that with the bull having an inch thick hide covering its forehead and with its tough thick skull, the bolt had just penetrated the skull and had temporarily stunned it without damaging the brain. If the animal had not fallen over on to the wrong side, if it had been pithed quick enough, then the thing would never have happened. Mat felt that he himself had been at fault for if instead of brooding about Wullie and thinking about bloody literature he had been paying attention, noticed that it was a bull that was being felled, he would have shoved the hindquarters against the wall and given the tail a pull as the pistol was fired. Then it would have fallen away from the wall in a position where it could have been pithed right away.

To think that he had pretensions to being an artist. He blethered away to Jimmy Aitken about writing whenever he had the chance. Yesterday he had written a story and Helen had believed in him. The day before he had spent spouting about art to Sam Richards and his friends. If he really was an artist then surely one of the things he should be more sensitive to and more responsible for was the suffering of others, especially the innocent. Instead of mauling words about inside his head he should be paying attention. This attentive explicit attitude towards his surroundings and others should be part of his nature as an artist, part of his duty. It was surely enough that the animal had to be slaughtered for men's sake without having to suffer this messy painful end as well. And besides, there was the innocence of the animal. It shouldn't have suffered through any defection on his part.

The edges of Mat's knives had been turned when they fell on the floor and Mat started to put a new edge on them as quickly as he could. He held the hone at the end and used the ball of his thumb as a stop for the knife. He got a certain grim satisfaction out of the thought that if he didn't pay attention while he was doing *this* that he'd take the fingers off himself. While he was honing the knives Jimmy had stuck both the beasts and was now working the crane lifting up the carcases to bleed. He was looking at Mat and smiling, making rueful grimaces and clicking with his tongue.

"Tch! Tch! Matthew Craig! I thought you were a goner."

They looked at one another and shook their heads commiseratingly. Jimmy laughed.

"These things can happen."

Archie Hind, *The Dear Green Place*

The Mole-catcher

The mole must have got into the news, for when I went across one of the low fields the other evening to where the mole-catcher was busy setting his traps he asked me if I had listened in to a broadcast by an English mole-catcher last night. I hadn't, and he proceeded to tell me that the Englishman had said that once out of forty traps he had taken forty moles. "I have never done anything like that," he admitted. "My best is fourteen out of fifteen traps." I remembered some of the lush lands in the southern counties of England and suggested that a lot must depend on the number of moles about. A mort of moles finding plenty of food would become fat and unsuspecting, and accordingly forty out of forty might be less of a feat in the south than fourteen out of fifteen in the north where the mole from necessity might be a warier animal. He spat on the small ball of earth in his left palm and then kneaded it with his right thumb.

"There may be something in that," he allowed, as his eyes lifted and looked away. His eyes were an impersonal greeny-grey, like glass or shallow sea-water. His face was lean and his hair neither fair nor dark, but somewhere in between, as the dusk comes between day and night. The kneading of his spittle into the earth had held my eye, and I was vaguely haunted by the notion of a remote creative act, as if in some far primordial age this had happened before, but when or where I could not exactly remember.

Presently, as we went on talking, I thought of moles as I had never thought of them before. We stood not far from a ditch with running water and a thick low-set thorn hedge. There they stayed in the hard weather, but now, with the frost gone from the ground and spring's stir of generation and awakening life, they adventured out into the field. I could see their paths coming from the hedge, all along the earth like swollen veins. A curiously secretive underground life, this of theirs — underground, yet, as it were, not dark, for in the countryman's proverb "a mole wants no lanthorn".

"Yes," said the mole-catcher, "I think the barrel trap is the best." All the time he explained its workings I was wondering what the earth in his palm was for. The trap is like a tiny barrel, with two grooves inside, one near each end where in a real barrel the head would be slotted. But into each groove now he introduces a noose of strong twine and fixes it in position with the kneaded clay, smoothing it all round with the ball of his thumb until noose and groove disappear. From the centre of the barrel protruded internally a tiny peg of wood. Knock out the lightly held peg, and the nooses leap from the clay by the swift action of an external spring.

In the chill of the evening his face looked cold, as though a drop of water might form any moment at his nose. Easy thought about life and death held no relation to his purpose. His intelligence was calmly remote from it, inevitably distant, and his actions had a craftsman's deliberation.

Had I not been struck by the kneading of spittle and clay I should not have had any special thoughts myself, for if the mole-catcher's job is necessary at any time, to-day it is very important — for us. These swollen veins that were the moles' tracks would spread over all the field in intricate formation like the veins in a human body, and the scores of molehills would multiply into an immense rash of countless warts, until the fructifying and growth on which our lives depend would be imperilled to the point of disaster.

"See that field up there," said the mole-catcher, pointing to a twenty-five-acre field on a slope. "The year before last I took one hundred and fifty moles off it."

I nodded, for I had seen the moles impaled in long lines on the wire fencing. "How," I asked him, as his impersonal eye slowly went over the ground about our feet, "do you find your spot for setting the trap?"

"Always look out for a new run," he answered, "because that's where she is working. See this one — it ends there. I'll set the trap here."

Round his left knee he had tied a piece of rubber tubing from a motor-car tyre, and now getting down on his knee he very neatly, with his mole-spade, cut out a section of earth the size of the barrel trap, and exposed the run.

"Always make sure," he said to me, "that your trap is deep enough," as he pounded the bottom of the run with the reverse end of his spade. "Once," he continued, "I was bedding the trap when I saw her working at the end of the run — as it might be over there. She heard me hitting the earth and came back, and, before my eyes, went clean under the trap and away. It was a lesson to me."

His fingers felt each end of the exposed run to make sure the passage was clear. All his motions were slow and deliberate and precise. There was no air about him of trusting to luck or chance. To say that this intelligence which the mole was up against was cool and ruthless would be to colour it emotionally. This intelligence did not sport with moles as the old Greek gods sported with men, or, for that matter, as many think God sports with men to this day. He was not a jealous mole-catcher, this man.

When he had bedded the trap to his satisfaction he lifted some of the dislodged earth and rolled it into a rounded lump in his palms. Long bony fingers placed the lump lightly over one end of the trap. They had a delicate touch. When at last the trap was hidden without being choked, the fingers spread a final loose covering of soil against the light. Then he switched his bag round and from it drew an arrow with a white cotton rag tied to the unpointed end. Into the earth he stuck this arrow upright.

"Yes," he answered, "it is to mark the trap. You might think it would be easy to find your trap on level ground like this, but it is often not easy. Once some sheep got in and rubbed themselves against my flags and knocked them down, and it took me a long time to find all my traps, a long time."

"I thought you would see the wire of the spring above the ground fairly easily?"

"You don't. Look back."

I looked back, and here and there saw the little white flags, but could not pick up the grey wire against the old grass.

In the gathering dusk the ground, when thus looked at closely, was suddenly like the relief map of a continent. It was not a flat, dull, uninteresting corner of a field, as any casual eye like my own might hitherto have thought. A continent reduced to this scale would be no more uneven. Myriad lines of communication, tunnelling, mountains, great valleys . . . .

"Do you see that big molehill over there?" He pointed to a mountain of a molehill, a veritable fortress and citadel among molehills.

"Yes," I said,

"Well, do you see where it is placed?"

"How do you mean?"

"Look at the lie of the ground. You can see it is placed on the highest spot."

My eye was not so keen as his, but when I bent down I saw that in truth here was a city set on a hill.

He nodded at my questioning surprise, and a gleam came into his eye, faint but clear. "Oh, they know what they're doing. They know all right. They put it up there so that the flood water won't reach them." There was something impersonal even in his speech. No trace of dialect thickened his meaning. Here was the voice that within a generation had turned from its rich native Gaelic into school-book English. Only the rhythm remained, quietly fluent as the land. The gleam in the eye was a tribute to the mole's wisdom. It passed like a momentary reflection of light.

I saw now the earth below the surface, from the cities of birth on the hills to the hollows where the choking water might entrap and drown. Was water the eternal enemy?

"No, water is the one thing they must have. You'll always find their runs making for water, and water indeed when a burn rises will sometimes come down their runs and do harm to the land."

When, in the darkening, I left him and from the thorn hedge turned round to have a last look he was moving over the earth with bent head. The short-sighted moles in their underground world had never seen that figure. And it seemed unlikely that even a Lewis Carroll among their philosophers could come within glimmering range of the dispassionate, but not blind, intelligence which presently paused, got down on one knee, and, taking some earth on a palm, kneaded it with spittle.

Neil Gunn, *Highland Pack*

Suggestions for Further Reading

For comparison with the Carlyle passage, other treatments of the relation between work and self-respect may be found in *Thirty Bob a Week* by John Davidson (in *The Albatross Book of Longer Poems*) and *Sunset Song* by Lewis Grassic Gibbon.

For studies of the Scottish economy in operation that make very engaging reading, see Bailie Nicol Jarvie's many monologues in Sir Walter Scott's *Rob Roy* and the later chapters of *Annals of the Parish* by John Galt.

Some sidelights on the kind of 'job satisfaction' enjoyed by the mole-catcher can be observed in *The Twa Dogs* by Robert Burns and *The Farmer's Ingle* by Robert Fergusson.

Neil Gunn's novels, of course, are much concerned with men (and boys) at work, and some of those already mentioned, such as *The Silver Darlings* and *Highland River*, could profitably be read.

Another writer much concerned with the way of life and therefore the economy of his own area is the Orcadian poet and short story writer, George Mackay Brown. The life of the crofter and the fisherman, both in the present day and in the distant past, is a common feature of his work. *A Time to Keep* and *Hawkfall* both offer stories of this kind.

Several modern Scottish dramatists have written plays about people at work in the industrial society. Among others there are *Willie Rough* by Bill Bryden and *The Bevellers* by Roddy Macmillan.

5   Death

The theme considered in this section is Death generally, but the passages, which show a variety of attitudes and treatment, are arranged to allow comparison and contrast.

'Weepers and Mourning Strings' is from *The Entail* by John Galt (1779–1839). First published in 1832, the novel deals with a favourite theme of the period — the divided family — and delineates two facets of Scottish life — pride of family and desire for possessions. As the passage shows, Galt portrays reality totally without squeamishness; character is emphasised by manner of speech; failings are treated with tolerance, not condemnation. The blunt realism (sometimes bordering on the coarse) of the Scots vernacular and its juxtaposition with the Standard English of the 'genteel' characters and the narration make the work almost symbolic of the attitude of post-Union Scotland to its native language.

Memoirs of a Highland Lady (1898), written by Elizabeth Grant of Rothiemurchus for her own family, gives a vivid picture of life in Edinburgh and the Highlands and of travel abroad. Scenes of early life are recalled with accuracy and a wide range of events is described. The selected chapter, 'The Captain's Death', sheds considerable light on burial customs. Written as it is in a dignified English, it is linguistically a complete contrast with Galt. Yet both passages are, in a way, similar since they are more concerned with the mourners than with the dead.

The two passages following upon these are chosen from writers of the inter-war years and are examples of genres enjoying considerable popularity at that time. The short story, *Beattock for Moffat*, by R. B. Cunninghame Graham (1852–1936) is concerned with the dying moments of an ordinary individual — an exile returning to die in his native country. This passage is evocative of Galt in the blunt, forthright attitudes expressed.

The passage from *Montrose* by John Buchan (1875–1940) on the other hand, being the biography of a national figure involved in matters of State and Religion, and dying for a cause, is more concerned with moral issues, with philosophical and spiritual aspects of death. The language of the two passages is appropriately contrasted — the colloquial tone of the one with its wry humour and pathos; the almost Biblical dignity of the other.

The final two excerpts from the modern period — both short stories — move on from death's incidentals to illustrate the skill with which apparently simplistic narrative can be endowed with a deeper symbolic meaning.

From Ian Hamilton Finlay (born in 1921) comes the story of the potato planters with its simple rural setting, yet it emphasises the incapacity of man to absorb the concept of death.

The collection of short stories by George Mackay Brown (born in 1921), *A Calendar of Love* (1970), depicts Orcadian society with sensitivity and vividness, and contains deep echoes of distant history and custom. In 'The Dead of Generations' from *Five Green Waves* these echoes bring us to an awareness of the universality of death and the cyclic pattern of human existence. In both stories there is an insistence upon tight patterning — of number, of linguistic repetition, of ritual movement. The earlier concentration on mourning 'rites' is replaced by a deeper awareness of the symbolism implicit in the actions and observations of the characters.

Weepers and Mourning Strings

The sorrow of Walter, after he had returned home, assumed the appearance of a calm and settled melancholy. He sat beside the corpse with his hands folded and his head drooping. He made no answer to any question; but as often as he heard the infant's cry, he looked towards the bed, and said, with an accent of indescribable sadness, "My Betty Bodle!"

When the coffin arrived, his mother wished him to leave the room, apprehensive, from the profound grief in which he was plunged, that he might break out into some extravagance of passion, but he refused; and when it was brought in, he assisted with singular tranquility in the ceremonial of the coffining. But when the lid was lifted and placed over the body, and the carpenter was preparing to fasten it down forever, he shuddered for a moment from head to foot, and raising it with his left hand, he took a last look of the face, removing the veil with his right, and touching the sunken cheek as if he had hoped still to feel some ember of life; but it was cold and stiff.

"She's clay noo," said he, — "There's nane o' my Betty Bodle here."

And he turned away with a careless air, as if he had no further interest in the scene. From that moment, his artless affections took another direction; he immediately quitted the death-room, and, going to the nursery where the infant lay asleep in the nurse's lap, he contemplated it for some time, and then, with a cheerful and happy look and tone said — "It's a wee Betty Bodle; and it's my Betty Bodle noo." And all his time and thoughts were thenceforth devoted to this darling object, in so much that, when the hour of the funeral was near, and he was requested to dress himself to perform the husband's customary part in the solemnity, he refused, not only to quit the child, but to have anything to do with the burial.

"I canna understand," said he, "what for a' this fykerie's about a lump o' yird? Sho'elt intil a hole, and no fash me."

"It's your wife, my lad," replied his mother; "ye'll surely never refuse to carry her head in a gudemanlike manner to the kirkyard."

"Na, na, mother, Betty Bodle's my wife, yon clod in the black kist is but her auld bodice; and when she flang't off, she put on this bonny wee new cleiding o' clay," said he, pointing to the baby.

The Leddy, after some further remonstrance, was disconcerted by the pertinacity with which he continued to adhere to his resolution, and went to beg her husband to interfere.

"Ye'll hae to gang ben, gudeman," said she, "and speak to Watty. — I wis the poor thing hasna gane by itsel wi' a broken heart. He threeps that the body is no' his wife's and ca's it a hateral o' clay and stones, and says we may fling't, Gude guide us, ayont the midden for him — We'll just be affrontit if he'll no carry the head."

Claud, who had dressed himself in the morning for the funeral, was sitting in the elbow-chair, on the right side of the chimney-place, with his cheek resting on his hand, and his eyelids dropped, but not entirely shut, and on being thus addressed, he instantly rose, and went into the nursery.

"What's t'ou doing there like a hussy-fellow?" said he. "Rise and get on thy mournings, and behave wise-like, and leave the bairn to the women."

"It's my bairn," replied Watty, "and ye hae naething, father, to do wi't. Will I no tak care o' my ain baby — my bonny wee Betty Bodle?"

"Do as I bid thee, or I'll maybe gar thee fin' the weight o' my staff," cried the old man sharply, expecting immediate obedience to his commands, such as he always found, however positively Walter, on other occasions, at first refused; but in this instance he was disappointed; for the widower looked him steadily in the face, and said, —

"I'm a father noo; it would be an awfu' thing for a decent grey-headed man like you, father, to strike the head o' a motherless family."

Claud was so strangely affected by the look and accent with which this was expressed, that he stood for some time at a loss what to say, but soon recovering his self-possession, he replied, in a mild and persuasive manner, — "The frien's expeck, Watty, that ye'll attend the burial, and carry the head, as the use and wont is in every weel-doing family."

"It's a thriftless custom, father, and what care I for burial-bread and services o' wine? They cost siller, father, and I'll no wrang Betty Bodle for ony sic outlay on her auld yirden garment. Ye may gang, for fashion's cause, wi' your weepers and your mourning strings, and lay the black kist i' the kirk-yard hole, but I'll no nudge the ba' o' my muckle tae in ony sic road."

"Tou's past remede, I fear," replied his father thoughtfully; "but, Watty, I hope in this t'ou'll oblige thy mother and me, and put on thy new black claes; t'ou kens they're in a braw fasson, — and come ben and receive the guests in a douce and sober manner. The minister I'm thinking will soon be here, and t'ou should be in the way when he comes."

"No," said Watty, "no, do as ye like, and come wha may, it's a' ane to me: I'm positeeve."

John Galt, *The Entail*

The Highland Widow

We were still in the middle of our books when the poor old Captain died. He had been subject for many years to violent attacks of *tic* in some of the nerves of the face. He had had teeth drawn, had been to Edinburgh to undergo treatment both surgical and medical, to no purpose. Twice a year, in the spring and fall, violent paroxysms of pain came on. The only relief he got was from heat; he had to live in a room like an oven. His good wife was so tender to him at these times; what a mass of comforts she collected round him!

He had been longer than usual without an attack; we were in hopes he was to be relieved during his decline from such agony, and so he was — but how? by a stroke of paralysis. It took him in the night, affected one whole side, including his countenance and his speech. He never recovered, even partially, and was a piteous spectacle sitting there helpless, well-nigh senseless, knowing no one but his wife, and not her always, pleased with the warmth of the fire and sugar-candy; the state of all others he had had the greatest horror of falling into. He always prayed to preserve his faculties of mind whatever befell the failing body, and he lost them completely; not a gleam of reason ever again shot across his dimmed intellect. This melancholy condition lasted some months, and then the old man died gently in the night, either eighty-four or eighty-six years of age.

The news was brought to the Doune early in the morning, and my father and mother set out immediately for Inverdruie. They remained there the greater part of the day. In the evening my father and I were occupied writing the funeral letters, and the orders to Inverness for mourning. Next day Jane and I were taken to Inverdruie. We had never seen a corpse, and the Captain had died so serenely, his vacant expression had disappeared so entirely, giving place to a placidity amounting to beauty, that it was judged no less startling first view of death could be offered to young people. The impression, however, was fearful; for days I did not recover from it. Jane, who always cried abundantly when excited, got over it more easily. The colour — the indescribable want of colour, rather — the rigidity, the sharp outline of the high nose (he had prided himself on the size and shape of this feature), the total absence of flexibility, it was all horror — him, and not him. I longed to cry like Jane, but there came only a pain in my chest and head. My father preached a little sermon on the text before us. I am sure it was very good, but I did not hear it. He always spoke well and feelingly, and the people around seemed much affected; all *my* senses were absorbed by the awful image on that bed. We were led away, and then, while conversation was going on in the chamber of the widow, my mind's eye went back to the scene we had left, and things I had not seemed to notice appeared as I must have seen them.

The body lay on the bed in the best room; it had on a shirt well ruffled, a night-cap, and the hands were crossed over the breast. A white sheet was spread over all, white napkins were pinned over all the chair cushions, spread over the chest of drawers and the tables, and pinned over the few prints that hung on the walls. Two bottles of wine and a seed-cake were on one small table, bread, cheese, butter, and whisky on another, offered according to the rank of the numerous visitors by the solitary watcher beside the corpse, a natural daughter of the poor Captain's married to a farmer in Strathspey.

A great crowd was gathered in and about the house; the name of each new arrival was carried up immediately to Mrs. Grant, who bowed her head in approbation; the more that came the higher the compliment. She said nothing, however; she had a serious part to play — the Highland widow — and most decorously she went through it. Every one expected it of her, for when had she failed in any duty? and every one must have been gratified, for this performance was perfect. She sat on the Captain's cornered arm-chair in a spare bedroom, dressed in a black gown, and with a white handkerchief pinned on her head, one *side* pinned round the head, all the rest hanging over it like the kerchief on the head of Henry of Bolingbroke in some of the prints. Motionless the widow sat during the whole length of the day, silent and motionless; if addressed, she either nodded slowly or waved her head, or, if an answer were indispensable, whispered it. Her insignia of office, the big bright bunch of large house keys, lay beside her, and if required, a lady friend, first begging permission, and ascertaining by the nod or the wave which was the proper key to use, carried off the bunch, gave out what was wanted, and then replaced it.

All the directions for the funeral were taken from herself in the same solemn manner. We were awestruck, the room was full, crowded by comers and goers, and yet a pin could have been heard to drop in it; the short question asked gravely in the lowest possible tone, the dignified sign in reply, alone broke the silence of the scene — for scene it was. Early in the morning, before company hours, who had been so busy as the widow? Streaking the corpse, dressing the chamber, settling her own, giving out every bit and every drop that was to be used upstairs and down by gentle and simple, preparing the additional supplies in case of need afterwards so quietly applied for by the friendly young lady, there was nothing, from the merest trifle to the matter of most importance, that she had not, her own active self, seen to.

I shall never forget her on the day of the funeral, the fifth day from the death. Her weeds had arrived, and remarkably well she looked in them. She, a plain woman in her ordinary rather shabby attire, came out in her new "mournings" like an elderly gentlewoman. She sat in the same room, in the same chair, with the addition of just a little more dignity, and a large white pocket-handkerchief. All her lady friends were round her, Miss Mary and Mrs. William from the Croft, Mrs. Macintosh from the Dell, Mrs. Stewart from Pityoulish, two Miss Grants from Kinchurdy, her own sister Anne from Burnside, Miss Bell Macpherson from Invereshie, my mother, Jane, and I. There was little said; every gig or horse arriving caused a little stir for a moment, hushed instantly.

The noise without was incessant, for a great concourse had assembled to convoy the last of Macalpine's sons to his long home.

A substantial collation had been set out in the parlour, and another, unlimited in extent, in the kitchen; people coming from so far, waiting for so long, required abundance of refreshment. They were by no means so decorous below as we were above in the lady's chamber, though we had our table of good things too; but we helped ourselves sparingly and quietly.

At length my father entered with a paper in his hand; it was the list of the pall-bearers. He read it over to Mrs. Grant, and then gave it to her to read herself. She went over the names without a muscle moving, and then, putting her finger upon one, she said, "I would rather Ballintomb, they were brothers in arms." My father bowed, and then offered her his hand, on which she rose, and every one making way they went out together, a few following.

They passed along the passage to the death-chamber, where on trestles stood the coffin, uncovered as yet, and with the face exposed. The widow took her calm last look, she then raised a small square of linen — probably put there by herself for the purpose — and dropping it over the countenance, turned and walked away. It was never to be raised. Though Jane and I had been spared this solemnity, there was something in the whole proceedings that frightened us. When Mrs. Grant returned to her arm-chair and lay back in it, her own face covered by a handkerchief, and when my father's step sounded on the stairs as he descended, and the screws were heard as one by one they fastened down the coffin lid, and then the heavy tramp of the feet along the passage as the men moved with their burden, we drew closer to each other and to good Mrs. Mackenzie from Aviemore, who was among the company.

Hundreds attended the funeral. A young girl in her usual best attire walked first, then the coffin borne by four sets of stout shoulders, extra bearers grouping round, as the distance to the kirkyard was a couple of miles at least. Next came the near of kin, and then all friends fell in according to their rank without being marshalled. Highlanders never presume, their innate good-breeding never subjecting them to an enforced descent from a too honourable place; there is even a fuss at times to get them to accept one due to them. Like the bishops, etiquette requires them to refuse at first the proffered dignity. What would either say if taken at his word?

The Presbyterian Church has no burial ceremony. It is the custom, however, for the minister to attend, generally speaking, and to give a lengthy blessing before the feast, and a short prayer at the grave. Mr. Grant of Duthil did his part better than was expected; no one, from the style of his sermons, anticipated the touching eulogy pronounced over the remains of the good old Captain — not undeserved, for our great-grand-uncle had died at peace with all the world. He was long regretted, many a kind action he had done, and never a harsh word had he said of or to any one.

My father gave the funeral feast at the Doune; most of the friends of fit degree accompanied him home to dinner. All sorts of pleasant stories went the round with the wine-bottles, and very merry they were, clergy and all; the parsons of Alvie and Abernethy were both there, coming in to the library to tea in high good-humour. The rest of the people, who had been abundantly refreshed at Inverdruie, dispersed.

Elizabeth Grant, Memoirs of a Highland Lady

The Run Home

The talk inside the carriage had given place to sleep, that is, the brother-in-law and wife slept fitfully, but the sick man looked out, counting the miles to Moffat, and speculating on his strength. Big drops of sweat stood on his forehead, and his breath came double, whistling through his lungs.

They passed by Lancaster, skirting the sea on which the moon shone bright, setting the fishing boats in silver as they lay scarcely moving on the waves. Then, so to speak, the train set its face up against Shap Fell, and, puffing heavily, drew up into the hills, the scattered grey stone houses of the north, flanked by their gnarled and twisted ash trees, hanging upon the edge of the streams, as lonely, and as cut off from the world (except the passing train) as if they had been in Central Africa. The moorland roads, winding amongst the heather, showed that the feet of generations had marked them out, and not the line, spade, and theodolite, with all the circumstance of modern road makers. They, too, looked white and unearthly in the moonlight, and now and then a sheep, aroused by the snorting of the train, moved from the heather into the middle of the road, and stood there motionless, its shadow filling the narrow track, and flickering on the heather at the edge.

The keen and penetrating air of the hills and night roused the two sleepers, and they began to talk, after the Scottish fashion, of the funeral, before the anticipated corpse.

"Ye ken, we've got a braw new hearse outby, sort of Epescopalian lookin', wi' gless a' roond, so's ye can see the kist. Very conceity too, they mak' the hearses noo-a-days. I min' when they were jist auld sort o' ruckly boxes, awfu' licht, ye ken upon the springs, and just went dodderin' alang, the body swinging to and fro, as if it would flee richt oot. The roads, ye ken, were no nigh hand so richtly metalled in thae days."

The subject of the conversation took it cheerfully, expressing pleasure at the advance of progress as typified in the new hearse, hoping his brother had a decent "stan' o' black", and looking at his death, after the fashion of his kind, as it were something outside himself, a fact indeed, on which, at the same time, he could express himself with confidence as being in some measure interested. His wife, not being Scotch, took quite another view, and seemed to think that the mere mention of the word was impious, or, at the least, of such a nature as to bring on immediate dissolution, holding the English theory that unpleasant things should not be mentioned, and that, by this means, they can be kept at bay. Half from affection, half from the inborn love of cant, inseparable from the true Anglo-Saxon, she endeavoured to persuade her husband that he looked better, and yet would mend, once in his native air.

"At Moffit, ye'd 'ave the benefit of the 'ill breezes, and that 'ere country milk, which never 'as no cream in it, but 'olesome, as you say. Why yuss, in about eight days at Moffit, you'll be as 'earty as you ever was. Yuss, you will, you take my word."

Like a true Londoner, she did not talk religion, being too thin in mind and body even to have grasped the dogma of any of the sects. Her heaven a music 'all, her paradise to see the King drive through the streets, her literary pleasure to read lies in newspapers, or pore on novelettes, which showed her the pure elevated lives of duchesses, placing the knaves and prostitutes within the limits of her own class; which view of life she accepted as quite natural, and as a thing ordained to be by the bright stars who write.

Just at the Summit they stopped an instant to let a goods train pass, and, in a faint voice, the consumptive said, "I'd almost lay a wager now I'd last to Moffat, Jock. The Shap, ye ken, I aye looked at as the beginning of the run home. The hills, ye ken, are sort o' heartsome. No that they're bonny hills like Moffat hills, na', na', ill-shapen sort of things, just like Borunty tatties, awfu' puir names, too, Shap Fell and Rowland Edge, Hutton Roof Crags and Arnside Fell; heard ever onybody sich-like names for hills? Naething to fill the mooth; man, the Scotch hills jist grap ye in the mooth for a' the world like speerits."

They stopped at Penrith, which the old castle walls make even meaner, in the cold morning light, than other stations look. Little Salkeld, and Armathwaite, Cotehill, and Scotby, all rushed past, and the train, slackening, stopped with a jerk upon the platform, at Carlisle. The sleepy porters bawled out "change for Maryport", some drovers slouched into carriages, kicking their dogs before them, and, slamming to the doors, exchanged the time of day with others of their tribe, all carrying ash or hazel sticks, all red-faced and keen-eyed, their caps all crumpled, and their great-coat tails all creased, as if their wearers had lain down to sleep full dressed, so as to lose no time in getting to the labours of the day. The old red sandstone church, with something of a castle in its look, as well befits a shrine close to a frontier where in days gone by the priest had need to watch and pray, frowned on the passing train, and on the manufactories, whose banked-up fires sent poisonous fumes into the air, withering the trees which, in the public park, a careful council had hedged round about with wire.

The Eden ran from bank to bank, its water swirling past as wildly as when "the Bauld Buccleugh" and his Moss Troopers, bearing the "Kinmount" fettered in their midst, plunged in and passed it, whilst the keen Lord Scroope stood on the brink amazed and motionless. Gretna, so close to England, and yet a thousand miles away in speech and feeling, found the sands now flying through the glass. All through the mosses which once were the "Debateable Land" on which the moss troopers of the clan Graeme were used to hide the cattle stolen from the "auncient enemy", the now repatriated Scotchman murmured feebly "that it was bonny scenery'' although a drearier prospect of ''moss hags'' and stunted birch trees is not to be found. At Ecclefechan he just raised his head, and faintly spoke of ''yon auld carle, Carlyle, ye ken, a dour thrawn body, but a gran' pheelosopher,'' and then lapsed into silence, broken by frequent struggles to take breath.

His wife and brother sat still, and eyed him as a cow watches a locomotive engine pass, amazed and helpless, and he himself had but the strength to whisper, ''Jock, I'm dune, I'll no see Moffat, blast it, yon smoke, ye ken, yon London smoke has been ower muckle for ma lungs.''

The tearful, helpless wife, not able even to pump up the harmful and unnecessary conventional lie, which, after all, consoles only the liar, sat pale and limp, chewing the fingers of her Berlin gloves. Upon the weather-beaten cheek of Jock glistened a tear, which he brushed off as angrily as if it had been a wasp.

''Aye, Andra,'' he said, ''I would hae liket awfu' weel that ye should win to Moffat. Man, the rowan trees are a' in bloom, and there's a bonny breer upon the corn — aye, ou aye, the reid bogs are lookin' gran' the year — but, Andra, I'll tak ye east to the auld kirk-yaird, ye'll no' ken onything aboot it, but we'll hae a heartsome funeral.''

Lockerbie seemed to fly towards them, and the dying Andra' smiled as his brother pointed out the place and said, ''Ye mind, there are no ony Christians in it,'' and answered, ''Aye, I mind, naething but Jardines,'' as he fought for breath.

The death dews gathered on his forehead as the train shot by Nethercleugh, passed Wamphray and Dinwoodie, and with a jerk pulled up at Beattock just at the summit of the pass.

So in the cold spring morning light, the fine rain beating on the platform, as the wife and brother got their almost speechless care out of the carriage, the brother whispered, ''Dam't, ye've done it, Andra', here's Beattock; I'll tak ye east to Moffat yet to dee.''

But on the platform, huddled on the bench to which he had been brought, Andra' sat speechless and dying in the rain. The doors banged to, the guard stepped in lightly as the train flew past, and a belated porter shouted, ''Beattock, Beattock for Moffat,'' and then, summoning his last strength, Andra' smiled, and whispered faintly in his brother's ear, ''Aye, Beattock — for Moffat!'' Then his head fell back, and a faint bloody foam oozed from his pallid lips. His wife stood crying helplessly, the rain beating upon the flowers of her cheap hat, rendering it shapeless and ridiculous. But Jock, drawing out a bottle, took a short dram and saying, "Andra', man, ye made a richt gude fecht o' it," snorted an instant in a red pocket-handkerchief, and calling up a boy, said, "Rin, Jamie, to the toon, and tell McNicol to send up and fetch a corp." Then, after helping to remove the body to the waiting-room, walked out into the rain, and, whistling "Corn Rigs" quietly between his teeth, lit up his pipe, and muttered as he smoked, "A richt gude fecht — man, aye, ou aye, a game yin Andra', puir felly. Weel, weel, he'll hae a braw hurl onyway in the new Moffat hearse."

R. B. Cunninghame Graham, *Beattock for Moffat*

The Curtain Falls

On Tuesday morning, the 21st of May, he rose for the last time. Like the Spartans before Thermopylae, he combed his long locks for death. The usual concourse of ministers and politicians was in his cell, and Wariston reproved him for his care of the body. "My head is still my own," was his answer. "Tonight when it will be yours, treat it as you please." Presently, he heard the drums beating to arms and was told that the troops were assembling to prevent any attempt at a rescue. He laughed and cried: "What, am I still a terror to them? Let them look to themselves; my ghost will haunt them."

He was taken about two in the afternoon by the bailies down the High Street to the Mercat Cross, which stood between the Tolbooth and the Tron Kirk — that dolorous road which Argyll and Wariston and James Guthrie were themselves to travel. He still wore the brave clothes in which he had confronted Parliament; nay, more, he had ribbons on his shoes and fine white gloves on his hands. James Fraser, who saw him, wrote: "He stept along the streets with so great state, and there appeared in his countenance so much beauty, majesty and gravity as amazed the beholder, and many of his enemies did acknowledge him to be the bravest subject in the world, and in him a gallantry that braced all that crowd." Another eye-witness, John Nicoll, the notary public, thought him more like a bridegroom than a criminal. An Englishman among the spectators, a Commonwealth agent, wrote an account to his masters. "It is absolutely certain that he hath overcome more men by his death, in Scotland, than he would have done if he had lived for I never saw a more sweeter carriage in a man in all my life.''

The scaffold was a great four-square platform, breast-high, and on it a 30-foot gallows had been erected. On the platform stood the ministers Mr. Robert Traill and Mr. Mungo Law, still bent on getting a word of confession or penitence. They were disappointed, for Montrose did not look at them. He was not allowed to address the mob, which surged up against the edge of the scaffold — a privilege hitherto granted to the meanest criminals; but he spoke apart to the magistrates and to a few of the nearer spectators. A boy called Robert Gordon sat by and took down his words in some kind of shorthand and the crowd, with that decency which belongs to all simple folk, kept a reverent silence. The Estates were afraid lest he should attack the king and spoil their game, but he spoke no word of bitterness or reproach; rather — *splendide mendax* — he praised Charles's justice. It was the testament of a man conscious of his mortal frailty, but confident in the purity of his purpose and the mercy of his God.

"I am sorry if this manner of my end be scandalous to any good Christian here. Doth it not often happen to the righteous according to the way of the unrighteous? Doth not sometimes a just man perish in his righteousness and a wicked man prosper in his wickedness and malice? They who know me should not disesteem me for this. Many greater than I have been dealt with in this kind. But I must not say but that all God's judgments are just, and this measure, for my private sins, I acknowledge to be just with God, and wholly submit myself to Him.

"But in regard of man, I may say they are but instruments: God forgive them and I forgive them. They have oppressed the poor and violently perverted judgment and justice, but He that is higher than they will reward them.

"What I did in this kingdom was in obedience to the most just commands of my sovereign, and in his defence, in the day of his distress, against those who rose up against him. I acknowledge nothing, but fear God and honour the king, according to the commandments of God and the just laws of Nature and nations. I have not sinned against man but against God; and with Him there is mercy, which is the ground of my drawing near to Him.

"It is objected against me by many, even good people, that I am under the censure of the Church. This is not my fault, seeing it is only for doing my duty, by obeying my prince's most just commands, for religion, his sacred person, and authority. Yet I am sorry they did excommunicate me; and in that which is according to God's laws without wronging my conscience or allegiance, I desire to be relaxed. If they will not do it, I appeal to God, who is the righteous Judge of the world, and will, I hope, be my Judge and Saviour.

"It is spoken of me that I should blame the king. God forbid! For the late king, he lived a saint and died a martyr. I pray God I may end as he did. If ever I would wish my soul in another man's stead, it should be in his. For his majesty now living, never any people, I believe, might be more happy in a king. His commandments to me were most just, and I obeyed them. He deals justly with all men. I pray God he be so dealt withal that he be not betrayed under trust, as his father was.

"I desire not to be mistaken, as if my carriage at this time, in relation to your ways, were stubborn. I do but follow the light of my conscience, my rule; which is seconded by the working of the spirit of God that is within me. I thank Him I go to heaven with joy the way He paved for me. If He enable me against the fear of death, and furnish me with courage and confidence to embrace it even in its most ugly shape, let God be glorified in my end, though it were in my damnation. Yet I say not this out of any fear or mistrust, but out of my duty to God, and love to His people.

"I have no more to say, but that I desire your charity and prayers. I shall pray for you all. I leave my soul to God, my service to my prince, my goodwill to my friends, my love and charity to you all. And thus briefly I have exonerated my conscience."

There is a tradition that during the morning there had been lowering thunder-clouds and flashes of lightning, but that as Montrose stood on the scaffold a burst of sunlight flooded the street. When he had finished speaking, he gave money to his executioner and prayed silently for a little. His arms were pinioned, and he ascended the ladder with that stately carriage which had always marked him. His last words were: "God have mercy on this afflicted land!" Tears ran down the hangman's face as he pushed him off, and we are told a great sob broke from the crowd. They had cause to sob, for that day there was done to death such a man as his country has not seen again.

John Buchan, *Montrose*

The Potato Planters and the Old Joiner's Funeral

The potato planters had only just started work again after having their dinner. They were spread out in almost a straight line across their first drills in the middle of the field.

There were seven planters, two men, two women, and three young tinker girls. The old tinker who was carrying the potatoes to them had filled their sack-aprons, and was opening more sacks with his clasp-knife farther down the drills.

The old tinker grimaced when he discovered that all the sacks he opened were filled with big potatoes. That was bad for whoever was carrying to the planters. Before he had got three sacks open, the seven planters had emptied their aprons and he had to walk back up the drills and fill them all over again. He staggered across the drills, between the planters and the sacks, with the heavy wire basket held at arm's length against his belly.

As soon as they had got their potatoes, the three young tinker girls started to plant them out. They held up their rough heavy sack-aprons as if they were pinafores filled to the brim with pretty flowers. The two men went on planting methodically while the other two women began to move away out in front as if there was a race down to the fence at the bottom of the field.

It was a hot spring day. The seven planters were sweating already. As the old tinker said, it was far too hot a day for working; they ought to have been fast asleep under some trees where it was shady and cool. A white heat-haze hung on the hills. The sun was like a huge marigold in the blue sky right above their heads. Away on the far side of the field one of the tractors was droning. The potatoes fell with little thuds into the hot, dry earth where spiders scurried among the grains of the potato manure like cooking-salt.

The planters moved slowly down the field, repeating their mechanical movements below the fiery sun that stung their necks. The old tinker filled their sack-aprons with the big potatoes as quickly as he could.

Before the planters had reached the bottom of their first drills they all stopped work for a time and stared down the field to the main road. They all stared at the motor hearse going up the road to collect the body of an old joiner who had died that week. They all stared till the black, shiny vehicle went out of sight behind the blue pine trees. The old joiner, they remembered, was to be buried that afternoon at 2.30 in the cemetery on the far side of the village, three miles away. When they had thought about this for several seconds, they all called to have their sack-aprons filled — all seven of them at once.

The tinker ripped open a fresh sack with his clasp-knife. His face was thickly coated with pale dust; it was almost the colour of candle-grease. He leaned his weight on the heavy sack to spill a basket-load of potatoes into the basket at his feet. Before he could get the heavy sack righted again the potatoes had overflowed the basket and spilled on the ground. He had a sudden desire to beat his breast.

Suddenly, while they waited for the old tinker to come with potatoes, the seven planters noticed that the other old man, who had been carrying potatoes in the morning, was not there. They thought about him not being there and each one, secretly, arrived at the conclusion that he was away at the funeral of the old joiner who was being buried that afternoon at 2.30 in the cemetery on the other side of the village, three miles away. They went on noticing that the old man was not there each time they ran short of potatoes and had to wait for the old tinker to hurry along to them, with his heavy basket.

The seven planters reached the bottom of their first drills. They moved into seven new drills and started back up the field. Now they had their backs to the main road and they had an awful feeling that the funeral would sneak by silently without them seeing it. But they had reached the top of the field and turned around again before the funeral went by.

There were more cars than anyone had expected there would be. There were seven cars, not even counting the hearse with the old joiner laid in it, on his way to be buried in the cemetery on the far side of the village, three miles away. The minister's small, stream-lined car was in the middle of the line. Because of its shape — like a pullet's egg — it was easy to pick out, and with its bright blue colour it looked very gay among all the other cars that were mostly black. The seven cars kept the same distance apart, and it looked at first as if the hearse was towing them along slowly on one long rope. Then the minister's car started to catch up on the car in front, and the cars in behind it had to hurry to catch up too.

The seven planters stared fixedly at the funeral. Being Protestants they did not cross themselves, or say or do anything whatever. They just stared. The two men did think of raising their caps but it seemed to them that the habit of doing that must have died out. The two women thought of saying something but they were each afraid to speak in case they said the wrong thing. The one in the green apron had a growing feeling that the funeral would have to hurry if it was to be down at the cemetery on the far side of the village by 2.30, as it ought to be.

There was silence for several moments after the funeral had gone out of sight behind the trees. Then there were seven small thuds because all the seven planters dropped the potatoes they had been holding when they stopped to watch. They started to move on again in a crooked line, under the hot sun like a huge marigold in the sky.

Suddenly the old tinker stopped, and laid his wire basket down on the earth. He bent his knees slightly, and raised his right arm, pointing upwards. The seven planters looked questioningly at him.

"Death!" said the old tinker, waving his left arm about. "'Tis terrible what Death will do to a man . . ."

The seven planters stared at the tinker with vacant expressions on their sweaty faces.

"Take that man there," said the tinker, lowering his arm to point after the funeral. "I was speaking to that man, there, only on Saturday . . ."

"No," said the woman in the green apron, breaking in on the tinker. "Not that man. Another man. It was a different man you were speaking to."

The old tinker let his arm drop down to his side. He turned his face towards the woman in the green apron. Trickles of sweat had drawn tragic lines down his grey cheeks.

"A different man!" he said. "And is *he* dead as well?"

"They are both dead," said the woman in green, lowering her sack-apron a little.

"They are both dead. But the man you were speaking to was a different man. I know he was a different man because I saw you speaking to him. I happened to see you speaking to him last Saturday morning, about 10 o'clock, and it was not the same man."

"A different man!" exclaimed the old tinker, shaking his head sadly. He lifted his basket and staggered towards the planters with it held against his belly.

The half-past bus came out from behind the pine trees with a sudden flash of windows. The planters all stopped planting and looked at the bus going along the main road.

"I thought that," said the woman in green. "I knew that all along. It will take that funeral all its time to be down at the cemetery by half-past two."

One of the two men planters took out his watch slowly, looked at it intently, then put it away. The seven planters moved down the field in the intense heat. They reached down to the bottom of the drills and turned up again.

A few minutes later there was a further interruption as a tractor came racing into the potato field through the far gate. The trailer was loaded high with more potato-sacks and on top of the load stood the gay young tinker, the old tinker's son. He stood with his legs wide apart, lashing the tractor with a long, imaginary whip. Plainly he was imagining himself to be a cossack or something.

"Tallyho! Crack! Crack! Yipee!" he kept on shouting at the top of his voice.

The old tinker scowled when he discovered that the new sacks, too, were filled with big potatoes. He seemed to see two old men stretched out under shady trees, and though one of them, he knew, was different he could not think why that was the case.

The hot sun, like a huge marigold, beat down on the field.

The other old man, who was away at the funeral, did not get back to the potato field till almost four o'clock. The old tinker asked him where he had been.

Ian Hamilton Finlay,
The Potato Planters and the Old Joiner's Funeral

The Dead of Generations

The grave-digger had finished making Moll Anderson's grave. He was sitting on the shaft of his barrow, smoking a clay pipe. As I turned in at the gate he wagged his beard at me, for he did not associate this shy decently-clad boy with the naked insolence he had seen running out of the sea half an hour before. I wandered away from him among the branching avenues of tomb-stones — the tall urns and frozen angels of modern times; the fiery pillars with the names of grandfathers on them; the scythe-and-hourglass slates of the eighteenth century; and the lichened leprous tombs of a still earlier age. This small field was honeycombed with the dead of generations — farmers with stony faces; young girls rose-cheeked with consumption; infants who had sighed once or twice and turned back to the darkness; stern Greek-loving ministers; spinsters with nipped breasts and pursed mouths. I stood on the path, terrified for a moment at the starkness and universality of shrouds; at the infinite dead of the island, their heads pointing westward in a dense shoal, adrift on the slow tide that sets towards eternity.

My dreaming feet brought me to a low tombstone set in the east wall:

HERE LIES BURIED
A FOREIGN SEAMAN,
OF UNKNOWN NAME AND NATIONALITY
WHOM THE SEA CAST UP ON THIS ISLAND,
JUNE THE SIXTH, 1856

'Though I take the wings of the morning,
and flee to the uttermost places of the sea.'

I closed my eyes and saw a little Basque town between the bay and the mountains.

The feast of Our Lady of the Sea was over. The nets and the oars had been blessed. The candles were still burning in their niches among the rocks.

Now the young people are dancing in a square that lies white and black under the moon.

The musician slouches, as if he were drunk or half asleep, against the fountain. Only his hand is alive, hovering over the strings like a vibrant bird.

The young people are dancing now in long straight lines. The partners clap their hands and bow to each other. They shout; the dark faces are lit up with a flash of teeth. They move round each other with momentarily linked arms. They incline towards each other, their hands on their knees, and stamp their feet. It is all precision, disciplined fluency, a stylized masque of coupling.

Older men and women sit gossiping on the door-steps. Occasionally they sip from tall glasses. One, a fat man with a yellow beard, looks often through a gap in the houses, at a ship anchored in the harbour.

An old shawled woman stands alone, in the shadow of the church. No one speaks to her; the seal of separation is on her. She is the guardian of the gates of birth and death. In this village she comes to deliver every wailing child, she goes to shroud every quiet corpse. Her eyes are in the dust, from which all this vanity has come, and to which it must return.

The hand over the guitar moves into a new swirling rhythm. Now the square is all one coloured wheel, a great wavering orange blossom.

Suddenly there is an interruption. A tall bearded sailor appears at an alley-opening and walks slowly across the square. The guitar falters. The dance is frozen. The old dark woman raises her head. The officer points to one of the dancers and crooks his finger: he must come, immediately, the ship is sailing tonight.

The seaman — he is only a boy — turns once and looks back. A girl has raised her apron to her face. The yellow-bearded man rises from his doorstep and makes a gesture of blessing: "Lady of Waters, guard him this day and all days till the sail returns to the headland."

Above the village a cross stands among the stars. Through a long silence comes the sound of the sea. The last votive candle gutters and goes out among the rocks.

The little town of moonlight and music will never see that sail again. Her voyage has ended on a northern rock. All her sailors have vanished down the path of gull and lobster, scattered in a wild Atlantic storm. One broken shape only was lifted out of the seaweed. Curious hands have carried the nameless thing in procession across the fields. They have clipped the rags from it and combed its hair, and covered the crab-eaten face. And though there was no priest to sing Latin over it, a Calvinist minister said, 'All flesh is grass, and the glory of flesh is as the flower thereof' — the orange-blossom of Spain and the little blue Orkney primula, whose circles of beauty are full and radiant for a short time only; and then, drifting winterward, or broken with June tempest, lay separate shining arcs in the dust . . .

My slow circuitous walk had brought me to the new gaping hole in the earth. The grave-digger was still sitting on his barrow. He bored a sidelong glance into me and said: "There's only one way of coming into the world, but ah, God, there's two or three ways of going out."

"That's a fact," I said.

"Would you like," he said, "to see what a man *truly* is?"

Not understanding, I gave a quick nod. He groped with his hand into the small hill of clay beside the open grave, and brought out a skull. Carefully he wiped it on his moleskin trousers. ''That's you,'' he said, ''and me, and the laird, and Frank the idiot. Just that.''

He laughed. ''There's nothing here to make your face so white. It's as harmless as can be, this bone. It's at peace, and not before time. When it lived it had little rest, with its randy eyes and clattering tongue. This skull belonged to Billy Anderson, Moll's grandfather. He was twice in jail and fathered three illegitimate bairns. O, he was a thieving, drunken, fighting character, and it was a good day for him when we threw him in here. Wasn't it, Billy?'' he said to the skull, blowing smoke into its eye-hollows. ''Wasn't it, boy?'' . . . The skull grinned back at him.

From the other side of the loch the school bell rang the dismissal.

Over the hill from the village, like a procession of beetles, came the mourners.

George Mackay Brown, *Five Green Waves*

Suggestions for Further Reading

Death is a common theme in all literatures and Scots is no exception. David Daiches in *The Paradox of Scottish Culture* makes interesting comments in this connection.

George Douglas's *The House with the Green Shutters* shows a proud man absorbed with material possessions whose treatment of his family leads inexorably to violent death, and to suicide as the answer to despair.

Neil Gunn once again deserves mention, dealing as he does with a whole way of life and being therefore concerned with death as well as life. Any of the novels previously mentioned would be appropriate.

Robert Louis Stevenson is another writer much concerned with death. One of his short stories, *Thrawn Janet*, is in the ghost story genre, and captures brilliantly the horror which superstition can attach to death. His novel *Dr. Jekyll and Mr. Hyde* deals with death of the most violent kind, but is more concerned with the Scottish paradox of the dual identity. In this respect it is often compared to James Hogg's early nineteenth-century *Confessions of a Justified Sinner*.

Two modern novels which deal with the Highland Clearances are Iain Crichton Smith's *Consider the Lilies* and Fionn MacColla's *And the Cock Crew*. These are more than mere historical novels, however. They, too, are much concerned with some of the paradoxes of the Scottish character (in this case within the Gaelic culture), with the struggles of conscience and religious belief, and with coming to terms with death.

Finally, Edwin Morgan's short poem *King Billy* opens with what seems like a straightforward description of funeral rites. As we read, however, we discover that the rites have been applied to someone we would not normally associate with such rites: a Glasgow gang leader, reduced in his later years to a lonely and empty life, at whose death memories of him as a folk hero returned and thousands turned out to mourn him — paradox yet again.

6 Some Older Passages

The Scots language, as used before the Union of the Crowns, was a dialect of English closely related in its origins to the Northumbrian dialect. To say this is in no way to detract from its distinctive national flavour. As far as Lowland Scots of the early sixteenth century were concerned, the linguistic term 'Scots' meant Gaelic, for they considered their own language to be 'Inglisch'. Dunbar pays tribute in 'The Golden Targe' to 'reverend Chaucere, rose of rhetoris [eloquent writers] all', who wrote in 'oure tong' and was 'of oure Inglisch all the lycht', thus proclaiming his belief that they spoke and wrote the same language.

The passage from the New Testament in Scots is from the version made by Murdoch Nisbet about 1520 from Purvey's revision of Wycliffe's translation. The short extracts from the Burgh records of Glasgow are included to illustrate the colloquial vigour of the language that shines through the legal terminology. The excerpts from George Buchanan's *Chamaeleon* (1570), from the diary of James Melville (1584) and from *The Basilicon Doron* ('The Kingly Gift') of James VI are examples of lively writing of various kinds. Buchanan is satirising his political opponent, Maitland of Lethington; Melville gives an account of a precarious voyage undertaken to escape from religious persecution; while King James offers advice to his son Prince Henry on how to rule his future kingdom. The paragraph from the dedication to Allan Ramsay's *Proverbs* (1737) reveals the poet's delight both in the homely wisdom of the proverbs themselves and in the use of the familiar Scots for literary purposes.

from Murdoch Nisbet's Scots version of the *New Testament,* c. 1520

Ye have herde that it has bene said, e for e, and tuthe for tuthe: Bot I say to yow, that ye aganestand nocht ane evile man; bot gif ony man strike thee on the richte cheke, schaw to him alsa that uthir. And to him that wil stryve with thee in dome, and tak away thi cote, leife thou to him alsa thi mantil. And quhaevir constrenyeis thee a thousand pasis, ga thou with him uthir twa. Gefe thou to him that askis of thee, and turn nocht away fra him that will borow of thee. Ye have herde that it was said to aldmen, Thou sal lufe thi nechbour, and hate thin ennimy: Bot I say to you, lufe your ennimyes, do ye wele to thame that hates you, and pray ye for thame that persewis and sclandiris you; That ye be the sonnis of your fadir that is in hevinis: that makis his sonne to rise uponn gude and evil men, and raynis on just and unjust men. For gif ye lufe thame that luvis you, quhat mede sal ye have? quhethir gif publicanis dois nocht this? And gif ye salus your brethir anlie, quhat sald ye do maire? quhethir gif hethinmen dois nocht this? Tharfor be ye perfite, as your hevenlie fadir is perfite.

Matthew 5.38 to end

from the *Burgh Records* of Glasgow

22nd November, 1588

The quhilk day anent the trublance persewit be James Scott, painter, burges of Glasgow, againis Adame Elphinstoun glasin-wright, David Reid, Thomas Reid, Arthour Fischour, and Andro Bucklis — The said Adame is fundin in the wrang and amerciament of court, for the streking of the said James Scott on the breist with ane pistolat, throw the force quhairof he dang the said James to the eird, and effusioun of his bluid in grit quantitie. And siclyk the same Adame is fundin in the wrang and amerciament of court, for cumin to the said James Scottis hous at Lambes last, and sutting of George Scott, sone to said James, with ane drawin sword, and say-ing, gif he had him, he suld lay his pudenis about his feete, and biddin of the said George Scott come furth or ellis he suld haif ane cauld armefull of him.

21st January, 1588

The quhilk day Jonete Bogyll, spous to James Craig, is decernit in ane wrang and amerciament of court, for the hurting of Jonete Clogy, spous of Johne Cuthbert, on the heid with ane stane to the effusioun of her bluid in grite quantitie; and sickly the said Jonete Clogy is decernit in ane wrang for streking of the said Jonete Bogyll on the halfatt, and ruiging of courch af hir heid, and dume gevin thairupon.

29th May, 1590
The quhilk day Alspaith Clogy, dochter to Thomas Clogy, is decernit in ane wrang and amerciament of court for casting of stanes at
Christiane Sauchie, and byting of hir throuch the airme, and latting
the piece flesche quhilk sche bait fall in the water.

from George Buchanan's *Chamaeleon,* 1570

Thair is a certane kynd of beist callit chamaeleon, engenderit in sic
cuntreis as the sone hes mair strenth in than in this yl of Brettane,
the quhilk, albeit it be small of corporance, noghttheless it is of ane
strange nature, the quhilk makis it to be na les celebrat and spoken
of than sum beastis of greittar quantitie. The proprietie is marval-
ous, for quhat thing evir it be applicat to, it semis to be of the
samyn cullour and imitatis all hewis except onelie the quhyte and
reid, and for this caus ancient writtaris commounlie comparis it to
ane flatterare, quhilk imitatis all the haill maneris of quhome he
fenyeis him self to be freind to, except quhyte, quhilk is takin to be
the symboll and tokin gevin commounlie in divise of colouris to
signifie sempilnes and loyaltie, and reid signifying manlines and
heroyicall courage. This applicatioun, being so usit, yit peradven-
ture mony that hes nowther sene the said beist, nor na perfyte pro-
traict of it wald beleif sic thing not to be trew. I will thairfore set
furth schortlie the descriptioun of sic ane monsture not lang ago
engendrit in Scotland in the cuntre of Lowthiane not far frome Had-
ingtoun to that effect that, the forme knawin, the moist perstiferus
nature of the said monsture may be moir easelie evitit: for this
monstre being under coverture of a mannis figure, may easeliar
endommage and wersid be eschapit, than gif it wer moir deforme
and strange of face, behaviour, schap and memberis. Praying the
reidar to apardoun the febilnes of my waike spreit and engyne, gif
it can not expreme perfytelie ane strange creature maid be nature,
other willing to schaw hir greit strenth or be sum accident turnit be
force frome the commoun trade and course.

from the *Diary* of James Melville, 1584

Thus my cusing, being a mariner, conducit a bott to carie a town of his portage wyn about to Carell, and decking me upe in his sie attyre betymes in the morning, about the simmer solstice, tuk me in down under Dondie as a shipbroken sie-man; and rowing about, behovit to go to the heavin of St Androis, to lose a certean of skleatt steanes; and because it was law water, we behoved to ly a whyll in the road till the water grew, whare, the bott wanting ane owerlaft, the seall was cassen ower hir ta end, and ther I leyed upe, lest I sould be spyed of sum shipes rydding besyde. Bot within schort space, partlie be rokking in the sie, and partlie for want of care, I grew sa extream seik, that manie a tyme I besaught my cowsing to sett me a-land, schosin rather anie sort of dethe, for a guid cause, nor sa to be tormented in a stinking holl. And yit, whowbeit it was extream peanfull, I gatt ther notable medicin of vomitine, quhilk was a preservative to my helthe all that yeir. Sa, coming hard to the steppes of the Archbishopes peire at St Androis, we loste our skleattes, and tuk in vivers, and rowit out agean immediatlie, and cam that night to Pitmillie-burn-mouthe, wher I gead a-land, and reposit me in my sie abbat. And efter offers of grait kyndnes be the Lard, and furnitour of a rubber of starke Merche eall, betymes in the morning we rowit out about the Nes. The day was hat. Ther was bot twa men in the bott, by twa cusings of myne, with my self. Of these twa, we haid an at our devotion. The uther was the awner of the bott, and verie evill-affected; bot the hat rowing, and the stope with the stark eall hard besyd him, maid him atteanes to keave ower aslipe. And it pleased God to send a prettie pirlye of wound, wherby getting on a seall upon hir, or ever our schippar wakned we was a guid space besouthe the May; wha, seing he could nocht mend him self, was fean to yeild and agrie with his merchant for a hyre to Berwik. Bot being af and on with Dumbar, about ane efter noon comes af the hilles of Lamermure-age a grait mist with a tempestuous schoure and drow, quhilk, or we could gett our sealles taklit, did cast us about, and, or my cusing was awar, caried us bak almaist to the May, with such a how wa and spene drift, that the bott being opin, he lukit for grait danger gif the stormie schoure haid continowed. Bot the young man being verie skilfull and able, starts to his kist, and tuk out a compas, and finding us contrare our course, with mikle ado, wanting helpe, and schipping of mikle water, he cust about and pykit on the wind, halding bathe the helme and scheit, susteining in the mean tyme evill langage of the schippar in stead of helpe, till it pleasit God mercifullie to luik upon us, and within an houre and an half to dryve away the schoure and calm the drow, sa that it fell down dead calme about the sune drawing leache.

To keipe the sie all night in an opin little bott, it was dangerus, and to go to Dumbar we durst nocht, sa, of necessitie, we tuk us toward St Tab's Heid. Bot we haiving, but twa eares, and the boot slaw and heavie, it was about alleavin houres of the night or we could win ther. Whowbeit, na man was ydle. Yea, I rowit my self, till the hyd cam af my fingars, mair acquented with the pen nor working on ane are. Coming under the crag, we rowit in within a prettie lytle holl betwix the mean and the head, whare easelie going a-land, we refreschit us with cauld water and wyne; and returning to our boot, sleipit the dead of the night, bot neidit nan to wakin us, for soon, be the day light piped, ther was sic a noyse of foulles on the crag, and about us, because of thair young annes, that we war almaist pressed to launche out. Now we haid Cawdingham Bay and Hay-mouth to pas by, and that but slawlie, rowing be the land, whar the residence of Alexander Home of Manderston, an of our cheif confederat enemies, and wha haid intercepted a boot of the Earle of Angus coming about from Tamtallon to Berwik nocht lang befor. This put us in grait feir; but our guid God gardit us, making a sweik thik mist till aryse, wherby we might bot skarslie gis at the sight of the land, and thairfra nane could sie us. Sa we cam on hulie without fear till we wan within the bounds of Berwik, whar we was in graitest danger of all, umbesett in the mist be twa or thrie of the cobles of Berwik, quhilk war sa swift in rowing, that they ged round about us. Bot we being fyve within burd, and haiving twa pistolets, with thrie swords, and they na armour, they war fean to let us be, namlie, when they understud that we was making for Berwik.

Thus gratiuslie protected by my guid God, I cam to Berwik.

from **The Basilicon Doron** of James VI, 1591

Heere nowe speaking of oppressoures and of justice, the purpose leadeth mee to speake of Hie-land and Bordour oppressions. As for the Hie-lands, I shortly comprehend them al in two sorts of people: the one, that dwelleth in our maine land, that are barbarous for the most parte, and yet mixed with some shewe of ciuilitie: the other, that dwelleth in the Iles, & are alluterlie barbares, without any sorte or shewe of ciuilitie. For the first sorte, put straitly to execution the lawes made alreadie by mee against their Ouer-lords, & the chiefs of their Clannes; and it will be no difficultie to danton them. As for the other sort, followe foorth the course that I haue intended, in planting Colonies among them of answerable In-lands subjects, that within short time may reforme and civilize the best inclined among them: rooting out or transporting the barbarous and stubborne sorte, and planting ciuilitie in their roomes.

But as for the Bordours, because I knowe, if ye injoy not this whole Ile, according to Gods right & your lineall discent, ye wil neuer get leaue to brook this north and barrennest part therof; no, not your owne head wheron the Crowne should stande; I neede not in that case trouble you with them: for then they will be the middest of the Ile, & so as easily ruled as any part thereof.

from the Dedication to Allan Ramsay's *Proverbs,* 1737

As naithing helps our happiness mair than to have the mind made up with right principles, I desire you, for the thriving and pleasure of you and yours, to use your een and lend your lugs to these good auld saws that shine with wail'd sense, and will as lang as the warld wags. Gar your bairns get them by heart; let them have a place amang your family-books; and may never a window sole through the country be without them. On a spare hour, when the day is clear, behind a ruck, or on the green howm, draw the treasure frae your pouch, and enjoy the pleasant companion. Ye happy herds, while your hird-sells are feeding on the flowry braes, you may eithly make yoursells master of the haleware. How usefou will it prove to you, who have sae few opportunities of common clattering when ye forgather with your friends at Kirk or market, banquet or bridal? By your proficiency, you'll be able in the proverbial way, to keep up the saul of a conversation, that is baith blyth and usefou.

7   **Scottishness**

What is it that makes Scottish prose Scottish? All the writers in this book are Scots by birth. That might be the basis of an answer, but it would beg too many questions. Does the 'national' characteristic lie in the language used; or the theme treated; or the tone adopted? Or does it come out of particular combinations of these elements?

When we read the older passages, which form one section of this book, we hear a rich, strong tongue that is no mere dialect of English; yet, with Lord Cockburn, writing only a century after Ramsay, we are in another linguistic world. The consequences of the Union of the Crowns and the Treaty of Union were crippling for Scottish prose; increasingly, the Southron way with words came to dominate the Scottish literary scene. Poetry fared better — it always does. And, of course, the vernacular speech, on a regional basis, survived — and survives — political and cultural discouragement. In an essay called 'Registering the reality of Scotland' Edwin Morgan observes, 'Lowland Scots today may be only the shreds of a language, but they are remarkably tenacious and expressive shreds which show no signs of disappearing.' David Daiches in 'The Paradox of Scottish Culture' considers the state of the nation after 1707:—

> It was too late to do anything for Scottish prose, which was later to find some attenuated prolongation of life in dialogue in Scottish novels.

If language is thought of as expressing a nation's soul, then Scotland will be hard put to it to find national identity. Hugh MacDiarmid in poetry returned a magnificent answer to the doubts of Stevenson and others concerning parochialism in language. But in prose, despite the shining examples of Lewis Grassic Gibbon and Sidney Goodsir Smith, we have lost linguistic ground since the time of Scott, the North British wizard.

In matters of theme and tone, Daiches sees the eighteenth century again as being the watershed:—

> The very fact that the [Jacobite] cause was lost helped to turn Scottish national feeling into something elegiac and literary, and is one reason — the other is the unassimilated effects of the industrial revolution on the Scottish imagination — for the incurable nostalgia of much Scottish literature especially in the nineteenth century.

Even today, in the world of North Sea oil and promised parliaments, we still will hanker after the past, for we are as Edwin Muir points out, 'a myth-making people; and we do not always go honestly about constructing our myths.'

Accompanying the hero-worship and the nostalgia, there is a sentimentality about us that flourished in the Kailyard school which Douglas and Gibbon, in their different ways and generations, were out to destroy. But as well there is a shrewdness, a hard sense of realism which Douglas shows us as 'caution' in conflict with 'imagination'. Evidence of this 'cultural schizo-phrenia' is abundant in Scott. The dying outlaw adjures the young man,

> Remember the fate of our race, and quit not the ancient man-
> ners of the Children of the Mist.

Bailie Nicol Jarvie knew perfectly well that those 'ancient manners' were bad for trade and social stability, and yet part of him responded to their primal dignity. In many ways, Jarvie is the quintessential Scot. He is the Lowland, urban businessman who respects the trade-despising, pastoral Highlander; the Protestant, Hanoverian Whig who has time for the Catholic, Jacobite Tory; the believer in progress who regrets the passing of an older culture. About Jarvie too there is a smack of the sturdy democrat, and in this collection the democrat makes several quiet, but telling, appear-ances. In *The Field of Sighing*, the peasant lad keeps his self-respect by not envying the folk at the Big House — only despising them:

> May the Lord on His throne above keep me poor and sane.

And again, Hugh Miller in *My Schools and Schoolmasters* gets in his polit-ical dig:

> Masons had reason at times for not touching their hats to gent-
> lemen.

Men at work, even hard, unpleasant work, can hold on to their self-respect. The mole-catcher, the farm-worker, the slaughterman are all unemotionally proficient; it is the idle men — and masters — who get sentimental, Blake's Clydesiders with no ships to build. 'It was a tragedy beyond economics.' Here the 'imagination' outweighs the 'caution'. This is not the stuff of which 'Red Clydeside' legends are built.

Perhaps the most persistent theme in this anthology is that of struggle, the dour response of human beings to a harsh environment. In the world of the family the conflict is most often between father and son, and, although not peculiarly Scottish, that particular conflict is liable to be more bitter in a patriarchal society where emotion is often repressed. Then there is the struggle of human beings to survive in an urban situation. In Hanley's case, a nicely observed social adjustment, the outcome is happy; in the Changeling's it is tragic and shaming.

Even against death there is a struggle. In *Memoirs of a Highland Lady* the rituals, more social than religious, are serenely observed. But in Galt, the conventions are astonishingly and piercingly questioned. 'Beattock for Moffat' is a snell counterblast to 'the English theory that unpleasant things should not be mentioned, and that, by this means, they can be kept at bay.' The paradox of Calvinism is acted out here; the fight is to be fought although the outcome is known beforehand. Out of the dourness of landscape and personality Cunninghame Graham creates an austere spirituality. 'Caution' and 'imagination' are fused.

To round off the anthology, a few more extracts are now offered, each shedding some light on the Scottish character both past and present. With the exception of the last, all the extracts are by writers already represented in earlier sections. The last extract, from Robert McLellan's play *Jamie the Saxt*, is offered as a sample of Scottish drama. In it we have a modern re-creation of the character of the Scottish king (and prose writer!) who, by moving to London on his accession to the throne of England, started the movement which brought about the disappearance of a distinctive Scottish prose style.

The Lion and the Lamb

"These Hielands of ours, as we ca' them, gentlemen, are but a wild kind of warld by themsells, full of heights and howes, woods, caverns, lochs, rivers, and mountains, that it wad tire the very deevil's wings to flee to the tap o' them. And in this country, and in the isles, whilk are little better, or, to speak the truth, rather waur than the mainland, there are about twa hunder and thirty parochines, including the Orkneys, where, whether they speak Gaelic or no, I wotna, but they are an uncivilised people. — Now, sirs, I sall haud ilk parochine at the moderate estimate of eight hunder examinable persons, deducting children under nine years of age, and then adding one-fifth to stand for bairns of nine years auld, and under, the whole population will reach to the sum of — let us add one-fifth to 800 to be the multiplier, and 230 being the multiplicand —"

"The product," said Mr. Owen, who entered delightedly into these statistics of Mr. Jarvie, "will be 230 000."

"Right, sir — perfectly right; and the military array of this Hieland country, were a' the men-folk between aughteen and fifty-six brought out that could bear arms, couldna come weel short of fifty-seven thousand five hundred men. Now, sir, it's a sad and awfu' truth, that there is neither wark, nor the very fashion nor appearance of wark, for the tae half of thae puir creatures; that is to say, that the agriculture, the pasturage, the fisheries, and every species of honest industry about the country, cannot employ the one moiety of the population, let them work as lazily as they like, and they do work as if a pleugh or a spade burnt their fingers. Aweel, sir, this moiety of unemployed bodies, amounting to —"

"To one hundred and fifteen thousand souls," said Owen, "being the half of the above product."

"Ye hae't, Maister Owen — ye hae't — whereof there may be twenty-eight thousand seven hundred able-bodied gillies fit to bear arms, and that do bear arms, and will touch or look at nae honest means of livelihood even if they could get it — which, lack-a-day, they cannot."

"But is it possible," said I, "Mr. Jarvie, that this can be a just picture of so large a portion of the island of Britain?"

"Sir, I'll make it as plain as Peter Pasley's pikestaff — I will allow that ilk parochine, on an average, employs fifty pleughs, whilk is a great proportion in sic miserable soil as thae creatures hae to labour, and that there may be pasture eneugh for pleugh-horses, and owsen, and forty or fifty cows; now, to take care o' the pleughs and cattle, we'se allow seventy-five families of six lives in ilk family, and we'se add fifty mair to make even numbers, and ye hae five hundred souls, the tae half o' the population, employed and maintained in a sort o' fashion, wi' some chance of sour-milk and crowdie; but I wad be glad to ken what the other five hunder are to do?"

"In the name of God!" said I, "what *do* they do, Mr. Jarvie? It makes me shudder to think of their situation."

"Sir," replied the Bailie, "ye wad maybe shudder mair if ye were living near-hand them. For, admitting that the tae half of them may make some little thing for themsells honestly in the Lowlands by shearing in harst, droving, hay-making, and the like; ye hae still mony hundreds and thousands o' lang-legged Hieland gillies that will neither work nor want, and maun gang thigging and sorning* about on their acquaintance, or live by doing the laird's bidding, be't

---

* *Thigging and sorning* was a kind of genteel begging, or rather something between begging and robbing, by which the needy in Scotland used to extort cattle, or the means of subsistence from those who had any to give.

right or be't wrong. And mair especially, mony hundreds o' them come down to the borders of the low country, where there's gear to grip, and live by stealing, reiving, lifting cows, and the like depredations! A thing deplorable in ony Christian country — the mair especially, that they take pride in it, and reckon driving a spreagh (whilk is, in plain Scotch, stealing a herd of nowte) a gallant, manly action, and mair befitting of pretty men (as sic reivers will ca' themsells) than to win a day's wage by ony honest thrift. And the lairds are as bad as the loons; for if they dinna bid them gae reive and harry, the deil a bit they forbid them; and they shelter them, or let them shelter themsells, in their woods, and mountains, and strongholds, whenever the thing's dune. And every ane o' them will maintain as mony o' his ane name, or his clan, as we say, as he can rap and rend means for; or, whilk's the same thing, as mony as can in ony fashion, fair or foul, mainteen themsells — and there they are wi' gun and pistol, dirk and dourlach, ready to disturb the peace o' the country whenever the laird likes; and that's the grievance of the Hielands, whilk are, and hae been for this thousand years by-past, a bike o' the maist lawless unchristian limmers that ever disturbed a douce, quiet, God-fearing neighbourhood, like this o' ours in the west here.''

Sir Walter Scott, *Rob Roy*

So Be It

But still there was enough in our old society to justify the affection with which all who knew it always remember it. It was excellent in itself, and curious in its position.

It contained many good, and several bright, names both professional and literary, and was graced by a far greater intermixture of resident rank and family than either Edinburgh or any provincial town can boast of now, when everything of the kind is sucked into the London whirlpool. The successive throes of the old town for deliverance had gradually produced St. John Street, Brown's Square, Argyle Square, George Square, and gardened Nicolson Street, each of which, with its new-lighted swarm, was fashionable in its day. Yet even with these aids there was very little elbow-room, and the quarters of the gentry were always clustered together. Chambers, in the beginning of his interesting *Traditions of Edinburgh*, gives some curious statements of places and residents. They exhibit a picture of society which is incomprehensible now, and indeed was scarcely credible even to such survivors as lived in it. They imply that those of the upper class must have all been well acquainted, and must have associated with the familiarity of village neighbours. What else could people do who pigged together in the same "Land", and had their main-doors within a few feet of each other on the same common stair? This must certainly have occasionally given rise to the petty quarrels and factions that keep small sets awake; but on the whole the local concentration was favourable to kindliness and mirth.

The Learning and Elegance of the scene must have been set off by its contrast with the very recently softened barbarism of the country. Ceremony still kept the field against the levelling tide of what was thought modern vulgarity. It was still an age in which powdered bag-wigs, embroidered coats, hooped brocades, and rules and formalities, gold buckles, high heels, higher head-gear, and other picturesque relics, were not unnatural, and were looked upon with the greater interest from the obvious nearness of their final disappearance. There was no public, and very little local, schism. The seeds of religious dissent had been sown, and the crop was even above the ground; but it was unbrairded and unfelt. There were fanatics in those days, but they let good society alone; and there was a race of agreeable and rational clergymen whose sense of decorum was not shocked by polite company, nor their piety deemed wasted if it was not all given to the poor, or the pulpit, or the Presbytery. The violence of Jacobitism had abated, and after that of the French Revolution began, it created no discord among the upper ranks, which were all of the same opinion. Those of that class, therefore, lived well together. The people had not arisen. There was no Public. The single upper class that existed included the nobility, the gentry, the Law, the College, the Church, and Medicine — the whole station and learning of the place, and formed an aristocracy which shone undisturbed.

This "local aristocracy" is the true key to the understanding of the interest and the peculiarity of that society. It was a club, which recognised members of every description who were respectable and agreeable, especially from learning and rank. Nor were even tradesmen, called merchants, absolutely rejected, provided their trade was adorned by personal or family eminence. One good effect of rank or high family is that it confers respectability on its remoter members without wealth, and enables them to be poor, or to follow humble avocations, without degradation; and this feeling brought some even of our deserving shop-keepers within the privileged class, which thus formed a little world of itself.

This community has been made more interesting to a later generation by the fame of some of its members, which always elevates the whole body. And the interest is deepened by its being now seen that the society was shedding its lustre on the last purely Scotch age. Most of what had gone before had been turbulent and political. All that has come after has been English. The eighteenth was the final Scotch century. We, whose youth tasted the close of that century, and who have lived far into the Southern influence, feel proud of a purely Edinburgh society which raised the reputation of our discrowned capital, and graced the deathbed of the national manners. No wonder that we linger with affectionate respect over the deserted or degraded haunts of our distinguished people, and that we feel as if we could despise ourselves if we did not prefer the memory of those scenes to all that is to be found in the commonplace characters of modern men, and in the insignificance of modern refinement.

The change that has taken place was inevitable. It is the same change that has effaced peculiarity everywhere, and has cast all habit and character in one mould, of which London is the model. The comparative value of what Edinburgh has lost or gained is not difficult to be ascertained. In point of beauty, and everything connected with the economy of life, the improvement is immeasurable. A return to the old style for a single year would be thought a severe sentence by a criminal court.

Henry Cockburn, *Memorials of his Time*

Graven Images

The whole problem of the Burns cult in Scotland is a peculiar one, and I may as well animadvert upon it here, since no book about Scotland can avoid it. Burns was a great poet, and a character of great likeableness and charm. He was also a man whose life and poetry are very difficult to separate; for the best of his poetry sprang directly out of his life. He expressed more perhaps than any other poet his workaday character in his poetry, throwing into it his daily hopes, fears, humours, affections, lusts, repentances, despairs, sentimentalities. With such a figure to work on, it was easy for the popular imagination to substitute the man, or an idealised effigy of him, for the whole Burns, forgetting that the poet was an essential part of him and that his actual life could not have been what it was if he had not possessed genius. This is roughly what has happened. To every Scotsman Burns is a familiar figure, a sort of household god, and most Scotsmen, I suppose, could reel off a few proverbial tags of his poetry, and one or two of his songs set to music. But that is all. This public effigy, in which the lover, the boon-companion and the democrat are the main ingredients, with a hard-working farmer in the background, but all subdued to respectability by time, is the real object of worship of the Burns cult. It is not a literary cult, but a social one. It has very little to do with Burns, and is concerned chiefly with the perpetuation of a myth. In that myth Burns becomes an ordinary man like his devotees, which he was not. He also becomes a successful lover and a free and glorious companion, which everybody would like to be. His myth is thus based on a firm foundation of sanctified illusion and romantic wish fulfilment. This legendary figure is a Scotsman who took upon him all the sins of the people, not to redeem them, but to commit them as ideally as they should be committed, that is, freely and guiltlessly, in an imaginary world beyond good and evil, a Paradisal Kailyard with a harmless domesticated serpent; for even to the most respectable of Burns's worshippers, to elders and ministers of the Kirk, Burns's sins are in a special category, and his fornications have the prescriptive right of King David's. He was a scapegoat driven out to sweet pastures, while the people elected to remain in the wilderness; a god who sanctified the meagre indulgences of the many by unlimited loving and drinking.

This is not an unfair description of what Burns means to Scotland as a racial myth. The Burns of popular legend is an imaginative incarnation of a people's desires, unfulfilled in life. It has no fundamental resemblance to Burns himself. Burns was not, for the age he lived in, an immoderate drinker; nor was he a careless lover, and he perpetually cursed the weaknesses in himself which his admirers glorify. He had, like all poets of equal greatness, a keen and sure moral sense fed by a universal human sympathy such as no other Scotsman has possessed. His life was not a happy one, but filled with misery and disappointment, which he bore bravely. However, I am not concerned here with Burns, but with his legend, which is an important social phenomenon.

The myth of Burns would not have risen at all, however, if Scotsmen had not an exceptionally powerful myth-making faculty. The history of Scotland is filled with legendary figures, actual characters on which the popular imagination has worked, making them its own and by doing so transfiguring them. Wallace and Bruce, Mary Stuart and Prince Charlie are not so much historical characters as figures in an unwritten ballad: they have taken on an almost purely poetical reality, and are semi-inventions like Mary Hamilton and the Bonny Earl of Moray, the originals of whom we know to have existed historically, but who are now part of a song. Sometimes the basis on which these legends arose was paltry enough, but that did not affect the stability or the beauty of the legend. These myths never took as their foundation a moral hero: Knox, the most important figure in Scottish history, and one of the greatest, has had many lies told about him, but he has never been the theme of a poetical fiction. It is heroism, beauty and grace, generally heightened by weakness or misfortune, that the communal poetic faculty of Scotland prefers to work upon. At the beginning, when Scotland was conscious of its growing power, the theme of legend was successful heroism against odds; later, when it felt its power slipping from it, or quite vanished, its imagination turned to the spectacle of beauty in misfortune and the tragedy of a lost cause. These legends signified more than they said, like all legends, and though the theme might be Wallace and Bruce, or Mary Stuart and Prince Charlie, the mood which chose them was the mood of a nation, a nation in the first case conscious of power and in the second of weakness.

Edwin Muir, *Scottish Journey*

Here's Tae Us! Wha's Like Us?

I trust I have made myself clear. The majority of Glasgow pubs are for connoisseurs of the morose, for those who relish the element of degradation in all boozing, and do not wish to have it eliminated by the introduction of music, modernistic fitments, arty effects, or other extraneous devices whatsoever. It is the old story of those who prefer hard-centre chocolates to soft, storm to sunshine, sour to sweet. True Scots always prefer the former of these opposites. That is one of our principal differences from the English. We do not like the confiding, the intimate, the ingratiating, the hail-fellow-well-met, but prefer the unapproachable, the hard-bitten, the recalcitrant, the sinister, the malignant, the sarcastic, the saturnine, the cross-grained and the cankered, and the howling wilderness to the amenities of civilization, the irascible to the affable, the prickly to the smooth. We have no damned fellow-feeling at all, and look at ourselves and others with the eye of a Toulouse Lautrec apprais-ing an obscene old toe-rag doing the double-split. In short, we are all poets (all true Scots — that is, all Scots not encased in a carapace of conventionality a mile thick) of *l'humour noir* and, as William Blake said, "All poets are of the devil's party".

There is a well-known story about Carlyle and Emerson spending several hours together without exchanging a word. Carlyle declared it was one of the best nights he ever spent with anybody. A lot of us spend many nights in Scottish pubs in the same way and we agree with Carlyle. Scotland produces a type of man who can dis-pense more completely than any with what James Joyce called "the atrocities of human intercourse".

There is nothing less exportable than a national sense of humour. The Scottish temper I am writing about is little known abroad. Our internationally famous comedians purvey a very different account of us. The sorry joke is that so many Scots believe the latter and model themselves all too successfully on it. Yet what I am trying to express is well-enough known about us in other connections. It is this that has for centuries made the Scottish soldier famous as a bayonet-fighter. A similar preference for naked steel runs through every phase of our life. It is summed up in the old Gaelic proverb: "Fingal's sword never needs to cut twice." Burns says in one of his poems that you need not be "nice" with him. No one need be "nice" with any true Scotsman — in fact, he will not allow it at all. The only kind of friendships one makes — or wishes to make or could tolerate at all — in such pubs was well described by my Irish friend, the late W.B. Yeats, when he wrote:

> I called him a knave and a fool —
> But friendship never dies!

In other words, the injunction which is as one with the very mar-

row of our bones is "Woe to him of whom all men speak well."
We have no use for emotions, let alone sentiments, but are solely
concerned with passions.

Our attitude is not inhuman. We are experienced men of the
world. We like what we like to be a little grim — in keeping with
the facts of life, and loathe facile emotions. We cherish no illu-
sions, and consequently prefer a mutual taciturnity to any sort of
social joy, standing shoulder to shoulder with other men we do not
know from Adam and do not want to know. We feel no necessity
whatever to indulge in any airs and graces, are not fond of promis-
cuous conversation, at least of any sustained sort, and if our risible
faculties are moved at all by the human spectacle, that movement
only adorns our faces intermittently with some sort of *risus sar-
donicus* that in flickering across our features barely interrupts the
emission of the dense smoke of the black tobacco going well in our
clay pipes.

Hugh MacDiarmid, *The Uncanny Scot*

'Feed My Sheep'

The day she went to see the minister she dressed as carefully as she
could. It was a long way to go and she was very nervous. She
hardly got any sleep the night before, wondering what she would
say and how she would act, for he had a big house and servants. It
might be that when the moment came she wouldn't be able to say
anything at all. She might just stand there completely tongue-tied:
for it wasn't an easy thing to speak to the minister. In fact she had
never spoken to him before. True, he might say "Good day" to her
but there had never been any conversation. The minister had a lot
on his mind.

That night she thought about him and didn't sleep well. He was a
big burly man who kept himself to himself in the huge manse.
Apart from being the minister he was said to be clever and to write
little books. She didn't much approve of this for she didn't think it
was a minister's job to be clever. After all, hadn't Paul said that to
be a Christian you didn't need to be clever? But she had to admit
that he made a good sermon, though now and again he was inclined
to show his cleverness and explain how certain words could have

different meanings. This only confused her but he could get a lot out of a text. She remembered a particularly good sermon on the text "I will arise now and go to my father" in which he had shown that the father of the Prodigal Son was meant to be God. This text had made a strong impression on her for he might have been speaking of her son who had gone to Canada. She often thought that he was speaking to her personally.

So all that night she was thinking of what she would say and do and was tired when the morning came, beautiful and innocent and calm with its bluish mist concealing the power of the sun. She could hardly eat anything and her stomach seemed to have gone to her mouth. But she did manage to cram something down. It would be better for her to go in the morning because she was at her strongest and best then and she was sure he would be at home. If she waited till the afternoon she might change her mind. There was no way of locking the door and she wouldn't have dreamed of doing so anyway. No one ever locked a door in the village, no matter how long he or she was away from the house. There was nothing to steal and anyway no one stole. She could not remember anybody stealing anything and if anyone did he wouldn't last long in the village. For stealing was a great crime. Who could hold up his head again if he stole anything?

She walked slowly along the road not meeting anybody at first for they would be out at the corn. In the distance she saw the sun flashing on silver. It would be a sickle or a scythe. However, she was not destined to reach the minister's house unaccosted. At the very end of the road she saw Mrs Macleod stacking peats near the fence. She didn't particularly care for Mrs Macleod but at the same time she couldn't pass her without speaking.

"Why, Mrs Scott, what a surprise."

She couldn't think of anything to say but: "It's a fine morning."

"It's that indeed," said Mrs Macleod coming towards her, carrying a peat in her hand almost absentmindedly. Her dark eyes were glinting, curious to know why Mrs Scott dressed in her Sunday black was walking along the road at that hour. But she didn't ask directly.

"You get a lot of dust on the road in summer," she said, looking at the long black skirt.

The road was blinding white and pitted with holes, now dry and dusty. Mrs Scott walked on the grassy verge of the road by the ditch in which there was a little water, green and slimy.

"You wouldn't like to come in for a minute?" asked Mrs Macleod.

"No, thank you just the same," said Mrs Scott.

All around her the air was fresh and new. She hadn't been out as far as this for a long time. She pulled her hood down over her brow. Said Mrs Macleod:

"I hear you had the man on the white horse to see you."

"Yes, I had that," she said.

"Ay, he was in most of the houses."

There was a silence, Mrs Macleod finally breaking it in a worried manner:

"You never know what will happen do you?"

"No." No indeed.

The house at the back seemed unusually quiet. There wasn't much water in the barrel at the door. A few hens scrabbled in the dust. A cock suddenly raised its head and crowed for no reason. Her husband must be away again in Edinburgh, thought Mrs Scott. He didn't seem to look after his own house though. There was no look of fresh paint about and the door was cracked and starving for paint.

"It's worrying, isn't it?" said Mrs Macleod, looking at her in a scattered way. But she looked worried too, as if she would cry any minute. She was supposed to be really helpless in outside work.

"I don't know what to do if they put us out," she said. "With so many children."

Mrs Scott wasn't feeling very tolerant that morning. It was the same for everyone, wasn't it, and anyway Mrs Macleod had a husband she could rely on. She was sure that Donald Macleod would be all right. He was the sort of man Patrick Sellar would like, a man who wasn't interested in the church and spent most of his time in Edinburgh. In fact he might help Sellar to pull the church down. It was the sort of thing he would do, laughing and making jokes.

Mrs Macleod looked as if she was about to say something else but didn't. She looked down helplessly at the peat in her hand as if she had just noticed it, then hearing the crying of children said quietly:

"Well, I suppose I must get back. I have the dinner to make. Be careful when you're crossing the bridge. They say it's not very steady."

Mrs Scott said nothing and walked on till she came to the river where the wooden bridge was. There was still some water in the river but she didn't look at it much for it would dazzle her eyes with the sun flashing on it like that. There was no hand rail and though it was a reasonable width the bridge seemed to have rotted and was swaying a bit. One of the planks had a hole in it and all of them were slimy. She managed to cross, breathless and frightened, keeping her eyes away from the water and looking only at the wood of the bridge. Below her she knew there would be little darting trout but she had no time for that. She reached the other side, her shoes sinking in the dampness, and stopped for a little time, collecting herself again. Then she set off across the moor, red with heather. She found herself thinking of the days when as children they used to go out and collect the purple blaeberries into jars. For hours they moved from clump of heather to clump of heather, heading northward all the time, their mouths becoming more and more purple: and they jumped peatbanks under the great bowl of the sky till finally they lost sight of the village altogether and were in a strange new world without boundaries, crawling along, filling the jars.

Steadily she tramped on, some yellow flowers fluttering slightly at her feet. A lark flew up startled in front of her and climbed into the sky twittering. She didn't look up. Once she was startled by the whirr of a larger bird, like a clock being wound up. No animal, however, moved around her, no hare and no rabbit. Up above her, though she didn't see it, a crow was hanging. Once a wasp sped angrily past her face and she flicked at it with her hand. Bees were humming round the heather flowers. In the old days she would have looked for white heather.

Seen from above she was a diminutive figure in black plodding steadily across the moor alive with yellow and wine-red, her shoes sinking into the moist earth. To the south of her there rose gently lazy smoke from the village, a thin blue into a bluer sky. In the distance she could hear someone hammering, perhaps repairing a fence. But she was alone on the moor. Not quite alone, for she came suddenly upon an object which at first she took to be a piece of dirty cloth. As she approached it she could hear a thick buzzing sound which puzzled her, a buzzing as of a great number of flies, almost like the sound of a sleepy saw sawing fresh wood. When she came to the object she looked down and almost turned away with disgust and sickness. It was the carcass of a thin sheep, soiled white with a black head, one of the Highland sheep of which people owned one or two. But nevertheless she stayed there for a

while, fascinated with feelings of revulsion and pity. The sheep
stared up at her, both its sockets empty and yet liquid as if with
tears. The crows could have done that and indeed as she looked she
saw a crow some yards off, staring at her stonily with fixed eyes as
if there was real intelligence behind them. There was a gash in the
sheep's side at which the flies were buzzing in a domestic sort of
way. In fact it all looked very homely. The buzzing reminded her
of the humming of Sunday pots on boil. All the living beings she
could see — which were the flies — were busy, all except the
sheep whose black legs were twisted under it and the crow which
was waiting for her to go, as if it had staked a claim to the place.
Now that she could see it more clearly she noticed that its thin
black head was twisted on its neck at an unnatural angle. It was
quite quite dead and yet in a disturbing way it seemed to be appeal-
ing to her out of its empty sockets. The flies of course didn't notice
she was there. They hummed fatly and richly at the wound.

She stared at them for a long time, then continued towards the
manse. The crow stayed there till the last moment, then with an
angry ''caw'' rose into the air, flapping its wings and gently hovering till she had gone. After that it would return to the sheep again.
Already it had picked the eyes out cleanly like gems from an old
brooch. She hated crows for they used to swoop and take the chickens from the ground. She had lost many chickens that way, as
well as to the gales which lifted them up and blew them towards
the moor. She looked back but the crow had settled again, still a
yard or two from the sheep. She continued walking, deliberately
avoiding the lochside where her mother had once screamed on a
moonlit night long ago. She could see the sun dazzling among the
reeds and the blue of the water but she kept a good distance from
it. There wasn't long to go now.

When she came to the manse the first thing she noticed was the
garden. Villagers, of course, didn't have gardens and in general
didn't think of flowers as things which had to be nursed into existence and considered in an aesthetic way. In fact they didn't think
of them at all as separate from the earth in which they grew. To
plant and cosset flowers into existence would be considered an
effeminate and silly activity. You couldn't eat flowers; and as for
beauty — what was that? Nevertheless, she stopped and stared at
the flowers, which were all different colours from red to purple.
She saw a green plant writhing its way up one wall of the manse.
She had never seen ivy before.

"Good day, Mrs Scott."

She turned and there was Mr Macmillan coming towards the minister's peatstack with a wheelbarrow. All gathering of peats and planting of potatoes and practically everything else was done for the minister by the villagers.

Mr Macmillan had an old bedridden sister who had been ill for years and whom he looked after with an almost womanly tenderness. He was a very religious man but would not become an elder because he didn't think himself worthy of such a position. Most days you could see him working at the quarry, carrying stones about endlessly in a wheelbarrow, and covered with white dust. In fact, you couldn't think of him apart from his wheelbarrow, bent over it as if he had been born with one in his hands and was pushing it towards a horizon which he would never reach. He was always working except when you would see him spitting on his hands to make the wooden handles of the barrow softer, or when he was eating a piece of bread sitting by himself on a gravelly slope above the quarry.

"And how are you keeping, Mrs Scott?" he shouted without halting in his stride, as he made towards the stack to tip the wheelbarrow over.

"Not too bad, Mr Macmillan."

"I am glad to hear it. Just pull that rope."

And he was absorbed in his work again.

She went up the stony path and pulled the rope at the door, causing a bell to jangle in the hollowness inside, so great a noise indeed that she was frightened that she had pulled it too hard. Written in front of her on a door more massive than any she had ever encountered were the letters, in gold, STRATHNAVER MANSE. The bell's jangle seemed to prolong itself indefinitely till finally, as it was fading away in short irresolute waves, a young girl wearing a black apron and a white pinafore came to the door, opened it and looked at her in some surprise. She didn't recognise the girl and thought that possibly she might be one of the minister's relatives.

"Is it the minister you want to see?" the girl asked in a kind of impudent tone to which Mrs Scott was not used.

"If the minister would see me for a minute," she heard herself saying. Behind her she could hear Mr Macmillan humming a psalm tune as he worked at the peats, and this comforted her.

"I'll see if he will speak to you," said the girl, turning on her heel and leaving her at the door.

Mrs Scott felt a vague unease stir in her, like a snail under a cold stone. She didn't know what she had expected. Perhaps to find the minister himself come to the door and draw her inside in a kind manner. But the impersonal nature of this encounter frightened her a little. She found herself staring through the open door into a hall and saw directly above her a deer's head nailed to the wood, the eyes glassy under the spreading antlers. Behind it a stairway rose, darkly spiralling, and on the curving wall could be seen a portrait of a minister in dark robes. She couldn't see the face, however, and was trying to make it out when the girl returned to say:

"Follow me, please."

She followed her down the hallway till they came to a door. The girl knocked and the minister said "Come in" and she found herself in a room with tall windows and shelves crammed with books. She had never thought the whole world could contain so many books.

The minister was sitting at a tall desk. She had evidently interrupted him in his writing — perhaps Sunday's sermon. Rays of sunlight fell across the desk, catching in a mesh the huge Bible he had been consulting. She didn't know what she ought to say or do. The girl had gone but the door remained open.

"Would you please shut the door?" said the minister, coming from behind his desk and standing in front of the fire, quite a large one even though it was a fine day. On the mantelpiece were glass ornaments, some in the shape of animals though she didn't know their names. She shut the door.

"Have a seat Mrs . . . Macleod, isn't it?"

"Mrs Scott," she got out.

"Oh, of course, Mrs Scott. Such an inexcusable mistake."

She sat down, very delicately, her hands folded in her lap.

"And now," he said, gathering the skirts of his long coat behind him, "what can I do for you, Mrs Scott? I trust that you are well?"

"Yes, thank the minister. I hope the minister is well himself."

"Oh, I am quite well, Mrs Scott, thank you, quite well. But I must say that I have a lot of cares these days, Mrs Scott, and many responsibilities. To win over souls to the Lord is a wearying task, Mrs Scott."

She was aware that he was looking at her keenly while his mouth was speaking these words.

"And what is it, Mrs Scott, that you came about exactly?" The clock on the mantelpiece struck sharply, startling her for a moment and seeming to add urgency to the minister's words. At the same time he went and sat down at the desk, looking at her over it as she had once seen the schoolmaster do when she had gone to ask how Iain was getting on with his lessons. She had to pull the chair round a little to face him. His head was caught in the light, the Roman nose, the face which was still plump without being round, the full lips, which were very red, the fine forehead under the fringe of grey hair. She didn't know how to start, and was aware that his fingers were tapping restlessly on the desk in front of him.

"I came to see the minister about the man on the white horse."

"Man on a white horse?" he echoed richly, leaning back in his chair, his hands folded across his stomach.

"Yes. He came two days ago. He said he was going to put me out."

She thought his eyes narrowed slightly.

"Oh, you mean Patrick Sellar?"

"The minister will know his name better than me," she said, and was surprised to see his blue eyes flash a little before he smiled again.

"Let me get this clear," he said, leaning forward. "You came to see me about Patrick Sellar who came to your house and said he was going to put you out?"

He walked over to the fireplace and stood there, legs straddled. She had to turn round in the chair again.

"Well, Mrs Scott," he said good-humouredly, "and what do you want me to do about it?"

She looked down at the floor and then at the fire which she could see between his legs.

"I was thinking . . . that the minister might write . . . might write to him to tell him that . . ." She stopped.

"To tell him what, Mrs Scott?"

Irrationally she said:

"He was saying that they were going to pull down the church."

"Yes, Mrs Scott. That is perfectly true."

Something was going on in her head, though she couldn't tell what it was. The strange surroundings and the tension of going to see and speak to the minister in his own manse, the sunlight and the fire were having an effect on her. She swayed a little.

"Are you all right, Mrs Scott?"

"Yes," she said, gritting her teeth. "I am all right, thank the minister."

"I'm glad of that. I was going to say that they are going to build another church in the north. I had a long discussion with Mr Sellar about it."

He frowned, placed the tips of his fingers together and said:

"Have you ever thought, Mrs Scott, that this is a visitation?"

Still looking at her he clicked his fingers sharply, then continued with some anger:

"I mean that the people of this village, aye, the people of all the villages here, have deserved this. Have you ever thought that this came as a punishment for their sins?"

He walked over to the window and she followed him with her eyes. "Looking out into the bright light of summer, Mrs Scott, seeing the birds of the air and the flowers of the field it is not easy to remember and remind ourselves of our sins. It is not easy to remember those things that we ought not to have done, and the things that we ought to have done but haven't. Night after night I hear them dancing, Mrs Scott. Sometimes I cannot get on with my work because of it. Oh, I have spoken to them about it, but the young are not so responsible as they were — and whom must we blame but their elders?"

As he ceased to speak Mrs Scott sank into a daze at this new view of things. Was it perhaps true that Patrick Sellar, the man on the white horse, had been sent as their scourge? Was he a penance imposed by God Himself?

"I have served here for many years as the servant of God's servants," the minister said, standing at the window, his beautiful resonant voice filling the room, his handsome head haloed with sunlight. "And I can tell you of practices that a daughter of God would not believe." He nodded his head emphatically three times. "I speak of their carnality, Mrs Scott, and their music which is not the music of David. I speak of some who do not attend church at all. I speak of a growing lawlessness amongst my flock. I speak of a general lawlessness in the whole land. How many of them come to the tables of the Lord? How many of them are not thinking of the flesh and their worldly pleasures? How many of them are learning disobedience to their lawful master the Duke? Why, I have heard of some who refuse to serve in his army."

For a moment, entranced by the thrilling voice, Mrs Scott was nodding her head in agreement with what he had to say. It was true enough, what he was saying. Some of the words struck home to her, buried themselves in her heart. The music was ungodly, the young were disobedient, the world was changing, there was much lawlessness. Sin, all in scarlet, was striding the world like the huge soft round red flowers in the minister's garden. But when the minister began to speak about the Duke, and added:

"Do you know that when the Duke was asking them to join his regiment — to fight for their lawful king and country — not one of them volunteered?" the spell was snapped, she raised her head and looked up directly into the light.

The minister, sensing that he had made a mistake, continued as if he hadn't noticed.

"Not that that is the important matter. What is important is the attitude it shows. Where one is not loyal to one's earthly master one is not likely to be loyal to one's God. Didn't the Lord Himself say that we must be loyal to our earthly masters?"

He stopped, then said in a different tone:

"It is their land, Mrs Scott, and the law is on their side."

"Does the minister think that it is right for them to put me out?" she said daringly, squinting into the light where the head was golden.

"Mrs Scott, we are all going to be put out. I myself am going to be put out. I shall have to leave this manse which I have loved and this church which I have built with my own hands. Do you not think I will miss them though I have had to suffer much obduracy?"

Why had he said he had built the church with his own hands, which he hadn't done?

"Mrs Scott, I had a long talk with Mr Sellar. He struck me as a reasonable man, a man who must carry out his orders, albeit a man who will show humanity to the weak. I say I had a long talk with him. He promised us all houses, aye, better houses than we have at present. He told me of a place where you would all have a second chance, a chance to begin anew. Mrs Scott, do you know, can you imagine, what it is to be able to begin again? To have a second chance? How few of us in this world, Mrs Scott, are given a second chance."

Again the words struck home. Did she too not need a second chance? Could she begin again, miraculously transformed, be neither too hard nor too soft, learn to love and be loved, escape the voices screaming out of the darkness?

"No, Mrs Scott, they are not monsters. They are reasonable men."

Patrick Sellar a reasonable man? The minister was sitting behind his desk again watching her, his little eyes seeming to twinkle. And perhaps because of the eyes, which remained cold though they appeared to twinkle, or a trick of the light, or the way his head was cocked, or was it perhaps because of the buzzing of a fly on the window-pane, she was reminded of the crow which had stared unwinkingly at her, only rising at the last moment, as she had left the dead and dreadfully wounded sheep behind. The buzzing of the flies seemed still to be at her ears.

"Do not believe, Mrs Scott, that I do not see your difficulty. Nevertheless, I'm sure you will be helped to remove your furniture and ... er ... impedimenta. I'm sure that Mr Sellar will see to that."

"The minister ..." she began as he came over as if to take her by the arm and lead her out. She was about to say "The minister knows best" but the words stuck in her throat. She only managed to get out the two words "The minister" before she found herself being thrust towards the door, the darkness in the hall blinding and chilling her.

"And I am sure we will see you in church this Lord's Day as usual," said the minister startlingly. She almost caught a weakness in the voice. Eyes bent on the ground to find her way, she did not answer. Something was causing her to shudder, spasms of cold and fear were shaking her internally. When she reached the door she turned away from the blinding light, which rose straight at her face like a huge white door opening.

"You are quite all right then, Mrs Scott?" said the minister with a false tenderness in his voice, his hand on the door, to his right the red shine and fat glitter of garden flowers and behind him the mazy winding of the ivy like a long green snake clutching and weaving. Mr Macmillan was not to be seen. Endlessly cheerful, endlessly industrious, he would be away with the barrow and loading it with another burden of peats.

Leaving the manse she felt completely desolate. She heard the door shut behind her. The heady scent of the flowers was in her nostrils, like an obscene perfume. A picture of her mother stepped into her mind as if straight from a garish frame and stabbed her like a knife. Inside the barred creel she saw the caged bony face moving to and fro. She found herself half-running, having covered a good distance already. It was much hotter now and her hands were prickly with sweat. Ahead of her the ground seemed to be heaving and the air full of smoke and fire. Panic seized her. She wanted to be home. "I must get home", she thought, as if the house had disappeared in her absence. She had a dreadful fear that she was going to die on the moor like the sheep she had seen. She steadied herself and took another step into the sun. On and on she walked, following old paths impressed into her brain.

This must have been why when she passed by the loch she stopped and looked at it and at the reeds growing out of it. Midges were moving on the surface of the water in a thin cloud. The loch looked innocent, gentle, calm, without a tremor. This apparent tranquillity belied its depth. She looked at it, thinking of that night many years before. She saw again the twisted face sparking hate at her between bars of moonlight — not, she hoped recognising her — and she heard again the obscenities that poured out of the toothless mouth.

Staggering, she left the lochside and made her way across the moor. This time she didn't pass the sheep, nor did she see any crows. All she was set on doing was getting home. After that she would think again. With her head bent she noticed more and more living things among the heath and grass. An insect winged with light was fluttering about before her. She saw some ants and again something slithered quickly away with an eel-like motion through the crackling heather which was coloured a living blood red. A bee swung upside down on a yellow flower, palpitating. She came to the river and the bridge. Head bent, she saw small trout flashing deliriously in the sun, sparkling in spots of blinding white. What was that in the water? A jersey, a pair of woollen pants? A child's face smiling up at her slightly distorted? She leaned down to see more closely and fell into the sparkling water, what there was of it.

Iain Crichton Smith, *Consider the Lilies*

Sabbath Morn

DAVID DUNBAR: That's juist it. Ye hut the nail on the heid. I canna say that I'm fair convinced it *was* the real Mackay — I mean, the poo'er o' the Holy Ghost — mysel'. The de'il plays some unco tricks. But at ony rate, if it wasna the genuine article, it was a marvellous imitation, an' the maist impressive thing o' the kind I've seen since auld Dr Nixon afore Gilruth's time, said, *'Let everybuddy sing,'* wi' sic emphasis on the everybuddy that we'd nae sooner sterted than puir Jimmy Carruthers, who was born deef an' dumb, joined in wi' sic an unearthly timmer that half the congregation lost their voices wi' shock . . .

CHARLIE MEARNS: An' it minds me o' anither occasion when a verra peculiar effec' was conjured up — a verra peculiar effec' indeed. A veesitin' meenister — a long drink o' water frae Paisley wey — had just gi'en oot his text, when a cock outside gied aff wi' a tremenjous "Cock-a-doodle-do!" The haill congregation gapit like a'e man; like a boxin' referee or an auctioneer, somehoo or ither there was nowt i' their heids but the coont — yin — twa — three! When the cock crew thrice a sort o' spasm o' fear ran through the haill buildin'. Naebody kent whaur to look or what to dae. Then, daggont, if the doited fowl didna craw aince mair, an' the tension brak' an' we a' burst oot lauchin' in a helpless kind o' way, the veesitin' meenister leadin' off wi' a howl like a hyaena . . .

DAVID DUNBAR: But what did the man *mean*? That's the thing. It was like seein' something that was neither flesh, fowl, or guid reid herrin'.

CHARLIE MEARNS: Like the beast in Revelations!

DAVID DUNBAR: Ye canna gie ony name to it. Tak'n word for word, it was a rigmarole o' nonsense — every phrase seemed chosen because it was the unlikeliest possible phrase to tack on to the yin that gaed afore it. An' yit there's nae gainsayin' the terrific effec' he somehoo or ither produced . . .

CHARLIE MEARNS: It was something like the kind o' grand paralysin' feelin' that can sometimes be created by brakin' oot, wi'oot ony warnin', frae a plain everyday kind o' passage into a crashin' bit o' French or Latin . . . only fer stranger.

WILLIAM BEEDIE: Aye! It was stranger than French or Latin. It was a language that has lost a lot in Blawearie for mony years i' the coorse o' translation into what passes for English. It was the language o' God . . .

JOHNNY SOUTAR: Ye dinna mean he was speaking' i' Braid Scots?

WILLIAM BEEDIE (*savagely*): No! ye gowk! . . .

JOHNNY SOUTAR (*anxiously*): Oh, I didna ken. Dinna get angry wi' fowk less gleg i' the uptak' than yersel'! Only, if it had been Braid Scots, nae maitter hoo auld-farran', I'se warran' I'd hae kent a wird or twa here an' there at ony rate.

WILLIAM BEEDIE *(disregarding Soutar)*: Ye ken the text, "My words are not as your words." Weel, there ye are. God tak's oor words when he speaks to us, but he fills them wi' his ain meanin's, which are quite different to ony we gi'e them oorsel's. An' that's the wey they soon' half-familiar, an' yet entirely strange an' beautiful an' terrible...*But here he comes!*

MRS DUNBAR *(returning to the 'muttons')*: A prophet o' Israel wad hae been sair oot o' place an' a maist unprofitable objec' in Blawearie pulpit at this time o' day! We've made some progress durin' the past twa-three thoosan' years — although ye wadna think sae to hear some fowk talkin'! It used to be thocht great sport hereaboots to gang an' see a public hangin' an' it strikes me the feelin's no' deid yet, an' some fowks gang to the kirk to enjoy the thocht o' some o' their neebors bein' fried to death in hell. But I dinna think that Christ himsel' had muckle stammack for that kin' o' spectacle...

MISS FREW: Christ came to earth to seek an' to save...

MRS DUNBAR: I ken *(tartly)* — an' his meenisters 'ud dae weel to follow his example while the time lasts. They'll need it a'.

MISS FREW *(completing her sentence with ostentatious patience)*: But God'll judge at the hinder-en'.

MRS DUNBAR: It s'ud be left to God an' to the hinder-en' then. Mr McIlwraith (an' him an unmarriet man that disna ken what every man an' wumman born has meant to some mither) spak' wi' as muckle assurance the day as if he were God himsel' dividin' the sheep an' the goats at his appinted time. I wunner *(her temper rising)* God didna...

MRS ROEBUCK: *Wheesht, here he comes!*

TAM STODDART: Christ himsel' wisna averse to a wee drappie noo an' then, for his stammack's sake.

MRS ADAM PERT *(scornfully)*: Ye're no' the only elder o' the kirk wha's mair fu' o' Paul's clash than the gospel o' the livin' God.

TAM STODDART *(patiently)*: Weel, if that was Paul an' no' the Lord himself at ony rate it was Christ that cheenged the water into wine...

MRS ADAM PERT: To suit some fowk he'd hae ha'en to aboleesh water a' thegither — an' then ye'd ha'e been aye dookin'.

TAM STODDARD *(losing his temper)*: Hyech! I expec' a wumman'll ha'e the last word at the verra Judgment itsel'.

MRS ADAM PERT *(victoriously)*:   Nae doot; but mair than likely if she has, it'll be to plead for some sumph o' a man.

ADAM PERT: *Wheesht, here he comes!*

(The Rev. Mr McIlwraith and the veteran beadle, Heb Duncan, come slowly down the path from the church to the gate. All eyes are turned towards them. Coming alongside the folk:)

MR MCILWRAITH: Well, how did you like the sermon?

In Chorus: { A searchin' utterance.
Aye, sir, yon's the stuff to stir fowk up.
A whiff o' the pure Jerusalem, etc., etc.

MR MCILWRAITH *(patting little Roebuck girls' heads, and going off)*:   We must try all kinds of methods.

(The old beadle stands giggling away into his beard at a great rate, incoherently amused.)

Several Voices: What are ye lauchin' at?

THE BEADLE *(at last)*:   Lauchin'. It 'ud mak' a cat lauch. The method was mebbe his ain, but the sermon wasna. Dr Gilruth gied it frae the verra self-same pulpit here close on twenty years ago, an' I've heard it fower times since to my shair an' certain knowledge, an' bits o't at orra times forbye... Ye ken that muckle purple passage in the middle o't. Weel, when Dr Gilruth was writin't he found yin o' his bit sheets o' paper half-fu' to start wi' — wi' a passage he'd been copyin' frae that fantastical divine, Dr Donne — a great Yankee revivalist, if I remember rightly! — an', absent-minded-like, thocht that he'd juist written it as pairt o's sermon. So he tacked on the rest to the end o't. He never noticed it the first time he delivered it; but I spotted the cuckoo i' the nest, an' when he gied it a second time, I spiered why he keepit in a passage that had nae connection wi' the rest o' the sermon ava! "Man, I never noticed it," he said, an' then he tellt me hoo it must ha'e happened. "But I'll juist leave it there," he added. "It may be an accident, or it may be the hand o' God. It'll no' dae ony ill in either case. Them that comes to the kirk i' the richt frame o' mind'll never notice that onything's amiss, an' them that dae notice'll be puzzled to death to ken what to mak' on't..."

(A study in faces)

Hugh MacDiarmid, *The Uncanny Scot*

The Wisest Fool

THE KING: *(Reaching for the bottle)* Weill, Jock, it's been a grand efternune. Eh, Mistress?

MRS E: It has that, yer Grace. Sall I tak the airn?

THE KING: Leave it. I want it. I'm expectin Sir Robert.

MRS E: Very weill, yer Grace. I'll leave ye, I think, and hae the table laid. *(Knowingly)* Will ye bide for supper?

THE KING: *(Joyfully)* Mistress Edward, ye're the best friend I hae! I'll clap my sword to yer guid man's back and say "Arise, Sir Nicoll"!

MRS E: Na na, yer Grace, dinna dae that. The Kirk wad turn against him. Aa the tred in black claith wad gang to Tam MacDowell. Wait till he's retired.

THE KING: Aa richt, whateir ye please. *(Eagerly)* What's in the pat?

MRS E: Cock-a-leekie.

THE KING: Ye maun hae kent I was comin!

MRS E: *(Bobbing)* I ken ye like it.

THE KING: I dae that. (MISTRESS EDWARD *leaves*) Jock, I'm bothert aboot siller. It'll tak a lot to cairry on a raid in the Hielands.

MAITLAND: *(Who has been helping himself from the bottle)* Damn it, man, ye hae eneugh gowd at Stirlin to pey for a dizzen raids, if ye juist had the gumption to use it.

THE KING: Na na, Jock! Annie wadna hear o't! She wad flee oot at me! I wadna hae the life o a dug! Dinna stert that again!

MAITLAND: It's the ae wey oot.

THE KING: It canna be! We maun fin some ither! And it maun be sune. My haill hairt's set on stertin at ance. Man, think —

MAITLAND: Wheesht!

THE KING: Here they are! It's Sir Robert! By God, I'll gar him wriggle! Ye'll hae the time o yer life nou!

(NICOLL *enters*)

NICOLL: Here's Sir Robert.

(SIR ROBERT *enters*. NICOLL *withdraws*. THE KING *affects a heavy scowl.*)

SIR ROBERT: *(Puzzled)* Your Majesty?

THE KING: Weill?

SIR ROBERT: You seem hostile.

THE KING: Daes it surprise ye?

SIR ROBERT: It doth, your Majesty, immensely.

THE KING: What dae ye think o that, Jock? He's fair astoundit!

(MAITLAND *gives a little bark of laughter.*)

SIR ROBERT: *(Indignantly)* My Lord! Your Majesty!

THE KING: Ay ay, Sir Robert, wark up yer indignation! But ye dinna ken what's comin! Dae ye see that airn? Dae ye see that bit o flannel? Dae ye see this letter? Ay, Sir Robert, ye may weill turn pale. Ye may weill gowp like a frichtent fish. Ye're a proved plotter, a briber o traitors, a hirer o murderers! Whan I think hou ye hae leived amang us, respectit by gentle and simple in the Toun, treatit like a lord at Coort, honoured wi my ain freindship and invitit often to my very table, I tak a haill-hairtit scunner at human nature! There's nae kent form o tor-ture, nae way o inflictin daith, that isna ower guid for ye! Ye're waur nor the warst auld beldam witch that was eir brunt to cinders!

SIR ROBERT: Your Majesty, I am but an instrument of my coun-try's policy.

THE KING: Policy! Jock, he said policy! (MAITLAND *snorts*) Sir Robert, yer mistress daesna ken what policy is. She wantit to stop the plottin o the Papists, and aa she could think o was to mak Bothwell sic a terror to the country that I had to look to the Papists for help. Aa the siller she wared on Bothwell, gin it had been peyed to me at the stert, wad hae redd her o the Pap-ists at ance!

SIR ROBERT: I think she attributed your friendship with the Pap-ists, your Majesty, to your hatred of the Protestant Church.

THE KING: The Protestant Kirk! It's a Presbyterian Kirk! They winna acknowledge their Sovereign as their speeritual heid! They elect men o their ain to tak the place o my bishops in the Three Estates! I woner what the Queen yer mistress wad dae, Sir Robert, if the preachers o her ain Kirk in England denied her authority! Wad she show nae ill will? I ken she wad, for by God, there's nae sovereign in Christendom hauf sae shair o Divine Richt as her Majesty o England! My fecht with the Kirk, Sir Robert, is a fecht against government frae the pulpit, and yer mistress suld be the last to encourage that!

SIR ROBERT: Your Majesty, there was no question of such encour-
agement. My mistress feared Spanish invasion and the loss of
her throne.

THE KING: Spanish invasion! Did she think for a meenit that I wad
jeyn wi Spain to put Phillip on the throne o England and destroy my ain claim to succeed her! Ye wad think, Sir Robert,
that I had nae intelligence at aa!

SIR ROBERT: Your Majesty, I assure you.

THE KING: Oh ay, Sir Robert, try to win me roun, but I tell ye
that gin I had nae mair sense nor to waste guid siller on a
treacherous blaggard like Bothwell I wad droun mysell in the
nearest dub. Dae ye ken what he's dune? He's jeynt the Pap-
ists!

SIR ROBERT: *(Slightly startled)* I thought it possible.

THE KING: Ye thocht it possible!

SIR ROBERT: I did your Majesty, as you will realise from my letter.

THE KING: I realise frae yer letter that ye were gaun to try to force
my haund through the Kirk. Dinna try to mak oot, Sir Robert,
that ye thocht I wad need ony forcin if Bothwell turnt his coat!
Ye hae won what yer mistress wantit nou, but dinna try to tak
the credit for it!

SIR ROBERT: Am I to understand, your Majesty, that the Papist
Lords will be attacked?

THE KING: They will by God, as sune as I can fin the siller!

SIR ROBERT: *(Airily)* Then, your Majesty, all is well. I am certain
that the Queen my mistress, when she hath heard of your
resolve, will endow you with undreamt of wealth.

THE KING: *(Eagerly)* Dae ye think sae, Sir Robert?

SIR ROBERT: I am certain, not only because you intend to serve a
cause she hath at heart, but because she must regard you now
as sound in your religion, and therefore the most proper person, by your faith as by your birth and endowments, to succeed
her on the Throne.

THE KING: Ye think sae, Sir Robert?

MAITLAND: Sir Robert hauds the best caird in the pack, yer
Grace. He aye wins ye roun.

SIR ROBERT: *(In protest)* My Lord!

THE KING: Na na, Sir Robert, he's richt! Ye ken hou to play on
my hopes o the succession!

SIR ROBERT: Your hopes are brighter now, your Majesty, than the stars of heaven.

THE KING: Awa wi ye. Flaittery wins nae favour frae me. Ye'll hae to show yer guid will in mair solid form. Hou sune dae ye think I can hae some siller?

SIR ROBERT: As soon as the Queen my mistress hears of your resolve.

THE KING: Then let her hear at ance. And I'll write to her mysell. Ye may tak yer letter.

SIR ROBERT: Your Majesty, you are indeed merciful. Have you seen ought of my servant?

THE KING: Ye deil, ye're wrigglin oot aathegither! Yer servant's in the Tolbooth, and he'll bide there the nou! I maun dae something to assert mysell! Gin it werena for the turn things hae taen, Sir Robert, I wad be faur mair severe! Ye wad pack yer kist and mak for the Border! Ye bide on, ye understaun, for the sake o the guid will that maun exist atween mysell and yer royal mistress, but gin I fin ye up to ony mair o yer intrigues I'll ask her to remove ye at ance!

SIR ROBERT: Your Majesty, I understand.

THE KING: Awa and think shame o yersell!

(SIR ROBERT *bows to* THE KING, *then to* MAITLAND, *then leaves. They watch him go.*)

THE KING: I couldna be hard on him, for he's fired my hopes. Jock, I *will* pledge the bairn's praisents! They'll be safe nou. I can hae them back whan his mistress pays up. Oho, but fortune's favoured me the day! There's naething in my wey! Aa that I hae wished for is promised at last! Bothwell on the scaffold, the Papists houndit doun, the Kirk in my pouer, England ahint me, and then, in the end, the dream o my life come true! It gars my pulse quicken! It gars my hairt loup! It gars my een fill wi tears! To think hou the twa pair countries hae focht and struggled. To think o the bluid they hae shed atween them, the touns they hae blackent wi fire, the bonnie green howes they hae laid waste. And then to think, as ae day it sall come to pass, that I, Jamie Stewart, will ride to London, and the twa countries sall become ane.

(MISTRESS EDWARD *can be heard off calling* "Nicoll! Nicoll! Come for yer supper!")

MAITLAND: *(Coming out of his trance and reaching for the bottle)* Ay, yer Grace, it's a solemn thocht. But the auld bitch isna deid yet.

(He places the bottle before THE KING. THE KING *fills his glass.)*

THE KING: *(Raising his glass high)* Jock, here's to the day. May the mowdies sune tickle her taes.

*(*MISTRESS EDWARD *appears at the door of the dining-room.)*

MRS E: *(With a deep curtsy)* Yer Grace, the supper's ready.

*(*THE KING *and* MAITLAND *eye each other and drink the toast.)*

CURTAIN

Robert McLellan, *Jamie the Saxt*

Glossary

ae, *one*
aganestand, *offer resistance to*
ahint, *behind*
airn, *iron*
alleavin, *eleven*
alluterlie, *completely*
anent, *concerning*
atteanes, *soon*
atween, *between*
aughteen, *eighteen*
auld-farrant, *old-fashioned*
ava, *at all*
aweel, *well (exclamation)*
aye, *yes, always*
ayont, *beyond*

bailie, *magistrate*
bairnies, *children*
ben, *in, into*
bike, *hive, swarm*
bratty, *apron*
braw, *fine*
breer, *sprouting*
britchen, *part of the harness of a horse*

carle, *man*
chirt, *squeeze*
claes, *clothes*
claik, *tattle*
clarty, *dirty*
clash, *gossip, tittle-tattle*
cleiding, *clothing*
clour, *a blow*
coble, *flat-bottomed boat*
cock-a-leekie, *soup made from fowl boiled with leeks*
conducit, *hired*

corp, *corpse*
coup, *fall*
courch, *a woman's cap*
crowdie, *porridge, pure curd mixed with butter, food in general*
cusing, *cousin*

daggont, *confound it*
dang, *threw, knocked*
danton, *daunt, depress*
darg, *work*
doited, *foolish*
dome, *law-suit*
douce, *grave, sober, respectable*
dourlach, *short sword, dagger*
drow, *mist, shower, haar*
dub, *puddle, gutter*
dune, *done, finished*

eall, *ale*
eird, *earth*
eithly, *easily*
engyne, *genius, intellect, character*
eschapit, *escaped*
evitit, *avoided*

fash, *annoy*
fasson, *fashion, style*
feart (for), *afraid (of)*
fecht, *fight*
feint, *the devil (used in strong negations or exclamations)*
forbye, *besides, in addition to, with the exception of*
forkytail, *earwig*
fykery, *fuss*

gar, *make, compel*

gavelock, *broad black beetle, insect like an earwig but longer*

gear, *property, money*

gif, *if*

gillie, *clansman*

gin, *if*

gleg, *sharp, quick*

gowd, *gold*

gowk, *fool*

gowp, *gulp, gape*

greet, *cry*

grip, *seize*

gude, *good, God*

gudeman, *husband*

gurly, *surly*

habber, *stutter, talk continuously*

haill, *whole*

hained, *saved*

hairt, *heart*

haleware, *the whole thing*

halfatt, *the side of the face, the temple*

harst, *harvest*

hateral, *heap, large quantity*

haud, *hold*

heavin, *haven, harbour*

hird-sell, *flock of sheep*

hirple, *hobble*

hoast, *cough*

how, *hollow, deep*

howm, *holm, field*

hulie, *completely*

hurl, *ride, drive*

ilk, *each*

jawbox, *kitchen sink*

Jenny Hunderlegs, *centipede*

jeyn, *join*

kailyard, *kitchen-garden*

keave, *fall, topple*

keelie, *a street arab*

ken, *know*

kist, *chest, coffin*

kittle, *to become interested, to warm up*

Lambes, *Lammas*

ley, *grass-land*

limmer, *rascal*

lithe, *shelter*

loon, *youth*

loup, *leap, jump*

lug, *ear*

mair, *more*

manyplies, *part of the intestines of cattle*

maun, *must*

meal-ark, *a large meal-chest*

mear, *mare*

mercat, *market*

midden, *rubbish heap, dunghill*

mind, *remember*

moil, *to labour*

mowdie, *mole*

nodge, *jogging movement*

nowt, *cattle*

nowther, *neither*

or, *before*

orra, *occasional*

other, *either*

outby, *there, nearby, a short distance off*

ower, *too (much)*

owerlaft, *covering, superstructure*

owsen, *oxen*

parochine, *parish*

pend, *covered archway*

pirlye, *a small amount, a gentle breeze*

pleugh, *plough*

plew-stilts, *plough handles*

portage, *private luggage or cargo*
pudenis, *puddings; intestines*

quean, *girl, woman*
quhaevir, *whoever*
quhairof, *whereof*
quhat, *what*
quhilk, *which*

rap, *seize*
redd, *tidy*
reive, *plunder, rob*
remede, *remedy*
rubber, *cask*
ruckly, *rickety*
ruiging, *tugging*

sald, *should*
sark, *shirt*
schosin, *choosing*
scunner, *dislike, disgust*
seall, *sail*
shair, *sure*
sho'elt, *shovel it*
sic, *such*
sickly, *similarly*
siller, *money*
skeugh, *twisted, misshapen*
skleatt, *slate*
slater, *wood louse*
sole, *sill*
sorning, *sponging*
speir, *ask*
spreagh, *stolen cattle*
spreit, *spirit*
stammack, *stomach*
stan' o' black, *mourning suit*
stirk, *cattle*

stope, *flagon*
stot, *cattle*
sumph, *fool*
sweirty, *idleness*
syne, *then, since, ago*

tae, *toe*
tae, *the one (contrasted with the other)*
tatties, *potatoes*
thae, *those*
thigging, *begging*
thrapple, *neck, throat*
thrawn, *stubborn, ill-tempered*
threep, *insist*
timmer, *unmusical voice*
tolbooth, *town gaol*
tred, *trade*
tron, *market-place; public weighing machine*

umbesett, *surrounded*
unbrairded, *not yet sprouting*
unco, *strange; very*

vivers, *food, provisions*

wa, *wave*
wailed, *choice, select*
ware, *spend, squander*
wark, *work*
waur, *worse*
whilk, *which*
wis, *know, think*
wotna, *do not know*
wulks, *whelks*

yird, *earth*